Sustainability by Design

Sustainability by Design

A Subversive Strategy for Transforming Our Consumer Culture

John R. Ehrenfeld

Yale University Press

New Haven and London

"The Opening of Eyes," by David Whyte, from *From Songs for Coming Home*. Reprinted with permission from Many Rivers Press, Langley, Washington. www.davidwhyte.com.

"The Descent," by William Carlos Williams, from *Collected Poems 1939–1962*, Volume II, copyright ©1948, 1962 by William Carlos Williams. Reprinted by permission of New Direction Publishing Corp.

Set in Sabon by Binghamton Valley Composition.

Printed in the United States of America.

Library of Congress Cataloging-in-Publication Data
Ehrenfeld, John.
Sustainability by design : a subversive strategy for transforming our consumer culture / John R. Ehrenfeld.
p. cm.
Includes bibliographical references and index.
ISBN 978-0-300-13749-1 (hardcover : alk. paper)
1. Sustainable development. 2. Consumption (Economics) I. Title.
HC79.E5E346 2008
338.9'27—dc22
2008012032

A catalogue record for this book is available from the British Library.

The paper in this book meets the guidelines for permanence and durability of the Committee on Production Guidelines for Book Longevity of the Council on Library Resources.

10 9 8 7 6 5 4 3 2 1

To my grandchildren

The Opening of Eyes

That day I saw beneath dark clouds
the passing light over the water
and I heard the voice of the world speak out,
I knew then, as I had before
life is no passing memory of what has been
nor the remaining pages of a great book
waiting to be read.

It is the opening of the eyes long closed.
It is the vision of far off things
seen for the silence they hold.
It is the heart after years
of secret conversing
speaking out loud in the clear air.

It is Moses in the desert
fallen to his knees before the lit bush.
It is the man throwing away his shoes
as if to enter heaven
and finding himself astonished,
opened at last,
fallen in love with solid ground.
—*David Whyte, From* Songs for Coming Home, *©1989 Many Rivers Press*

Contents

Illustrations

Tables

Foreword

PETER M. SENGE

Today, more and more people are waking to the realization that we cannot continue on our present path. What best personifies the deeper imbalance that exists? We could select any one of a number: carbon in the atmosphere and climate change, global insecurity, dwindling supplies of drinking water, the plight of poverty, lost topsoil, unhealthy food, or hundreds of millions of displaced farmers worldwide. But this deeper imbalance is felt more than thought. It shows up in a deep sense of alienation and pervasive anxiety. It shows up in the growing culture of fear and distrust—of large institutions, of political and business leaders, of media, of one another, and, ultimately, of life itself. It shows up, by implication, in the countless efforts to bring spirituality and meaning back into our daily lives. I believe that the only path toward a future worthy of our aspiration—one we would gladly cede to our children and grandchildren—is through confronting both the inner and outer unsustainability of our present ways of living, and seeing how the two relate to one another.

John Ehrenfeld, a pioneer in "industrial ecology," is an unusual academic. With one foot in the world of philosophy and the other in the world of manufacturing, product, and business design, he embraces the paradoxical position that the future path will require both radical new technologies and new ways of understanding humanness. In this book Ehrenfeld aims to stimulate a new and richer conversation around sustainability. Few conversations hold greater portent for the future.

This simple word, sustainability, has escaped from the clutches of academics and social activists and now shows up regularly in newspapers and political speeches. But what does it mean? Having been a leader in the field for decades, Ehrenfeld traces its evolution, both superficially and more deeply. At one level, sustainability has emerged through restating the concerns of environmentalists, and it also represents an opening to ask deeper and more personal questions—for example, what truly matters to us as individuals, as parents, and as a society? For Ehrenfeld, sustainability is ultimately about "flourishing," not just surviving. A sustainable ecosystem is one that generates a level of health, vitality, and resilience that allows its members to both live and evolve. For humans, it could open a door to rethinking core questions that have always guided societies that both endured and thrived—questions that have largely disappeared in this age.

For millennia, societies that have nurtured civilization, east and west, north and south, have honored the timeless quest after transcendent ideals: *the good, the true,* and *the beautiful;* to be guided by *Great Spirit,* the *Tao.* When such aspirations become replaced by the mindless quest for *more,* we fall out of alignment with our deepest nature. Is it any wonder that we then also fall out of alignment with nature as a whole? Economics is the science of means, the efficient use of resources; it has nothing to say, inherently, about ends. Yet, there is hardly a politician on the planet who does not believe that her or his job security does not hinge on economic growth.

This irony may prove to be the tragedy of our time. It is ironic, and perhaps tragic, that economics (from the Greek *eco-nomus,* the household) started as a science of means, the efficient use of resources, and today defines the accepted and virtually unquestioned ends of society, and as well provides virtually all the guidance we acknowledge about those ends.

Working with John Ehrenfeld for many years has helped all of us in the "change" community understand the differences between "reducing unsustainability" and creating true sustainability. The former encompasses a host of mostly technological fixes that hold the promise of somehow solving the profound problems we face without causing any major inconvenience to those of us who have created them. But even if you manage to slow down while heading south, you still have to figure out what it takes to turn 180 degrees to head north. And since most of culture's experience lies in ways to head "south," usually faster and more efficiently, how can the members of any society possibly imagine how to find the way to the "north"? Ironically, the more we succeed in reducing unsustainability—through greater eco-efficiency, more aid to the poor, more distractions for the rich—the less we feel we even have to think about creating sustainability, real flourishing.

John Ehrenfeld has spent decades thinking about *creating sustainability,* and he believes it hinges on crossing three thresholds of awareness and intention. First, we must see our situation and our role in creating this situation. "It is only through reflection that we can escape our past," says Humberto Maturana, a Chilean biologist whose insights into awareness and cognition form a cornerstone of Ehrenfeld's hope for the future. You could say that the power of reflection is needed now more than ever before.

Out of deep reflection, genuine visions of what we truly seek can also arise. Most visions are extrapolations from the past, plus or minus 5 percent. But genuine visions give voice to the cry of the heart: that which moves through us rather than from us, that which answers a call from the future rather than preserves a security from the past.

Lastly comes the long, patient work of reinventing the structures that shape our collective lives. These structures are not imposed upon us from on high; they are enacted from our daily ways of living. "First we shape the walls and then the walls shape us," said Churchill. In social systems, these walls arise from our deepest and most unquestioned habits of thought and action. If these remain in shadow, beyond our awareness, little can change—for we are always chasing after the manifest problems in front of us and not the habits and forces that compel us. On reflection, they start to be revealed, along with the genuine aspiration for what truly matters. Enacting new structures consistent with different visions then requires "artifacts," bits of the new that we can work with and use, following sociologist Anthony Giddens, to enact new structure.

Ehrenfeld examines four broad arenas where new artifacts can be created to lead us to think and act differently: technology, beliefs, norms, and authority. For example, Ehrenfeld's vision of technology is a radical break from ever more efficiency and convenience. Buckminster Fuller used to say, "If you want to change how someone thinks, give up; you cannot change how another thinks. Give them a tool, the use of which will lead them to think differently." Ehrenfeld shows in depth the subtle ways that tools and tool users interact, for good and ill, and shows how a new discipline of designing products could restore our sense of awareness both of being present in what we do and of our responsibility toward those we affect through using our technology.

This is not a book of simple answers to not-so-simple questions, but is instead an attempt to reveal the core questions that are the basis for our current global crises. In the growing glut of stories about dark futures and anesthetizing paeans to technologies that will somehow save us from such futures, this book comes much closer to tapping the real source of hope and possibility for a flourishing future life—ours and all those with whom we share our home.

Preface

We can no longer survive on refrigerators, politics, card games, and crossword puzzles. We can no longer live without poetry, color, love.
—*Antoine de Saint-Exupery, 1943 Letter to General X*

This book, which has been almost twenty years in the making, tracks my own personal journey. About the time many people start to think about retiring, I began a new career as an academic, joining the faculty at MIT, my alma mater. Until then I had spent about thirty years working in the broad field of environment, covering the conventional media—air, water, waste—and ranging from bench research to resource management to policy analysis. Soon after I arrived, my colleagues and I launched the MIT Technology, Business, and Environment program. We focused on technology because some technological device or process is almost always closest to environmental damage. We chose business because it appeared to us to be the most powerful institution with respect to technology. We spent the next ten years studying environmental management in selected industries and companies.

At some point, the notion of sustainability entered our lexicon. MIT had joined with two other universities to create the Alliance for Global Sustainability, and our research group was much involved. Something about the prevalent notion of sustainability, which, then and now, generally mirrors the theme of sustainable development, was deeply troubling to me. It seemed so obvious that the same notion of "development" that had dominated the modern world for decades, even centuries, was at the root of whatever problems people were willing to put into the bin of unsustainability.

I had a strong sense that something larger than carbon dioxide or economic maldistribution or any of the usual "causes" was at work. In the years since I retired from MIT, I have become more skeptical about the ability of business and other institutions to move forward effectively on the sustainability front. One key reason is that sustainable development—the conventional working definition of sustainability— is an empty idea and contains within it the seeds of further environmental, human, and social degradation.

I cannot claim that my journey started from some deliberate reasoned analysis. Several activities brought a new focus to my continuing thinking about the subject of sustainability. The first was my involvement in a consortium of mostly large corporations that had joined together, under the auspices of the Society of Organizational Learning, to discover if they could begin to work toward creating sustainability by learning together across organizational boundaries. I found a critical and generally welcoming audience here for trying out many of the ideas that follow.

The second was the result of some personal training. During the "graduation" exercise, all the participants took turns facing the group and announcing who each would be on leaving the program. Everyone followed a format that began with the words, "I am the possibility of . . . ," with each then supplying the rest of the sentence. When my turn came, I had no idea what I would say. But as I turned and faced the group I heard myself saying, "I am the possibility that human and other life will flourish on the Planet forever." Like the others, I proudly wore my unexpected utterance as my name tag for the rest of the day. This experience left me with both an idea of what sustainability is really all about and the commitment to seek a way to bring it into the world. This book is part of that commitment.

Long ago, I was taught to write in the third person because nonfiction should reflect the objectiveness of the world. I remember carefully scanning students' papers to expunge any use of "I." I never associated this practice with the Cartesian model of the world I had embodied. Now, as you will read, I have learned that this view of the world is only one kind of story we tell others and ourselves to make social life possible, and, further, that this particular story no longer works very well. Life takes place in language. Elie Wiesel once said that "people become the stories they hear, and the stories they tell." What happens in life depends on the language we use and how it is understood. But this simple, sophisticated philosophical statement is just a fancy way of saying that life shows up inside stories. I don't mean formula stories with a beginning, middle, and end, but, rather, a conversation that brings meaning to life. Now I no longer apologize when my own "I" shows up.

This book is a story about a world of care and flourishing. Sustainability can emerge only when modern humans adopt a new story that will change their behavior such that flourishing rather than unsustainability shows up in action. Flourishing is not something to *do* or to *have*. One can flourish only by *Being*. This story is very different from one about ecoefficiency, solving technological problems, or getting the price right. Some of the words I use here have a familiar ring to them, but they do not mean the same thing as in everyday conversations—in particular, the ways in which I will describe being, care, learning, and design. To create sustainability, we must first adopt new meanings for the words we use to tell our stories. Only then will we begin to act in a way to produce sustainability and not the opposite. I believe that this book offers such a new vocabulary and the beginning of a new, compelling story, one that I care about very deeply. I hope you will agree and begin to bring it into your own life.

Acknowledgments

The first inklings of this book arose through conversations with my long-time associate and collaborator at MIT, Jennifer Nash. Han Brezet, my friend and colleague at the Technical University of Delft, hosted me for a year on the heels of my retirement from MIT. It was there I learned about product design and the concepts that helped me find a practical way to bring the theory and philosophy of sustainability to life. I acknowledge the Bainbridge Graduate Institute and their unique MBA students who start with a deep belief in these ideas. Many of the ideas were sharpened during a course on "radical" sustainability I taught there. It was also there that I met and subsequently taught jointly with Tom Johnson, who has been a most helpful critic and supporter. I also recognize the Sustainability Consortium within the Society for Organizational Learning, where my participation has given me many opportunities to try out much of what follows here.

My son, Tom, who writes professionally, has given me

invaluable advice and encouragement, often pushing me along just when I was running out of steam. And last, without the support of my wife, Ruth Budd, I would have long ago abandoned this project as it has occupied much too much of the time we have left to enjoy our wonderful life together. Our shared life has taught me what possibility means and why, without it, sustainability will always be just out of reach.

In the course of doing research and background reading for this book, I discovered that authors coming from many perspectives had already concerned themselves with the central notion of flourishing and even sustainability, although often not in these exact terms. I owe a deep debt to so many of these thinkers for providing me with the intellectual threads that I have woven together in a book that, hopefully, will give life to their thoughts and words. Readers will recognize contributions from the work of Anthony Giddens, Martin Heidegger, Humberto Maturana, Erich Fromm, Abraham Maslow, Manfred Max-Neef, Peter Senge, and others. I also owe a debt of gratitude to Fernando Flores, who introduced me to the ontology of Heidegger and the biology of Maturana through an intensive program in ontological design. Looking back at my notes from this program from the late 1980s, I find many seeds that have sprouted after a very long incubation period.

I acknowledge the support of my editors at Yale University Press, Jean Thomson Black and Jeff Schier. Jean added much to the book with her critical comments, and she kept my spirits up during the excruciatingly long process of getting this book out into the world. Jeff helped me transform a techie's text to a readable and accessible book. And finally, I thank those friends and colleagues plus a few anonymous referees who read the text in its early incarnations and kept me on the straight and narrow with their suggestions for improvement.

Sustainability by Design

Chapter 1 Is the Sky Falling, and, If So, Does Anyone Care?

The year's at the spring
And day's at the morn;
Morning's at seven;
The hillside's dew-pearled;
The lark's on the wing;
The snail's on the thorn;
God's in his heaven—
All's right with the world.
—*Shelley*, Pippa Passes

Is Shelley's wonderful sentiment still valid in today's much-changed world? I think not. The world is different in a profoundly threatening way, and it would be difficult, if not impossible, to offer proof of his statement according to the rigorous standards of modern science. And proof—or at least considerable recognition of unease about the future—is important as a mover of change; human history suggests that social change comes slowly, and usually only after a crisis. I have chosen not to spend many pages pointing to the coming crisis simply because so many others have already done this.[1]

Instead, I begin by stating my strong belief that it is important to take action now, long before the unsustainable state of the world does indeed induce such a crisis. We cannot continue to ignore history and the obvious signs of trouble. There is still time, I hope, although the stresses on both the human and the natural worlds may be reaching a point whereby the system cannot retain its current structure, and it may jump into a new regime even less sustainable than the present. To build my case I will largely stand on the shoulders of many who have looked at our modern, industrial, technological world through a critical lens and found it sorely lacking in qualities essential to the survival of all living species—not to mention to the continuing unfolding and development of the human species.

At the same time, I am convinced that each human being, deep down, lives every day striving to produce a flourishing, sustaining world, such as is found in Shelley's lines. It is this fundamental, perhaps even biologically based, sense that part of what it is to be human means re-creating our selves at every moment—on and on until we die. But because we can be blind in certain areas, this fundamental, positive engine for unfolding human potential has become buried so deeply that it comes to the surface only when our lives are imminently threatened. We strive ever harder to realize the world of our deepest longings, only to find it receding further from our grasp, perhaps unconsciously counting on a crisis to wake us up.

Our cultural history is a series of relatively calm periods punctuated with often-violent social change. We adjust to these altered conditions relatively quickly, as new generations replace those who were vanquished in the violent transitions from one order to another. Meanwhile, the natural world continues inexorably along its slow and steady evolutionary path, with little or no notice of the upheavals occurring in the human sphere.

The world is different today. We have developed weapons of such power that humans no longer can recover their numbers so simply after these periodic hiccups of history. In addition, the rapid spread of modern technological, consumerist economies—a weapon of cultural, if not biological, mass destruction—is wiping out what little remains of cultures that once lived in harmony with the world and with themselves. Nor is evolution left alone to follow its marvelous journey of bringing forth creatures that fit the world they are born into. In

Enough environmental writer Bill McKibben raises the specter of losing the most central traits of our humanness, among which are choice and uniqueness, by inducing "designer" genetic modifications to create tailored individuals or to prolong life indefinitely.[2] Relentless demands for energy and materials are upsetting and destroying the habitats and communities of human and nonhuman species, creating a pace of destruction that appears to rival that of the dinosaurs' demise. Evolution no longer can proceed without the indelible markings of human activity.

Let me return to Shelley's poem and ask again whether all is right with the world. What are the signs from which we can draw our answer? Since cutting open the belly of a lamb and seeking answers in the entrails is no longer fashionable, perhaps, then, our news media can serve the same purpose. If so, the outlook is not wonderful. The media are filled with stories of bad things happening everywhere: natural disasters of all sorts; breakdowns of historic proportions in the business community; a war carried on at the cost of destroying the most precious records of our modern civilization's ancient origins; and entertainment media selling violence as diversion and humor, recognizable as humor only through the fake laughter that accompanies it.

But even more telling are breakdowns that are appearing in the social fabric of life: record numbers of people are seeking treatment for depression and other signs of mental distress. Obesity is endemic in America, with recent evidence that oversize portions—a consequence of competition—are a major contributor. Peter Whybrow, Director of the Semel Institute of Neuroscience and Human Behavior at the University of California, Los Angeles, writes that our compulsive need for ever more stuff is producing individual and societal sickness. One consequence is the fading of relationships with other people, which he claims are the only sources of genuine happiness.[3]

New forms of social pathologies are showing up: road rage; mass killings in our schools and offices; rapidly growing divisions between the rich and the poor, with the rich appropriating more and more of the world's natural and economic resources; and homelessness, a historic phenomenon in all cultures, but seemingly out of place in an extraordinarily affluent world that should be able to provide the basic needs of everyone.

The materials that cycle through our economy aren't the only excess; there is also the waste that never makes it to the market. In *Natural Capitalism* the authors write, "Only one percent of the total North American materials flow ends up in, and is still being used within products six months after their sale."[4] Juxtaposed against the poverty on the streets of affluent nations is the poverty of over half of the world's human beings, who are just barely eking out a living even as they toil to produce the cheap goods that quickly end up on the waste piles of the wealthy. Is this picture one of sustainability? What is it about modern life that requires ever-increasing quantities of goods to produce satisfaction? Can this ever-accelerating pattern of consumption and waste last?

Such concerns as these do not go unnoticed even in the consumerist paradise the United States has become. Our society is, however, largely unwilling to face up to the seriousness of these present problems—not to mention those looming larger in the future. Just as an addict is blind to the causes of his or her pathology, society as a whole exhibits the same pattern. The social conversation picks up problems like pollution, global warming, poverty, or terrorism, and we turn to the powerful and the experts to find a solution. But the conversation is always about getting rid of something bad, never or rarely about creating something good. When we do attempt to follow a positive route, we reduce the most basic human qualities to a simple formula equating economic output to goodness of life, welfare, or some other intrinsic measure of being human. It follows, unfortunately, that this formulation simply leads to striving for more and more without much thinking about whether this mode of living is actually satisfying.

Starting with pollution and waste as primary themes in the 1970s, social talk about environmentalism has broadened to include issues like global warming, ozone layer depletion, and the collapse of the world's great fisheries. In fact, as I began to plan this book some years ago, Canada had just announced the complete closure of its historic cod fishery. This once-rich fishery off the northeastern coast of the United States and Canada has fed people all over the world—it may even have drawn the first visitors to North America from Europe (when Cartier arrived in the New World, it is said that he observed more than a thousand Basque cod-fishing vessels from the Iberian

Peninsula).[5] Once a model for what nature can provide without technological intervention, this great fishery is now facing extinction. The loss of such resources raises the specter of unsustainability, the inability to maintain into the future the style of life we now lead.

Global warming is another problem that, in addition to upsetting natural phenomena, is likely to cause great upset to our social systems, unless, as claimed by powerful technocrats, it is properly managed by new, high-efficiency energy technologies.[6] World hunger and epidemics like AIDS are also problems that we in the more affluent nations again look to technology in one form or another to solve or mitigate. Similarly, new and improved psychotherapeutic drugs are seen to be the answer for rising levels of apathy and depression in the industrial world.

In the environmentalist's conversation, we almost always speak only in terms of problems to solve, and rarely in terms of nurturing possibility. Something is missing here. Better, many things are missing. Addressing our unease with the world around us largely as a set of problems to be mitigated through technology is itself a manifestation of modernity. Since the rise of the Enlightenment, with its optimistic ideas about knowledge and technology, change is normally thought to be fundamentally progressive—leading individuals and the societies they constitute to an always-rosier future that is bigger and better than its past. Our job as individuals is to help this movement along by overcoming problems that impede the forward motion—typically by applying what has worked in the past. But such talk and action only can keep us firmly rooted in the past, albeit in bigger and better surroundings.

To escape from the past we must think in radical terms. Martin Luther King Jr.'s dream foresaw a whole new world. King's vision of the future was not just better than the past; it was separated from that past by an enormous chasm that required a brand-new story to bridge: "I have a dream . . . I have a dream that one day little black boys and black girls will be able to join hands with little white boys and white girls as sisters and brothers . . ."

But unlike King's vision of a new future, the one notion related to sustainability that has received attention from powerful forces in government and business—sustainable development—is not actually a vision of the future. It is merely a modification of the current process of economic development. Sustainable development proponents claim that this path need not cause the terribly destructive consequences of past forms of development. Sustainable development is fundamentally a tool that suggests new means but still old ends—development remains at the core of this concept. At best, our current sustainable development strategies can barely cope with the forces of unsustainability—a state of the world that is unlikely to be able to provide either the biological life support for humans and other creatures or the social characteristics that make life meaningful.

In contrast, sustainability is a distinction perhaps as old as humanity and the emergence of human cultures. It springs from reflection on the awareness of the passage of time and the consciousness of the mystery of birth and death. It undoubtedly has formed the cultural basis for the emergence of magic and religion, which serve both to illuminate sustainability and to seek it as part of one's living experience. In our modern view of reality, the separation of mind from world hollows out the meaning of sustainability.

To recover the full meaning of sustainability, a radical stance is critical. I begin with a new and distinctive definition of sustainability: *the possibility that human and other life will flourish on the planet forever.* Flourishing is the key to a vision of a sustainable future, and this way of conceptualizing sustainability connects to every kind of audience I have addressed. We must shift back to the flourishing fullness of "Being" from its impoverished modern form of "having." Immersion in the modernist cultural paradigm has disaffected human beings in three critical domains of living.

• The human, arising out of our (lost) sense of what it is to be a human being,
• The natural, arising out of our (lost) sense of our place in the natural world, and
• The ethical, arising out of our (lost) sense of responsibility for our actions and our relationships to others.

Evidence of these lost senses abounds in the form of ever-increasing levels of unsatisfying and wasteful consumption, family and personal breakdown, litigiousness, and environmental degradation, and in what many see as banality and shallowness in public and private life in general. I will use capital *Being* throughout this book to point to the unique way of existence that human beings possess, and lowercase *being* for things in general in the everyday objective sense. Without recovering our sense of Being and ethical responsibility, it is virtually impossible to start to take care of the world and our own species in ways to produce flourishing.

Unsustainability springs from the cultural structure of modernity itself: the way we hold reality and ourselves as human beings, and the hegemony of technology as the solution to every problem facing individuals and the society at large. Unsustainability is an unintended consequence of the addictive patterns of modern life. *Almost everything being done in the name of sustainable development addresses and attempts to reduce unsustainability. But reducing unsustainability, although critical, does not and will not create sustainability.* The world is awash with books and news items touting the importance and advantages of "green" products, housing, and institutional practices, but such practices and artifacts are at best only Band-Aids, and at worse they divert our attention from sustainability.

Sustainability is an outcome of the way we choose to live our lives. Sustainability is an emergent property of living systems different from the functional properties of mechanistic systems and objects. To look at it another way, we would never describe a machine as possessing sustainability. We might speak about its durability or reliability, but never about its sustainability. To me the most basic symbol of sustainability is that of flourishing. It pertains to all natural systems, both human and other living systems. For humans, flourishing means more than just remaining healthy. It also means living the good life, following precepts handed down over the ages by sages and philosophers.

Can the kinds of stories we now tell about how the world works, coupled to our present ways of coping with its problems, sustain human cultures and individual lives? Given the history of progressive human development under circumstances that seemed just as unsustainable, it is difficult to answer "no" convincingly. But does this mean that we should put all of our eggs in the basket of modernity and take a chance that our modern systems of thinking and acting will continue to produce the progression toward enlightenment and the realization of the flourishing of human potential I spoke of? I think not.

Alternatives do exist; it is more a question of how deeply we are buried in our habitual ways of acting individually and socially. The popularity of self-help books and quick cures to all problems from obesity to terror strongly suggests that our cultural habits keep us mired. This book takes the stance that there is a direct but challenging way out of this stalemate. It springs from the tried and true practices that deal with other forms of addiction and routine pathological behavior. Yes, the patterns of modern, consumerist life are exemplars of addiction.

The first step, similar to that used in programs like Alcoholics Anonymous and in many forms of psychotherapy, brings destructive patterns into view, raising them from the unconscious corner to which they have been sent. Step two is to replace the modernist vision that has been maintaining the endless revolutions of the vicious cycle with an evocative vision of the world that can continuously pull one and all into new possibility. Spanish philosopher José Ortega y Gasset put a positive spin on this idea, saying, "Life is a series of collisions with the future; it is not the sum of what we have been, but what we yearn to be."

The third step is the replacement of the structures and strategies that, like our unconscious selection of the domains in which we seek satisfaction, also keep us spinning about in circles, with images of satisfaction always just out of reach. Steps one and two are nothing more than a shift in our consciousness and in the language we use to give meaning to the incoherent signals the world sends to our senses. The change is transformative and takes but an instant. This is not to say it is easy—quite the opposite is true, as those committed to pulling themselves out of addictive and circular patterns know all too well. This kind of transformation takes hard work and, often, intervention, but, when it comes, it does so in the blink of an eye. Help can come from many places, even in the form of a few words from a poet, friend, or trusted teacher, or from a visceral message conveyed during a walk in the woods.

This third step, changing the culture and its consequent pathologies, takes much longer. The cognitive and material structures that reproduce cultural life—the technology and tools we use, and the institutions and infrastructure that shape our social lives—must be reinvented; some will need to be replaced outright, while complementing others will be sufficient. Einstein said that just as our ways of thinking keep us from breaking out of our stalemates, so too do they keep us from escaping the tangible structures of our social worlds. This book envisions a new landscape in which many of the familiar concepts show up differently.

The way we think about the world—which results in the reality that grounds and justifies our actions—leads to unsustainability and impedes a move to sustainability, because virtually every answer to every question we grapple with comes out of our objective view of reality. In a sense, we are stuck in the system that has created our dilemmas. Until we begin to dwell in a new world of sustainability we will have lots of questions but few answers. If you read this book expecting or hoping to find detailed answers, you will be disappointed, although I do try to point to a way to a sustainable future. But if you can discipline yourself to live inside the questions that are raised here, then you will slowly be able to discard the old tried, but no longer true, answers and replace them with new, effective ways of building a sustainable future.

Although sustainability is a global and universal concern, the focus of this book is on the modern, industrialized world. I have not forgotten nor overlooked the needs of everyone alive today, or those who will follow. The human needs for many are immediate and substantial, but they are being swept aside or trampled by the force of modernization in the name of (sustainable) economic development. We must first transform the overwhelming economic and technological power of modernity at home. And we can turn to the task of repairing the world of both people and nature only after we who call ourselves moderns recover our own humanity and experience the care that makes us human.

Chapter 2 Solving the Wrong Problem: How Good Habits Turn Bad

Explanations exist; they have existed for all times, for there is always an easy solution to every human problem—neat, plausible, and wrong.
—*H. L. Mencken,* A Mencken Chrestomathy

About ten years ago I participated in a workshop on industrial ecology and the service sector. This was one of an annual series that was sponsored by the National Academy of Engineering to delve into the then-emerging field of industrial ecology and to look for opportunities to improve ecosystem health. Industrial ecology is based on the idea that healthy ecosystems can also serve as a metaphor for sustainable human socioeconomic systems. One of the central themes in this field is the closing of material loops—in other words, recycling most everything we use in the same way materials flow in natural systems.

At this workshop a speaker from one of the largest retail chains in the United States gave an impassioned presentation about all the good things his firm was doing for environmental improvement. The highlight was a discussion of the results

of a program he called "dumpster diving," in which personnel at selected stores periodically emptied the dumpsters they used and
sorted the contents. Cardboard packaging turned out to be a major
part of all the trash. The company realized that it could bundle the
cardboard and sell it to recyclers, thus avoiding an environmental
problem and making money at the same time. The speaker con-
cluded with a proud statement about his firm's new program and
then invited questions. After a few queries about the details of the
project, one of the attendees asked, "What you are doing is certainly
a step in the right direction, but have you ever thought about all the
stuff that goes out of the front door? What about its impact on the
environment?"

The question stopped him short, and, after a long pause, he responded, "Well, I see what you are getting at. You mean that the real
impact of our business comes in the use and disposal of what our customers carry out with them." After another long pause, he continued,
"Well, if we are going to have any influence on what our customers
buy, we would have to give them information about the environmental implications of their purchases. And wouldn't this be the same as
telling our customers that they are dumb?" Ironically, his presentation came on the heels of another by a different major retailer, who
had described his company's new program to provide just such information to its customers. Further, he had also talked about another
program the company had undertaken to eliminate products that
could not conform to his firm's own set of environmental standards.

The dumpster-diving company was stuck in a common pattern of
problem-solving that may appear to work but that has significant and
serious "side effects." Although I use the term "side effects" in the
usual sense here, the term itself is fundamentally misleading. These
outcomes are not "side" at all; they are as much a consequence of
acting as are the primary efforts. To emphasize this point, in this
book I will always put "side effects" in quotation marks. The term itself suggests a desire to minimize or to wish away these outcomes.

The company in the example had picked out just a small part of the
problem that it purportedly was committed to address and had missed
the big payoff. Such behavior is typical in our modern world and is very
hard to avoid. Our society is addicted to reductionist ways of solving
virtually all our problems. When confronting problems we tend to chop

them into small pieces and give each piece to a specialist familiar with that chunk. Over time, as we engage more and more in this practice, society's (as well as an individual's) competence to address the complicated, messy problems we confront has diminished. Unsustainability is just such a messy problem. Reductionism will not make it go away.

Examples of such partial solutions abound. Increasing fuel economy is a familiar one; historically it has been the main strategy for solving the environmental problems of the automobile. Although actual performance has improved over time, the desired end result has not been achieved because increases in vehicle miles have overwhelmed efficiency gains, and because many drivers have shifted to vehicles such as various sport utility vehicles that lie outside the regulatory ambit. This strategy is shortsighted and shifts the burden away from the development of alternate means of transport.

The early history of environmental management is full of examples in which pollutants were merely moved from one environmental medium to another because the legal structure governing regulation in the United States focused on only one medium at a time. Thus pollutants removed from air and water ended up in landfills. Lawmakers ignored the laws of nature, especially the conservation of mass law, which would have indicated that this reductionist approach was doomed to failure from the start. We cannot attain sustainability by following that path. Only a holistic stance can get us there.

Lewis Carroll wrote that finding a way to make Humpty-Dumpty's shell whole is a great challenge, but that is what it will take to turn us from the unsustainable path of addictive consumption and reductionist solutions to the problems (plural) that crop up in our individual and collective lives. The choice of the singular "problem" in the title of this chapter is deliberate. The stories just told may seem unique, but they are characteristic of general patterns of behavior that we fail to recognize because our reductionist ways of thinking and other cultural limitations hide the context of actions from us. When we focus sharply on the problems (plural) before us, we often fail to see much more fundamental issues. I mentioned the reductionist habit of seeing only a bit of the whole story, but the problem (singular) is even deeper. With the help of some (causal loop) diagrams from systems dynamics, the way of portraying complicated situations developed by Jay Forrester and

others at MIT in the 1970s, I will show how our common ways of acting hide the underlying causes of unsustainability and hinder our attempts to produce sustainability. Systems dynamics played a central
role in the analysis done in *The Limits to Growth,* which brought the
threatened state of the environment to the world's attention.[1] Causal
loop diagrams continue to be a very useful tool in revealing one's mindset and in enabling change to that mindset, or "mental model," as systems theorist Peter Senge calls it in *The Fifth Discipline.*[2]

But before getting to the problem that needs to be addressed at the
root, let us examine a few basic systems diagrams. These generalized
patterns follow from the work of Daniel Kim and others in the field[3]
and, along with a few other general patterns, are so ubiquitous that
they have the form of standard models, that is, archetypes.

Figure 1 shows the most basic of loops. We spend much of our life
going around and around this one, as it is the fundamental form of
everyday action. Whenever we encounter something that needs doing
or fulfilling (the "problem," in this figure), we take an action to solve
it (the symptomatic "solution"). If the problem is a hole (like a hungry stomach), we fill it. And if it is a barrier standing in our way, we
take it down. The solution we apply causes an opposite effect (o). The
more we eat, the less hungry we feel. Of course, if we overeat, then
another problem may show up, but we will come to that situation in

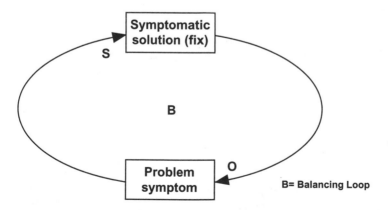

Figure 1. Basic problem-solving (balancing) loop

a moment. And as the problem lessens, so does the need for solution. The left-hand part of the loop indicates that the effect is in the same direction (*s*) as the action. The combination of opposite and same connection between action and effect forms a balancing loop and is an example of negative feedback. Because we spend most of our lives working to make our problems go away, this pattern of behavior is the most common. Some kinds of problems, like hunger, never go away, so we keep going round and round this loop. This pattern of behavior also describes our habits, which are nothing more than repeated problem-solving routines. They rise to the top of our toolboxes simply because they seem to work. Consequently, we use them over and over again and they become ingrained.

At this point things start to get more complicated. Everybody knows that many, if not most, of life's problems keep coming back where and when we least expect them. In Figure 2 I have added another loop to indicate that often the solutions we choose produce some sort of unwanted result or unintended consequence. One common outcome is that the original problem comes back at some later time: "fixes-that-fail." Another is that some unintended consequence shows up somewhere else. The side loop in this figure shows that the action and effects both flow in the same direction. The unwanted effects keep getting bigger the more we keep trying to solve the primary problem, which may also grow over time if our efforts fail to get at its roots. This kind of loop is called a reinforcing loop, and we term the process positive feedback. We usually try

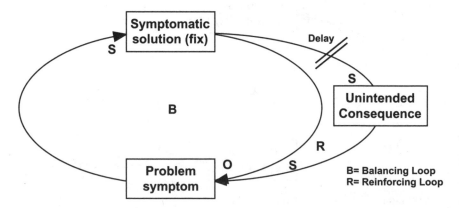

Figure 2. Fixes-that-fail archetype

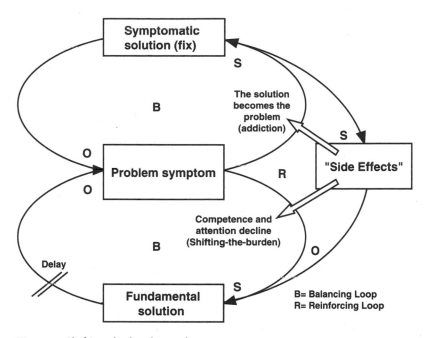

Figure 3. Shifting-the-burden archetype

to avoid this pattern, because nothing in life can grow without limits. The dangers of global warming could be magnified by positive feedback that causes the oceans to release previously dissolved greenhouse gases as they begin to heat up. This increase in emissions thereby contributes more to the rate of temperature rise.

Repeated attempts to solve the problems often have another serious negative "side effect." Figure 3 shows a new pattern that people fall into all too often. In this diagram, a presumed potentially effective solution appears in the lower loop. Such desirable action is hard to recognize, because our old habits can lead to two kinds of serious "side effects." The first, shifting-the-burden, is our tendency to lose sight of possible fundamental or more effective solutions while we remain stuck in our habitual ways, trying harder and harder to deal with situations that just don't seem to improve or otherwise go away. Our habits and fixation on the symptoms tend to blind us to the possibility of more effective and longer-lasting solutions. Our cultural impatience also turns us away from this realization. We shift the burden away from the more appropriate solution to the habitual one.

The story of Helen Keller and Annie Sullivan is often told to illustrate this pattern. After Helen's parents discovered that she was both blind and deaf, they found that the more they tried to do for her, the more obstreperous and difficult she became. When Annie Sullivan arrived, she forced Helen to begin to do everyday actions by and for herself. As Helen began to acquire basic skills and become responsible for her actions, her whole persona changed, ultimately producing one of the most remarkable human beings of our times. Her parents had been shifting the burden away from Helen, who needed desperately to learn for herself. Her story serves as an example of this type of danger and of the empowerment that can result by escaping its vicious circle. Table 1 shows some examples of typical shifting-the-burden behavior taken from business and life in general.

In some cases this pattern can lead to addiction. If the habitual solution has a negative impact on the system beyond simply defocusing attention, repeated efforts can severely damage the system itself. In this case, the solution becomes a new problem, as in alcoholism. Typically, alcoholism springs from attempts to mitigate pain and stress caused by an experience such as job stress or family troubles. At first alcohol seems to lessen the stress or anxiety, but the symptoms soon return because the cause is still lingering. After a while, alcohol begins to poison the body and cause a new set of symptoms that push the original set into the background. The chosen solution, alcohol, has become a new, more serious problem due to its deleterious physiological

Table 1. Shifting-the-burden examples

Problem Symptom	Symptomatic Solution	Negative Side Effects	Fundamental Solution
Bank failures	Federal insurance	Responsibility disappears	Prudent banking practices
Poor employee performance	Manager steps in	Erosion of confidence and relationship	Skills training
Oil scarcity and high prices	Create reserve supply of alternates	Inadequate development	New products, culture change
"Not enough time"	Eat fast foods	Obesity; sociability loss	Improve time management

and psychological effects. When this happens, the first problem can't be dealt with until the new one is addressed.

Habits that routinely produce satisfactory outcomes are everyone's primary tools for action. It is only when habits begin to produce either of these two patterns with pathological or negative "side effects" that we need to stop and take stock. Whether repeated attempts with fixes-that-fail create addiction or the lesser shifting-the-burden pattern, the result is the same. The individual or group becomes incapable of addressing the first problem in a fundamental way or, worse, cannot begin to touch it even if it is perceived as something that demands attention.

Such is the status of unsustainability. We can see these general patterns when we examine the primary framework for addressing unsustainability. Figure 4 is a repeat of the earlier one showing the general case of fixes-that-fail. Here I have explicitly substituted "all of our problems" for the general case and the technological solution (quick fix) for the symptomatic general solution as shown earlier in Figure 2. I am using "technology" here as a proxy for the normal, everyday choice of solution in today's modern context.

In our modern way of thinking and acting, we are accustomed to solving virtually every problem by some sort of technological means. By this I mean not only using some favorite artifactual device, but also by applying "scientific" theories when all of the alternative means held in reserve also fail to work. Although solutions to the

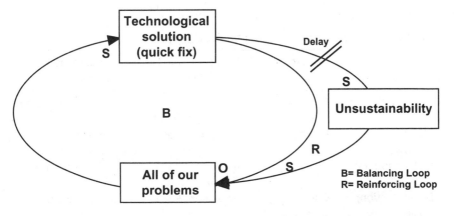

Figure 4. Unsustainability as an unintended consequence of modernity

immediate problem may appear, this habitual way of acting has the insidious "side effect" of producing serious deterioration of nature and our own humanistic capabilities. The long run of successes of the technological fix has also led to unjustified expectations that such solutions can always be found. Thomas Homer-Dixon, who has written extensively on threats to global security, calls this "technohubris," and he suggests that this route to solving today's complex problems such as global warming may not lead us to the place we seek.[4]

Table 2 shows some examples of such fixes to individual and social problems. Like other habits, these solutions do work for a while and can become part of the prevalent choices for dealing with the immediate problems of unsustainability. But to the extent that they are seen as "the solution," sooner or later the problems to which they have been applied will either reemerge or worsen.

To bring the argument closer to home, let us look at the dominant way of dealing with unsustainability today. Figure 5 puts the shifting-the-burden pattern into the context of efforts to produce sustainability. The more we follow the path of what has become commonly called sustainable development (the upper loop), the harder it becomes to jump from the top loop to the bottom one. In economic terms, we are spending our limited resources on the wrong things. We know that more fuel-efficient vehicles and fossil-fuel energy efficiency are not the long-term solution to unsustainability. We should be investing in radical new forms of transportation and energy generation, but instead we keep pouring our funds in the conventional direction.

Table 2. Examples of unsustainable practices

Problem Symptom	Symptomatic Solution	Negative Side Effects	Fundamental Solution
Global warming	CO_2 trading	R&D slips; irresponsibility	Renewable energy
Material use growth	Ecoefficiency	Ecosystem collapse	Industrial restructuring
Maldistribution	Tax policy	Irresponsibility; gated cities	Cultural change
Dissatisfaction; alienation	Commodity consumption	Addiction; loss of competence	Self-development

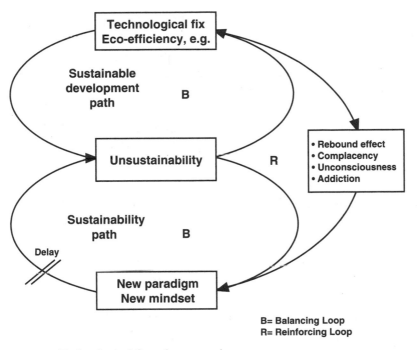

Figure 5. Technological fixes do not work

This might result in some success in the short run, but not if that strategy reduces longer-range efforts to a pittance. And in the matter of global warming, U.S. policy has been to do little, arguing we cannot even afford more efficiency without damaging the economy in the short term.

Attempting to address the symptoms of ecological stress rather than go to the root of the problem is a form of shifting-the-burden. The currently preferred policy to deal with greenhouse gas emissions and their relationship to global warming is through emissions trading and carbon taxes. These instruments are designed to bring about a reduction of global emissions that slows down, but does not stop, the buildup of solar energy–trapping gases. Such measures arguably are important and timely, but equally arguable is whether relying on these "solutions" shifts attention away from attacking the problem at its roots. In the long run, only the innovation and implementation of renewable energy sources will make this problem disappear. Arguments that it is economically preferable to do nothing at all and mitigate the effects are the worst form of shifting-the-burden, as they turn attention completely away from the causes. Such alternate paths to deal with complex social problems arise in part because we choose to compartmentalize expertise and reduce problems to fit into only a few of the boxes.

There is another, subtler problem hidden in this diagram. All of the existing efforts toward sustainable development simply equate more sustainability to less unsustainability. After all, that is the usual case in a linear, reductionist world. Even the Zen notion of a glass half full or half empty assumes that, as we reduce the bads or negatives, the goods will appear. In many cases this is true, but not in the case of sustainability. *Reducing unsustainability will not create sustainability.* Sustainability and unsustainability are not just two sides of the same coin or parts of the Zen glass contents. Our modern culture has led us to the wrong place by reifying sustainability.

The root cause of unsustainability is that we are trying to solve all the apparent problems of the world, large and small, by using the modernistic frame of thinking and acting that has created the metaproblem of unsustainability. Einstein is credited with only a slightly different observation: "The significant problems we face cannot be solved at the same level of thinking we were at when we created them." Modernity is a particular cultural form different from all that preceded it, and, in spite of those who argue we have gone beyond it, its culture dominates the West and increasingly is being imported by other nations trying to industrialize and adopt the cultural icons of the West, and especially those of the United States.

Given our total immersion in this culture, extraordinary steps are required even to recognize this form of habitual behavior, much less begin to try and change it. After all, that is what culture is: the ocean we all swim in and cannot sense ordinarily. Unlike fish, however, we can become conscious of the deep structures that drive our routines by stepping outside them and, with considerable effort, change them. If we do not, the world is likely to continue to degrade to a point where we truly cannot reverse the trend or, worse, where we suffer catastrophic and traumatic events.

Finally, it is very important that we look critically at the many programs that have come forth in the name of sustainable development or environmental management (one should always question whether we can really manage the environment). Sustainable development it-self is a technological, technocratic program. It epitomizes Einstein's statement and fits the shifting-the-burden archetype. Even its original parsing, as found in the United Nations' 1987 Brundtland report, which introduced this subject to the public at large, gives it away: "Sustainable development is a form of development . . ."[5] Then within sustainable development come programmatic prescriptions like ecoefficiency, Natural Capital, The Natural Step, Triple Bottom Line, and many others. All have some potential to mitigate or slow down the unsustainable trajectory of the globe, but all are only quick fixes. They are, as I have said, part of the problem, not the solution: they all will fail sooner or later and, worse, shift the burden away from more fundamental actions.

Chapter 3 Uncovering the Roots of Unsustainability

Lack of systemic wisdom is always punished.
—*Gregory Bateson,* Steps to an Ecology of Mind

In 1967, in what is now considered to be a classic article exploring the "roots of our ecological crisis," Lynn White, Jr., argued, "What people do about their ecology depends on what they think about themselves in relation to things around them. Human ecology is deeply conditioned by beliefs about our nature and destiny—that is, by religion."[1] He claimed more specifically that our environmental crisis was the result of our particular "Christian attitudes towards man's relation to nature. . . . We are superior to nature, contemptuous of it, willing to use it for our slightest whim." Perhaps this is enough to begin to explain why we have neglected the ecological system that we rely on for life itself, but it is not at all adequate to begin to explain the unsustainable state of the modern world.

The unsustainable state of the world needs explanation beyond White's focus on environment and religion. I offer three notions as very important causes: reality, rationality, and technology, which are also central factors when we turn to the redesign of the cultural structure and technological aspects of life. The omission of others' favorite causes of the sad state of the world should not be taken as an assessment that the redesign of the basic political economy or other aspects of social life today are of lesser consequence.

I will also point to other traits of our modern culture, such as its dominant norms (for example, efficiency) and beliefs (for example, technological progress), as being accessories after the fact. Other critics have argued that capitalism is the true culprit.[2] Still others point to the nature of human psychology and our genetic makeup.[3] Several readers of earlier drafts of the book commented that spirituality or, better, loss of spirituality wasn't mentioned as one of the roots of unsustainability. The literature on this subject is large. The notion of mystery and spirit suffers at the hands of modernity—philosophers and theologians have proclaimed that God is dead. Max Weber wrote, "The fate of our times is characterized by rationalization and intellectualization and, above all, by the disenchantment of the world."[4] I have not neglected this important factor, but, rather, include spirituality as part of the human domain. In my model of what it is to be human, caring for one's spirituality is one of the set of concerns that make us human. Turning to the spiritual at the expense of the others will not, however, produce sustainability.

The concepts of reality and rationality are closely coupled—inseparable, in fact, as reality underlies rationality as a ground. Splitting them as I have done is merely an analytic and editorial convenience for pointing out ways to redesign how we think and act. Technology, although a component of both reality and rationality, is treated as a separate category, as modern reality is shaped overwhelmingly by the presence of technology. And while it will be necessary to change our views of reality and rationality, it seems much easier to start with new forms of technology.

REALITY

Reality is merely an illusion, albeit a very persistent one.
—Albert Einstein (attributed)

The most taken-for-granted aspect of life is reality itself. We simply and unquestioningly accept that the outside world exists. Criticism of this naïve materialistic view (the idea that the external world is reflected as images in our minds) is left to philosophers and an occasional layperson facing an inexplicable situation. Further, we assume that the world we know is the same world everyone else apprehends, even if they might speak about it in another language. We assume all human beings have the same way of acquiring knowledge about the world, and of representing reality in the brain according to some yet to be completely understood mechanism. If anything worldly shows up as different when any two humans interact, it is usually attributed to a loss in translation or differences in cognitive content and ability. Although there are many names for this form of reality making—positivism is one such example—the one I will use is "objective reality."

Our everyday, objective way of holding reality is one of the root causes of unsustainability. This belief leads to the potential of domination at all levels of social interaction, from family to workplaces to whole societies. Chilean biologist Humberto Maturana claims that, in the objective reality way of thinking, "a claim of knowledge is a demand for obedience."[5] The idea of the separation of the mind from the world supports the idea of human mastery over nature, as we see ourselves as outside rather than as a part of the natural world. Objective reality disempowers the general public in favor of those in privileged professions, like scientists or economists who are consulted for solutions to life's "big" problems.

Just as I believe sustainability is the great challenge that humanity faces today, Maturana made a similar assertion about reality.[6] The two are intimately tied together, because the way we hold reality has much to do with the possibility of flourishing and the fullness of what it is to be human. In our conventional way of viewing reality—that is, the one into which we have been acculturated historically, including the learning we have received from our parents and formal teachers as well as from our own everyday experiences—we see the world as an external reality that we perceive and form through the workings of our nervous system.

Fortunately, there are other ways of thinking about reality that do not have the same consequences. The work of Maturana and others brings new perspective to how we construct reality. They point out that the properties of the observer produce the meaningful experience of the outside world, not vice versa as in the Cartesian model.[7] With the emergence of cognitive science and new aspects of evolutionary biology, talk about reality has moved outside the sphere of philosophy. Maturana comes from a biological tradition, and his arguments are based on his explanation of how living systems operate in the world. One of his main points is that human experiences of reality always involve an observer of the world.

In Maturana's worldview of reality, we view ourselves as interpreters of the actions in which we engage. The world becomes explicit as conscious experience only when our routinely effective actions break down or are interrupted by some event. When these interruptions occur, the world around us is revealed and those involved usually, perhaps always, render some assessment of what is happening (a story or explanation told to oneself or to others). Maturana states that "reality is an explanatory proposition [conversation] that arises in a disagreement as an attempt to recover a lost domain of coordination of actions or to generate a new one."[8] Those assessments become part of our historicity, the accumulated embodiment of our learned experience, and accrete to become the new basis for our interpretation of the next breakdown that occurs. Each experience builds a new foundation for interpreting and understanding everything that follows. We tend to forget these events along the way to the present so that "reality" seems to be timeless and context-free.

The cultural norm in the West follows the objective Cartesian paradigm in which the world is divided between an external, ahistorical reality and the human mind, which, through its rational powers, recreates that external world inside the brain. Some philosophers, such as Martin Heidegger and his followers, suggest that the world is mostly unavailable to us as human beings in that we act routinely and transparently and are generally unaware of our actions. Talking and walking, for example, are performed without thinking about them in the Cartesian sense and without a set of deterministic and explicable rules that would form a positivist's theory on the formulation of such actions. Indeed, if we were to try to explain what we were doing as we walked, we would very likely break the transparency of our action and stumble. It is clearly impossible to explain why we are saying what we are saying without interrupting ourselves and destroying the coherence of our conversation. The notion of theory as separate from practice is not consistent with this model of human consciousness. While acting in this transparent way, the world is concealed. In this way of viewing reality, Heidegger also suggests that humans construct the world through language, and act in that world to satisfy a deep-seated set of concerns.[9] He wrote, "Words and language are not wrappings in which things are packed for the commerce of those who speak and write. It is in words and language that things first come into being and are."[10]

How we see the world and respond to our everyday experiences come out of the fundamental presuppositions we hold. These presuppositions limit our possibilities and the subsequent actions we take. I believe that a worldview based on the presupposition of an interpretive, historical observer is more powerful than the conventional, everyday belief in a Cartesian observer. Power in this sense is the ability that reflection gives us to design and to redesign our lives, to reinterpret our experience as we learn to distinguish the several kinds of realities that we create, and particularly to be able to differentiate the things around us that are undeniable and unchangeable from those reified, abstract objects that live only in our linguistic assessments and interpretations.

RATIONALITY

> Reason is not what decides love.
> —*Molière*

Our view of reality is the basis for human action. It explains the world to us and for us, but it cannot explain the actions that we take within that world. In the Cartesian form of objective reality, action and reality are independent. Reality is simply out there; what we choose to do about it comes from some form of mental processing by which we try to make the most of the circumstances. The circumstances make up the external surrounding environment and our processing of it as two separate categories of objects.

This process of going from the reality of the moment to action follows our reasoning capability or our rationality. We often use these two terms interchangeably as independent properties of the human species, even of the human mind, but they have meaning primarily in the context of action. Rationality describes the basis of human actions and has a strong normative sense in that we expect people to act in a rational manner. Yet although we tend to think we have a clear idea as to what rationality is, there are many different ways to hold this distinction with significant consequences to the choice we make. Rationality has a strong tie to our interpretation of the world and what we should do about the immediate situation. It has both an ontological and a normative component.

The dominant notion of rationality in our modern world is that of economic man, *Homo economicus*. In this way of thinking, humans are always attempting to make the most of things, using their resources to maximize their well-being or happiness or pleasure or whatever word is used to speak about satisfying the self. The self is little more than a bundle of preferences that ebb and flow as they become momentarily satisfied or are pushed aside by another desire that mysteriously pops to the top of the heap. Individuals are always presumed to act in their self-interest, that is, to satisfy their needs. Acts that apparently are done for the benefits of others, such as heroism or altruism, are seen as manifestations of self-interest in this model, indicating that the individual has strong preferences for serving others.

The concepts of needs and satisfaction will reoccur throughout the remainder of the book. The economic model of rationality does not distinguish among different kinds of satisfaction nor does it set any bounds on individual fulfillment. The dominant utilitarian tenor of our and other modern political economies is the maximization of aggregate welfare. The more resources we have to expend and the more we do so, the better off will be the individual "I" and collective "we."

Rationality and reasonableness have very strong normative force attached to them. One of the worst things that can be said about a person is that the individual is acting unreasonably or irrationally. To the objective realists, this means that the person is doing something wrong. To others, it means that the subject of the observer's remarks is bucking the normal ways of doing things. In any case, this claim has strong negative social sanctions, calling for, in the extreme, separation from normal society. I will argue that acting according to prevalent norms is a root cause of unsustainability, and it will take a strong dose of unreasonableness to break the logjam of conventional thinking. The more that everyone believes that rationality is some sort of fixed capability of the human brain or some other aspect of human nature, the harder it will be to run up against the social tide.

TECHNOLOGY

> Alienation, if such an overused word still has meaning, is not only the result of social systems, be they capitalist or socialist, but of the very nature of technology: the new means of communication accentuate and strengthen non-communication.
> —Octavio Paz

The past thirty years or so have seen a growing consciousness and concern about the natural system in which human societies are embedded and which sustains us. These concerns are fundamentally different from those that arose during the early years of the Enlightenment, when thoughtful humans saw nature as hostile, alien, and harsh. They saw the new science and its manifestations in technology as means to protect humans and shield them from nature's exigencies. Now, some three centuries later, many thoughtful people have reversed their thinking.

Technology, as the instrumental means of empowering our actions, is a fundamental part of the structure of modern cultures. One common use of the term *technology* refers to the tools that humans use to produce satisfaction. This is the oldest way of looking at technology, because humans have been toolmakers from their very earliest origins. The origin of the word itself comes from the Greek word for craft—*technē*. This use is inclusive and comprises all sorts of tools, from the very simplest like a toothbrush to the most complicated like B-2 bombers or personal computers. The connection of technology (construed broadly as the resources we employ to bring about change in the world) to culture is important in that it can be one of several levers for change. Although technology thus plays a starring role in producing unsustainability, it can be just as important as a means to create sustainability. This apparent paradox can be resolved by considering how culture affects the way in which we design and use technological artifacts and institutions.

Technology also appears in a second linguistic form: as a way of holding the world. In this manifestation, technology belongs to one category of the structure of culture, or the beliefs we hold. Beliefs are the filters through which we construct meaning out of the incoherent signals with which the world constantly bombards our senses. Technology, in this manifestation, imparts a particular meaning to the world that shapes our experiences and determines how we go about our business, and it profoundly shapes our culture. Technological artifacts always act as filters for worldly phenomena and affect the meaning of the signals we process in our bodies. The world appears different through eyeglasses than it does without—fortunately so, for those with vision shortcomings. The silences between snippets of conversation that impart meaning in face-to-face encounters are taken as a warning of a dropped call when they occur during cell phone conversations, generally diminishing the richness of the interchange.

We have come to know nature as the source of human life both in an evolutionary sense and, more important, as the underlying support system for all forms of life on Earth. The demands that the technologies of modern, industrial societies place on the natural system have now reached a level where these supportive functions of nature, that same hostile nature of old, are feared to be in jeopardy. Technology serves the interests of humans in the positive sense of the Enlightenment, but also erodes the capacity of nature to sustain life. Technology, so it seems, also has a dark side.

But this is not the only way technology affects human life today. The pervasiveness of technology as the primary means of obtaining human satisfaction has a perverse effect on humanity. Great philosophers, psychologists, sociologists, and many others have argued that the essence of humanity is slowly becoming lost, as we turn over more and more of our modes of satisfaction to technology. Humanist philosopher and social psychologist Erich Fromm has argued that we have moved from a "Being" mode of life to a "having" mode of life.[11] Although always accepting that technology comes forth because it has some instrumental capability to do something someone wants to do in ways not known before, or to work much more cheaply or easily, critics such as Fromm see technology as eroding the meaning of what it is to be human. Here technology is not just the "high" technology of computers, automobiles, mobile phones, and the like, but it is a fundamental way humans take up with the world. It is a worldview that sees everything out there as having value only or predominately through its functional (instrumental) purposes. Heidegger called the world framed in this way as "standing reserve."[12] Human beings in such a modern world also take on the shape of utilitarian things, losing the unique capacity we alone possess among all living species—of Being-in-the-world, that is, living meaningful lives. But this modern way of Being is a trap because, in our striving for satisfaction, the predominance of technology stifles the noninstrumental, transcendent characteristics of what it is to be human. We are more than machines existing only to transform the material state of the world. Dignity and autonomy give way to a form of addiction to instrumentality—a machinelike existence—and to its relative, consumption.

A newspaper advertisement for a personal game device, the Nintendo DS, epitomizes this ubiquitous character.[13] Two men wait in a bus kiosk. One is slouched in a corner of the kiosk and is simply gazing out at the world through what appears to be a frown or otherwise unhappy look. The other, sitting upright and with a smile on his face, is playing with his electronic game. The accompanying text reads, "The average wait for a city bus is 12.8 minutes. Do something with your nothing." The implication seems clear. Any time taken merely to capture the world around oneself or to reflect for a moment is time wasted. *New York Times* columnist Tom Friedman told a related story describing a taxi ride from the Paris airport to his hotel.[14]

> After the car started to roll, I saw he had a movie playing on the screen in the dashboard—on the flat panel that usually displays the G.P.S. road map. I noticed this because between his talking on the phone and the movie, I could barely concentrate. I, alas, was in the back seat trying to finish a column on my laptop. When I wrote all that I could, I got out my iPod and listened to a Stevie Nicks album, while he went on talking, driving and watching the movie.
>
> After I arrived at my hotel, I reflected on our trip: The driver and I had been together for an hour, and between the two of us we had been doing six different things. He was driving, talking on his phone and watching a

video. I was riding, working on my laptop and listening to my iPod. There was only one thing we never did: Talk to each other. It's a pity. He was a young, French-speaking African, who probably had a lot to tell me.

I relate all this because it illustrates something I've been feeling more and more lately—that technology is dividing us as much as uniting us. Yes, technology can make the far feel near. But it can also make the near feel very far. For all I know, my driver was talking to his parents in Africa. How wonderful! But that meant the two of us wouldn't talk at all. And we were sitting two feet from each other.

Technology, both its development and its use, today seem to fit a vision of a world where we all go about our business detached, taking on a somewhat godlike nature in the sense that we do not need to be in touch with the things we use. Technology is like a slave—there to obey one's every command even if they are only thoughts. But this doesn't work well, because as such a slave technology lacks the meaning one brings to action. Automatic door openers are a good example. They open whenever one is within the range of the motion detector, whether that person was going to pass through or not. This becomes very distracting and irritating when one is simply waiting to be seated in a crowded restaurant, and the only place to stand is near the automatic door.

Technology has a third characteristic we need to examine. The late philosopher Hans Jonas has argued that modern technology renders ethical action and responsibility problematic.[15] The moral consequences of human action, in the times when notions about responsibility were shaped, always showed up proximately to the action. Ethics were connected to the immediate world of the actor. Responsibility could be defined in practical terms: knowingly avoiding harm. The forms of technology were such that the actors themselves could be expected to know all they needed to know to act in an ethical manner.

But modern technology has completely changed that context. The consequences of action now often take place over long distances and show themselves at much later times. The modern environmental movement got its start when Rachel Carson observed that DDT escaping into the environment was taken up later in avian food chains. Becoming concentrated in the animals at the higher end of the chain, brown pelicans and eagles for example, DDT caused the birds' eggs to become fragile, drastically lowering reproductive success to a point where these species became endangered.

Soldiers, whose knowledge of the actual battlefield comes through dim images on a cathode ray tube, are now fighting wars using radar screens and push buttons far from the scene of the action. The "pilot" flying the unmanned, missile-equipped Predator drone over Afghanistan or Iraq sits far from harm's way in a trailer just outside Las Vegas. The disappearance of the ozone layer was caused by the slow diffusion of chlorofluorocarbons into the stratosphere, where they are broken down and interfere with the process that maintains ozone at the levels that protect the Earth's surface from the sun's harmful ultraviolet radiation. Invented in 1931 by General Motors scientist Thomas Midgely, chlorofluorocarbons were held to be a wonderful new chemical species, displacing much less safe substances as refrigerants and solvents. Fifty-some years later, production of these same substances was banned under the Montreal Protocol.

Today some might argue that such inventions, even with great potential for good, should not be brought to the market if there is any question or doubt about their potential for harm. Given the many instances of unintended consequences such as those produced by chlorofluorocarbons, a new decision framework—the precautionary principle—has taken a place in environmental policy, explicitly in the European Union. But earlier, when the decision was made to market Midgely's new discovery, there was no context for precaution, because connections between chemicals and the environment were poorly understood.

On a more mundane level, consumers using devices like mobile phones or automobiles know virtually nothing about how they work. Modern technology exchanges the practical knowledge of the users for the detached knowledge of a disinterested set of experts. A Roman chariot driver knew all he had to about his machine to use it safely. A driver of a modern automobile knows little about how the whole system works, especially since hidden onboard computers control its key functions. The wells from which the gasoline comes are out of sight. The exhaust that causes global warming is invisible, and the connection between the two is technically so complex that even experts have a difficult time agreeing on the relationship. If and when we become conscious of signs of unsustainability and want to act to remedy the problem, it is virtually impossible to assign or accept responsibility. The Polluter Pays Principle, which underlies much environmental legislation in industrialized countries, attempts to assign responsibility to the "polluter," the agent producing the problem. In principle this seems to make ethical sense, but then who is the polluter—the firm that makes the things that cause pollution, the consumer who uses them, the stores that sell them, the government that permits them to be sold? This confusion is created in part by the unique properties of modern technology that Jonas describes.

The habitual usage of technological devices to solve deep-seated problems also leads to shifting-the-burden and its concomitant loss of responsibility. We hear much today about greening, riding the green wave, ecofriendly solutions, and so on. Virtually all of these are about some new device or practice that lessens the burden on the world. Nothing is really ecofriendly—perhaps some are ecofriendlier, but all human activities affect the environment in one way or another, changing what was the original state. All such actions are quick fixes; they fit the upper loop of the shifting-the-burden archetype, and consequently the problems of unsustainability will ultimately move out of the consciousness of the actors. Awareness that one is part of the problem gets lost. Responsibility for fixing the world will be seen as somebody else's, most likely the government's or some unseen industrial innovator's.

But it is not only technology that erodes responsibility. The dominant idea of a "free market" that maximizes the collective happiness by the working of an invisible hand leaves any moral outcome entirely to chance. One of my favorite quotes comes from American economic historian Robert Heilbroner, who wrote, "A general subordination of action to market forces demotes progress itself from a consciously intended social aim to an unintended consequence of action, thereby robbing it of moral content."[16]

This brief critique of modern life raises serious questions about the way we live in the affluent, technologically modern world. How long can we allow the natural world to become degraded and consumed without acting to avoid serious, untoward consequences? How long can we tolerate the inhumane conditions of the many who live in undignified if not unhealthy conditions in much of the world—and even in our own affluent countries? How long can we ignore our responsibility to them? Given the global interconnectedness of our economic system, do we not share responsibility? Or is it that we just cannot see our responsibility? Even if we tolerate or ignore their condition, can we call our own life sustainable? Questions like these have been raised in the public sphere in every historical era, but at this moment they seem more critical than ever. One reason again falls back on technology. Never before have humans possessed so much power to affect the world and all life forms with both positive and increasingly negative consequences.

These three distinctions—reality, rationality, and technology—are central to culture of modernity. Because they are so familiar and follow us everywhere, we have come to take them for granted as an immutable part of the world in which we live and work. We define ourselves through the way we understand them, and in so doing we create the context in which we act and, secondarily, the consequences of our actions, both intended and unintended. As long as we continue to hold our current beliefs as immutable, we cannot change the basic patterns of life that have become unsustainable. Nor can we make the tangible, material world disappear. We do, however, have power to change what we mean by reality and rationality by adopting a different approach regarding how we perceive worldly phenomena, and then converting our perceptions into action.

Technology, with its material artifacts and tools, is different from reality or rationality. Tools are real in the sense that we can pick them up and use them to change the immediate world to something we envision as missing in the present. Nevertheless, our understanding of what technology is, and the ways we design the tools we use, can be and need to be altered. Technology has led modern societies toward a lost sense of the place of humans within and as a part of nature, a lost understanding of what it is to be a human being, and a lost ethical ability to act responsibly. All three of these consequences are interlinked and must be recovered as stepping-stones toward sustainability.

Chapter 4 Consumption: A Symptom of Addiction

Denial ain't just a river in Egypt.
—*Mark Twain*

Modern living means the consumption of vast quantities of stuff. In the mid 1990s, Americans daily consumed approximately 120 pounds of resources such as coal, oil, metals, stone, and cement—an amount that was just about equal to their average body weight.[1] This statistic does not include the even larger, perhaps tenfold, quantities of wastes resulting from the production of these resources. Nor does it include the air and water used to produce the stuff they consume. For example, the authors of *Stuff* estimate that almost seven hundred gallons of water are required to put a cheeseburger on the table. If all six billion people on our planet consumed the amount of nonrenewable resources at the rate the average American does, about four Earths would be required to provide enough farmland and forests to support us.[2]

One obvious implication of such high levels of consumption is that the burdens placed on the Earth's ecosystem continue to grow and threaten to cause unpredictable consequences. But do we "need" to consume resources at these ever-increasing levels? Once again the answer may largely lie in the technological way of modern life. No matter how many artifacts we acquire to satisfy our needs, we always seem to require more and more, thereby following the patterns of addiction and shifting-the-burden described in previous chapters. But not only manufactured, lifeless artifacts fit this pattern; it also encompasses other human beings that one "acquires" to produce satisfaction.

In an interview British psychologist Oliver James said that "we have become addicted to having rather than being and confusing our needs with our wants." He claimed that consumerism has reached epidemic proportions, leaving "people richer but sadder."[3] An article in the New Yorker magazine accused American consumers of suffering from what it called "feature fatigue," meaning that we run out of patience and return purchases that have features that seemed desirable in the store but that lose their appeal once the package is opened.[4]

In seeking ways to understand this pathology of modern life, I turn again to the world of system dynamics for an answer. Figure 6 is the generic shifting-the-burden diagram redrawn with consumption as its focus. There is something about the way we consume that leaves us unsatisfied (fixes-that-fail) and, worse, that has shifted the burden and, worse still, created addiction. In the hurly-burly modern world we do not give ourselves time to search for the "right" answer to our wants and needs. "Not enough time" and "too busy" are ubiquitous complaints. We tend to follow the advertising messages that are omnipresent and that have just the right answer for whatever it is we think we need.

A few years ago I saw a TV news program reporting on someone's offer on eBay to place an ad on his forehead for thirty days. Curiosity piqued, I went to eBay and entered "forehead" in the search box. I found not just one but at least a dozen similar offers. I expected to find some responses to these and, sure enough, I did. The offer that caught the attention of the news story stood at an astounding bid of $22,000. Is there no place left on Earth without an ad?

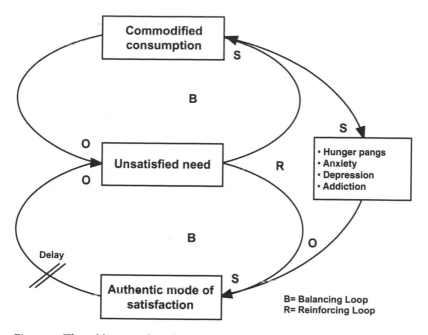

Figure 6. The addiction of modern consumption

AUTHENTICITY AND CHOICE

> Too many of us now worship self-indulgence and consumption. Human
> identity is no longer defined by what one does but by what one owns.
> But we've discovered that owning things and consuming things does not
> satisfy our longing for meaning.
> —*President Jimmy Carter*

The key to understanding the addictive nature of consumption today
is in the two words in Figure 6, *authentic* and *commodified,* though
neither term is used here in its usual sense. (Authenticity is a central
concept in the model that I use to define what it is to be human. I will
elaborate on this in Chapter 10.) Authenticity is related to one's sense
of wholeness and the degree to which the actions being performed
lead toward or away from one's sense of understanding of what it
means to be a human being. Authentic behavior is rare today, because
technology has turned our understanding of Being into an instrumental perspective from which we see the world, including the humans
that dwell therein, merely as standing reserve, waiting to be used for

the task at hand.[5] Inauthentic performance leaves a hole, something unsatisfied even if the task seems to have been successfully executed.

In this context *authentic* is related to the nature of choices one makes. Choice is possibly the most important notion in democratic societies,[6] as it is the essence of freedom in both a political and an economic context. Choice is related to the idea of free will, defined by René Descartes as "the ability to do or not do something."[7] Today, free will is generally accepted as a fundamental feature of the human self. The choice that Descartes poses is governed by the rationality of the mind. The utilitarians of the Enlightenment who constructed the moral philosophy that underpins our liberal (market-oriented, private) political economy claimed that the more choice available to human actors, subject only to moral restrictions on action, the better their lives would be.

Free will is, however, one of the problematic, perhaps even mistaken, beliefs of modernity that ultimately fuel the fires of consumption. Heidegger claims that actions follow from one's immersion in a culture that socializes individuals to relate to the immediate world according to their historical experience, rather than from some context-free and autonomous choice. Choices are more akin to habits. Unless the actor understands the process and "chooses" it over the idea that the "free self" is at work, the resultant choice of action is inauthentic and lacks meaningfulness for the actor. The more that choice is propelled by social forces, such as advertising and peer pressure, the less authentic the action will be, and the less satisfaction will show up at the root of Being.[8]

> You never know what is enough, unless you know what is more than enough.
> —*William Blake,* Proverbs of Hell

So far I have been arguing that the nature of technological delivery of satisfaction has led to two primary signs of unsustainability: excessive and threatening (to nature) levels of consumption and erosion of the core of Being (the meaning of being human). But there is another pathology buried in the way we consume that leads to domination—another source of unsustainability. The extraordinary number of choices available to consumers, especially in the United States, may not be the much-touted liberating means it is claimed to be. Consumer choice is constrained by the number of options available and the amount of money a consumer has to make purchases. I will focus on the former but will first make a few observations on the latter.

Many studies have shown that affluence beyond some point does not correlate with assessments of happiness or with other subjective measures related to well-being. This applies both to a single nation as well as comparisons across nations. In 1974 economist Richard Easterlin published his article titled, "Does Economic Growth Improve the Human Lot?"[9] He answered in the negative, and economists have been arguing about it ever since.

Barry Schwartz, a psychologist at Swarthmore College, has studied choice as the driver of freedom and self-determination. Schwartz claims that too much freedom (as choice), autonomy, or self-determination has negative and self-defeating effects and can become transformed to a kind of tyranny—just the opposite of what these attributes are supposed to produce.[10] For example, he cites a study concluding that shoppers prefer fewer rather than more choices for any particular product. Procter & Gamble saw sales increase by 10 percent after the company reduced the number of variations of one of its shampoos from twenty-six to ten. In another article he ticked off a list of items with "mind-boggling choices. . . . Eighty-five types of crackers. Two hundred eighty-five types of cookies. Eighty pain relievers. Thousands of mutual funds. Hundreds of cell phones, dozens of calling plans."[11]

I carried out an unplanned, one-person version of this test in my local supermarket. I went to buy a small container of yogurt and was so daunted by the more than one hundred different varieties that I decided to move on. There were yogurts with fruit on the bottom, fruit on the top, and fruit all over; low-fat and no-fat yogurts; yogurts of countless different flavors; and more. During a year we lived in the Netherlands, my wife and I noticed a great difference in the number of choices between the supermarkets there and those in the United States. For us, shopping in Europe was more comfortable than shopping here; although we had significantly fewer choices in the Netherlands, we never felt any loss of our autonomy or ability for self-expression.

Schwartz comes to the same conclusion as others studying the relationship between consumption (as a proxy for freedom and self-determination) and well-being: at some point increases in well-being slow down and reverse, leading to rising levels of clinical depression and falling or stagnant numbers in subjective surveys of satisfaction. His theory is that the sheer number of options overwhelms our cognitive mechanisms of rational choice. In the sense of the systems archetypes, this is another case of (quick) fixes that fail and, ultimately, of addiction. The quick fix here is embodied in the libertarian mantra that more and more choice, without the intervention of the regulative hand of government, is always better. Schwartz is a serious scholar, but it seems to me it doesn't take an academic to point out the signs of individual breakdowns all around, putting the central theme of the libertarian, free-market ideology in question.

Fromm extends Schwartz's critique from the effects on the individual to the societal scale.[12] Trying in the early part of the twentieth century to understand the rise of fascism, Fromm argued that freeing a society from the binding relationships that historically have provided them security produces the perverse, ironic effect of making the society more willing to accept tyrannical governments.

COMMODIFICATION

> Just as modern mass production requires the standardization of commodities, so the social process requires standardization of man . . ."
> —*Erich Fromm, The Art of Loving*

To understand commodification, I turn to the work of Albert Borgmann, a German-born American philosopher whose magnum opus, *Technology and the Character of Contemporary Life*, is a stunning, albeit dense, critique of the impact that modern technological products and services have had on human beings.[13] Borgmann argues that the artifacts and processes we employ for fulfilling our needs have taken on the nature of "devices" delivering commodities toward satisfying needs. The simplest way of thinking about a commodity is that it is "what a device is for." For example, a car is for providing transportation, and a furnace is for providing heat. Innovations in a device change its form, but the commodity tends to remain the same. Moreover, a commodity is something that can be consumed without regard to the device. Instant messaging is such a commodity. It is the same whether delivered by any of the many cell phone models or by a home computer. The cell phone may offer more convenience, but the commodity is the same.

One of Borgmann's examples is a cartoon about a couple shopping for their Christmas dinner. Standing by the frozen food section, the wife, holding up two boxes and apparently a bit puzzled, turns to her husband and asks, "For the big day, Harv, which do you want? The traditional American Christmas turkey dinner with mashed potatoes, giblet gravy, oyster dressing, cranberry sauce and tiny green peas or the old English Christmas goose dinner with chestnut stuffing, boiled potatoes, Brussels sprouts and plum pudding?"[14] Borgmann noted that Harv "looks a bit skeptical and morose. The world of bountiful harvests, careful preparations, and festive meals has become a faint and ironical echo. . . . The content, even when warmed and served, is a sharply reduced aspect of the once full-bodied affair."

What has happened to the notion of family and the process of being together associated with more traditional ways of getting ready for an event like Thanksgiving or Christmas? Harv's quandary points to the gap between our actions and what Borgmann calls our "values." Our actions do not correspond to what we seek in life. This term *values* is as elusive for me as is the concept of *need,* which I will explore later. Langdon Winner, another critic of modern technology, has pointed out the inadequacy of this term, noting that values is a useful catchall term for "cares, commitments, responsibilities, preferences, tastes, religious convictions, personal aspirations, and so forth."[15] I believe that all of these collapse into the notion of Being, which frames much of this book. All are manifestations of our humanness.

As Borgmann speaks of them, devices are means that fit into the upper loop. They handle the symptoms of our human needs for satisfaction in many domains but fail to address who we are in the process. Indeed it is the process, the relationships, and the experience itself that are essential elements of authentic human satisfaction. Borgmann does not believe the separation of means (the device) from the ends (the commodity) is all that positive in terms of its impact on human Being. The device becomes invisible and fades into the background along with any of the context associated with it. There is nothing present other than the commodified delivery of the fix. Addicts sometimes describe the experience that follows injection of any powerful drug as supremely narcissistic; they completely retreat from the world and into themselves. All sense of Being in a world disappears and with it any opportunity for reflection and presence. Whatever satisfaction gained is fleeting and lasts only until the user/consumer picks up the next device and awaits the commodity it is supposed to deliver.

CONSUMPTION AS SHIFTING-THE-BURDEN

> Many of the commonest assumptions, it seems to me, are arbitrary ones: that the new is better than the old, the untried superior to the tried, the complex more advantageous than the simple, and the fast quicker than the slow, the big greater than the small, and the world as remodeled by Man the Architect functionally sounder and more agreeable than the world as it was before he changed everything to suit his vogues and his conniptions.
> —*E. B. White, "Coon Tree,"* The Essays of E. B. White

Figure 6 illustrates the addictive pattern of this form of consumption. Addiction is, by definition, something bad and always means some loss of function or capability. In 1997 the television documentary *Affluenza* introduced a new term regarding the consumptive pattern of the United States. The originators of the film, KCTS/Seattle and Oregon Public Broadcasting, offer this somewhat facetious, but all too true definition:

> *Af-flu-en-za* n. 1. The bloated, sluggish and unfulfilled feeling that results from one's efforts to keep up with the Joneses.
> 2. An epidemic of stress, overwork, shopping and indebtedness caused by the dogged pursuit of the American Dream.
> 3. An unsustainable addiction to economic growth.
> 4. A television program that could change your life[16]

Although addiction is not good for the user, it is not so bad for those who supply the devices, whether they are controlled drugs, cell phones, or fast food. The scandal of the tobacco industry revolved about the issue of addiction and the efforts of those in the industry to hide their knowledge of their product's addictive power.

The point here, however, is that not just a few products and services have obviously addictive outcomes. Rather, independent of the particular device, commodified technological consumption as a ubiquitous cultural mode is fundamentally addictive. The capability being eroded lies at the very core of being human. In the human domain of sustainability, the most important task ahead is to reconstitute the human being from all of the pieces into which modernity has broken us. We must do what Lewis Carroll thought impossible: put Humpty-Dumpty back together again.

Commodified consumption does not always produce addiction. It can stop short and lead merely to shifting-the-burden. Perhaps that is better than becoming addicted, but it still causes undesirable consumption of material goods. This is shown as well in the central box in Figure 6, "unsatisfied need," often expressed as some problem to solve. A business example of this would be backlogs in order fulfillment. An example in private life is the desire for love. The upper loop represents the easy way toward satisfying this desire. In the business example, this might take the form of a manager stepping in and doing the job. In the second, it might be going on the Web and finding someone who is also looking for love. But in both cases, the problem or desire is not likely to go away no matter how many times one goes around the loop. The reason is simple: neither of these solutions produces authentic satisfaction, that is, makes the problem go away or fulfill the emptiness in a meaningful way. Each one simply treats the symptoms. Worse, they divert the actors from seeking fully satisfying solutions.

It is important to distinguish between these pathologies and repeated actions that actually work and produce the desired results so that the actor is authentically satisfied. These successful routines, or habits, are the fundamental evidence of *culture*, meaning observed behavioral patterns repeated over time and space. On the one hand, habits are the foundation of living successfully, but on the other they can slip into ineffectualness and pathology. One of the most important challenges for sustainability is the redesign of cultural underpinnings (the structure that shapes habits) such that actors will become more conscious of the "success" of their acts and move toward authentic choices when they find themselves slipping into the unsustainable patterns of addiction and shifting-the-burden.

The lower loop in the diagram represents just such an authentic path toward satisfaction, in which the underlying causes of the problem are addressed. In the case of poor performance in the order-taking department, the effective way might be to provide skills training for the staff so that their competence to complete the job matches the challenge. In seeking love, this might require much more work—the first step being to shift the whole notion of what love is all about. Love is one of those "things" that Fromm claims we now seek to *have* instead of to *be*. Because objective reality tends to turn common activities into objects, actions like loving have been reified, and consequently we believe we can acquire them. Such reification is so common today that I guarantee that everybody would be amazed by just how many of the "things" they talk about have no material reality at all. One simple test is to ask yourself if you could gather a bucketful of whatever it is you are speaking about. If the answer is no, then you are talking about something that does not have material reality and cannot be acquired in the same way that one buys an automobile or a pair of shoes. Sustainability is clearly something that one cannot gather in a bucket.

Love is also something that cannot be acquired, and so attempts to find it as an object are not likely to work. Love is found through loving, the set of actions that create a special kind of satisfaction in an ongoing relationship, and not mere feelings that disappear in the morning after a brief encounter with another human who is hungry for love as well. Loving takes commitment and much more; it is hard work, and the results do not often show up immediately. Neither does the outcome of personnel training. In most cases, the problem or the hunger persists for a while and the results of taking the path in the lower loop are delayed. The tendency in impatient, instant-gratification modern settings is usually to shrug one's shoulders and continue to pursue the symptom-relieving pathway, reinforcing the pattern.

My sense of the futility of pursuing meaningful relationships via technology was supported by a story in the *New York Times* about a large drop in usage of Internet dating services. Although some people reported successful outcomes, many who had abandoned this route complained that the matches simply did not produce the fullness needed for more intimate and lasting relationships. Something is missing from the system. Having been happily wedded for many years, I am certainly not one to offer a grounded comment to those still seeking a companion, but I suspect that it takes real people in real settings to work. Relationship is more than matching a set of profiles. The article makes the same point: "Many early adopters [of online services] . . . are moving on to the next big thing, which looks a lot like the last things on the dating front: bars, real-life matching services, setups arranged by friends."[17]

Another feature of contemporary life in America is the pervasiveness of fear, as was featured in filmmaker Michael Moore's provocative documentary *Bowling for Columbine*. Moore suggests that this is a characteristic unique to the United States. Fear is an assessment made when one feels unsafe. One result of a context of fear is that people seek to acquire safety, just like love, through having more devices, like guns and gated communities. But these "solutions" follow the upper loop and can only lead to an addictive pattern requiring more and more devices and resulting in less and less safety. Real safety can come only from a fundamental cultural shift that addresses whatever is causing the undesired symptoms.

The failure to find authentic satisfaction may be one of the root causes of our society's relentless preoccupation with speed. If one reads the tea leaves of popular culture, faster is almost always thought to be better. We cannot wait until the next model of a cell phone or computer hits the market. Items such as shoes that were once prized for durability now need to be replaced twice a year simply to keep up with the Joneses or to emulate one athletic icon or another. Automobiles are replaced long before they wear out. In some cases, one can make an economic argument that it is better to replace an aging item than to pay the costs to maintain it, but in most cases it is just impatience and boredom that lead to more consumption. The underlying cultural assumption in the United States that freedom is equivalent to choice in the marketplace certainly exacerbates this pattern of behavior. Even if whatever one has purchased does lead to satisfaction, isn't it good for our inner selves to get another one with more bells and whistles? Nowhere was this belief clearer than in President George W. Bush's "shopping solution" to the shock of 9/11.

Bush was, perhaps, unconsciously echoing an older theme about the centrality of consumption to the U.S. economy. Some fifty years ago economist Victor Lebow wrote, "Our enormously productive economy demands that we make consumption our way of life, that we convert the buying and use of goods into rituals, that we seek our spiritual satisfaction, our ego satisfaction, in consumption. . . . We need things consumed, burned up, worn out, replaced, and discarded at an ever-increasing pace."[18] If these words were true then, imagine the implications of an economy many times more productive.

There is virtually no patience left in the modern consumer world. And without patience there is no accepting that the fundamental satisfaction pathway almost always takes time to show results. In earlier times, when few devices (in Borgmann's sense) were available, people had no choice but to keep trying and to wait. The fundamental nature of competitive and open markets itself supports the addiction. Advertisements argue that satisfaction needs more and newer commodities. Like love, beauty is another reification; one cannot bring home beauty in a bucket. But as long as one is bombarded with messages that beauty can be had (*things* again), it is very difficult not to try to acquire whatever is said to produce it.

With this brief discussion of consumption, the answer should be apparent regarding the earlier question about the connection between this persistent outcome of current societal patterns of consumption and sustainability. Consumption keeps rising because the goods and services we purchase simply do not produce authentic satisfaction. We live in the upper loop every day. Our economy is predicated on ever-increasing output of material-based consumption. Our predilection to *having* (in Fromm's sense) even those non-things like love keeps us locked in the addictive pattern of the upper loop. We can never be satisfied. Authentic satisfaction, however, does not mean that our needs disappear. We must always feed our bodies. Our close relationships must be nurtured continuously. Our basic concerns persist. But what can happen is that the incessant seeking of commodified, technological—that is, material-oriented—solutions diminishes so that we can move on to address and fulfill other domains. Hopefully, in a sustainable world we will find that many concerns can be satisfied without material consumption.

Unsustainability is not caused just by the increasing consumption of stuff; it is the addictive patterns underlying that consumption. And it is the erosion of our capacity to move out of the upper loop so that we can begin to attack the root causes. We certainly need to do a better job of producing stuff that uses less energy and less material, but that approach is merely a temporary patch—a quick fix.

It should also be clear by now that producing sustainability will require a radical shift in our culture. We simply cannot again fall back on the optimism and teleology of modernity. New habits must replace the old; we cannot live successfully without habits, but if we are careful these new habits should be able to avoid the pathology of shifting-the-burden and addiction for a long and flourishing period.

Chapter 5 A Radical Notion of Sustainability

The same stream of life that runs through my veins night and day
runs through the world and dances in rhythmic measures.

It is the same life that shoots in joy through the dust of the earth in
numberless blades of grass and breaks into the tumultuous waves of
leaves and flowers.

It is the same life that is rocked in the ocean-cradle of birth and of
death, in ebb and flow.

I feel my limbs are made glorious by the touch of this world of life.
And my pride is from the life-throb of ages dancing in my blood this
moment.

—*Rabindranath Tagore,* Songs of Kabir

Missing almost completely from the problem-oriented activities of today is a vision of a world that is sustainable—even a definition of sustainability is missing. No wonder that we move forward only occasionally, instead drifting mostly sideways or backward. Perhaps it is because the very distinction, sustainability, is fuzzy and linguistically complex. Is it a property of a system? Perhaps, but even then one would need more information to understand its meaning. What is it about the system that is being sustained? For how long? Considered as a property, sustainability, like all "-ities," is not very satisfying. One always needs some other criteria to decide how much of the "-ity" is there. What makes flexibility flexible? The "-ities" almost always start as coined words describing some qualitative property of a system. Later our modern way of thinking reifies these terms and converts them into quantities we can measure and, ultimately, try to manage. The "-ities" are the reified aftereffects of qualitative assessments that have become so familiar that they seem to be things. It is not only the "-ities" that have become reified; many important qualities, such as love and happiness, also have become frozen and objectlike.

Even vision—foresight—has taken on thinglike properties. We now routinely create visions in formulaic processes as part of common strategic planning procedures. George H. W. Bush talked about the "vision thing" in this way. How can we avoid the same fate for sustainability? It is too important to be put into the same category as the other "-ities." To be a powerful force for redesigning the present, hurting world, sustainability needs to avoid becoming just another thing to measure and manage, and instead become a word that will bring forth an image of the world as we would hope it to be.

DEFINING SUSTAINABILITY

> Happiness is the absence of the striving for happiness.
> —*Zhuang Zhou*

I define sustainability as the *possibility* that humans and other life will *flourish* on the Earth *forever*. You will notice some circularity here since I use one "-ity" to define another. But *possibility* is perhaps the only "-ity" that cannot be made into a thing. It is just the opposite: possibility is *no-thing*. Possibility has no material existence in the world of the present. Possibility is always only a word. It means bringing forth from nothingness something we desire to become present. Possibility may be the most powerful word in our language because it enables humans to visualize and strive for a future that neither is available in the present nor may have existed in the past. Possibility is like a time warp, allowing one to escape from the limits of our past experience into an unshackled future. One might interpret Ortega y Gasset's words from Chapter 1 as the essence of possibility.

There is no plural for possibility as defined here; the idea of possibilities (plural) is a manifestation of the reification of which I just spoke. Most talk about possibilities in common conversation is better couched in terms of probabilities, the chances that something missing at the moment will show up in the next. In this way of thinking, the idea of chance suggests that the future, even if uncertain, is tied to the past. Even the concept of future is flawed. Our way of thinking about time has us believing that we can create it like the next frame in a motion picture. Of course, that is not so; we live only in the present. The past is nothing more than a story we tell ourselves about what has happened, incorporating everything we have ever experienced or heard about.

When one holds the idea of possibility as I have described it, future is a different concept. Future in this mode of living is a story of what one would want based on what has yet to be satisfied. Philosopher and sociologist Alfred Schutz wrote, "Our actions are conscious if we have previously mapped them out 'in future perfect tense.' "[1] Future is the possibility out of which one lives and acts in the present. The future as possibility arises and transforms your Being now. Aliveness shows up when future is a possibility coming from nothingness. And what is a better image of being alive than flourishing? Flourishing is the metaphor that brings life to this definition of sustainability and enables everybody to create their own image of what their flourishing world would be. Flourishing does not collapse into a thing or numerical measure of well-being to be managed.

Every culture and every age have conjured up images and sounds of flourishing. Even the ancient Greeks had a word for what I have called sustainability: *aephoria,* which is derived from *ae,* meaning forever, and *phoria,* meaning to bear fruit or to flourish. Flourishing is behind the acts and lives of great leaders like Gandhi, King, and Mandela. Flourishing is in the poetry of William Blake and e. e. cummings. It appears every time an infant first smiles. It unfolds in the blooming of a rose. It comes in the taste of water from a country spring or after a deep breath in the forest. All humans have had at least a moment when their senses revealed flourishing, but all too few live in circumstances where those precious moments reemerge over and over.

For living species other than humans, flourishing is about survival and maintenance of their species. It might mean more, but we cannot access the thoughts of these other species to discover what they are thinking. If we could, I imagine they would be speaking about air, soil, trees, water, or roses in much the same way we would talk about our place in the world. But flourishing means more to human beings. Human flourishing goes beyond our sense of belonging to and thriving in the natural world. It also involves the attainment of a few very special qualities that have come to be recognized as constituting our species as different from these other life forms. Hans Christian Anderson said, "Just living is not enough. . . . One must have sunshine, freedom, and a little flower."

Dignity is one of these qualities. The earliest philosophers recognized dignity as something special and essential to the "good" life. Speaking of the good life is another way of talking about flourishing peculiar to the human species and our own unique way of Being. Dignity is about living one's life according to one's values, free from domination. Dignity often manifests itself in negative situations, however, when one is forced into ways that belie those values. History is full of stories about people who have found dignity among the worst of dominating circumstances. Nelson Mandela survived decades of incarceration but emerged whole. But a world that requires everyone to become a Mandela certainly could not go by the name of sustainable. Social critics like Lewis Mumford have spoken eloquently of the danger that technology may erode dignity.[2] Jokes about the demeaning process of programming a VCR make light of the loss of dignity that technology can and does cause. The cultural voices impinging on our ears shout that we need more and more technology even as we feel a more than vague sense of loss. There is a strange sense of inevitability that drags us along.

Flourishing also consists of other distinctions of human origin that relate to the collective state. Justice, fairness, and equity come from our historical sense that flourishing has to do with more than our own selfish attainments. We accept, but fail to act accordingly, that there is a social dimension to living that recognizes in some way that all humans are interconnected and that the state of our individual lives is tied to the states of others with whom we share our only world.[3] Exploring these aspects of flourishing is the subject of philosophers and theologians. Even in a postmodern world, where many believe we cannot

Table 3. Maslow's attributes of Being

Attribute	Detail
Wholeness	Unity, structure
Perfection	Just-right-ness, suitability, completeness
Completion	Justice. Fulfillment
Justice	Fairness, oughtness
Aliveness	Spontaneity, non-deadness
Richness	Complexity, intricacy
Simplicity	Honesty, nakedness, essentiality
Beauty	Rightness, perfection, honesty
Goodness	Rightness, oughtness, honesty
Uniqueness	Individuality. Novelty
Effortlessness	Ease, absence of striving
Playfulness	Fun, joy, humor, exuberance, effortlessness
Truth, honesty, reality	Nakedness, simplicity, purity
Self-sufficiency	Autonomy (but not being alone in the world)

ground the meaning of these qualities on any absolute foundations, we still accept that they are critical to flourishing.

I have focused on the developed world in this discussion of flourishing, but I believe it also applies to the rest of the world as well, with these exceptions. Clearly those humans who do not have enough to eat, or who suffer from endemic illness, or who are forced to lead undignified lives, do not flourish. But poverty alone, as a relative measure, is not a barrier to flourishing.

The eminent psychologist Abraham Maslow turned to an examination of Being in his later years after establishing a seminal foundation for "need." Maslow's discussion of Being has the sense of flourishing that I portray here.[4] Table 3 presents his attributes. The items in the table can help reveal the presence of flourishing amid everyday activities.

I have been purposely vague in defining the attributes of flourishing. One reason is that flourishing is technically an emergent property of a complex living system. Such properties, like beauty, always emerge within the context of the observers or actors in the system and take on characteristics determined by that context. A second, related reason is that flourishing is treated differently by many of the disciplines that make up the humanities, the study of what makes us human as opposed to mere animals. Psychologists such as Maslow look for the kinds of signs shown in Table 3. Phenomenologists such as Heidegger probe the unique ontology of humans. We shall see that his primary tie to flourishing is the authentic satisfaction of a set of cares for oneself, other human beings, and rest of the world. Spiritual leaders offer very similar sets of attributes.

Rabbi Michael Lerner, writing from his concern for one of the fundaments of Judaism, *Tikkun Olam* (healing the world), offers the following description of what I would call flourishing: "Recognize that people hunger for a world that has meaning and love; for a sense of aliveness, energy, and authenticity; for a life embedded in a community in which they are valued for who they most deeply are, with all their warts and limitations, and feel genuinely seen and recognized; for a sense of contributing to the good; and for a life that is about something more than just money and accumulating material goods."[5] My point is that flourishing is the subject of the most central thinking of scholars and the public about what it is to be human. I believe that the vision of flourishing is the most basic foundation of human striving and, if properly articulated, can be the strongest possible driver toward sustainability.

Adding "forever" to this definition lends it the timelessness that is found in virtually all conversations about sustainability. Sustainable development is based on the idea that our generation's use of the resources left to us by our forebears will not compromise the ability of future generations to meet their needs. But is this not just a more complicated and indirect way of saying that flourishing is something that should go on forever? Sustainability makes little sense except as an everlasting condition. For those who would quibble with the use of "forever" as unrealistic or naïve in the face of evolutionary changes, and with the ultimate heat death of the world predicted by thermodynamics, its use here is connotative and metaphoric. It means simply that our actions need take account of the future in a meaningful way beyond the mere discounting of some economic calculus.

Consider again this definition: *Sustainability is the possibility that humans and other life will flourish on the Earth forever.* Doesn't this way of speaking raise a very different image and feeling from the notion of sustainable development? It doesn't say much about how to get there and it doesn't say how we will ever know that we are indeed there. Sustainability is only a powerful vision humans can use, individually and collectively, to design the world in which they live and act so that the possibility of flourishing is never closed off. As long as the door to the future remains open, even if only by a small crack, then that possibility exists.

But, as I have noted, our conversations about sustainability almost always take a negative tone. We can recognize many unsustainable aspects of the way we live in today's world. We can measure unsustainability and, through modern science, can even make predictions about it. And because we can observe unsustainability, we believe that we can make the world sustainable merely by mitigating or removing the conditions that cause it. This approach is like the story told about a fledgling artist with an assignment to make a horse out of a large piece of marble. After much struggle about how to start, she asked her master for advice. The response was, "Just remove everything that is not a horse." Having no idea of what a horse should look like in stone, the apprentice was just as stymied as before. The same goes for sustainability; without a vision, removing what is not sustainable will not work.

Not surprisingly, virtually all suggestions by the most powerful institutions of the modern world for solving the sustainability problem involve technology in some way or another. This is a great error and a sign of our unconsciousness and cultural immersion in modernity. Sustainability is *not* the obverse of unsustainability. They are not just two sides of the same coin. They are categorically different. And, as I have already said, reducing one does not automatically produce the other. Unsustainability is real and tangible and can be sensed, measured, and reduced to theory. Flourishing is real, although it may take metaphors to bring it to our consciousness. It is a qualitative, linguistic construction that describes the emergent properties of a living system as a whole. But sustainability is not real in the same sense. As noted above, flourishing, whenever we may see it in the moment, could also be found in the next moment, and the next, and on and on forever. Sustainability is a container for the highest set of human aspirations and associated cultural values.

From time to time psychology shifts away from its roots in explaining behavioral abnormalities and toward the positive. Maslow turned from a focus on deficiency and need to a positive psychology of Being, recognizing the presence of what he (and others) called peak experiences.[6] Since about 2000, psychologists have become explicit about examining life through a positive lens, calling their work positive psychology.[7] I found the title of the introduction to the book just cited particularly relevant: "Human Flourishing—The Study of That Which Makes Life Worthwhile."

I add this reference here for several purposes. I believe that flourishing is not definable or measurable in the sense that scientists ascribe to the objects they study. To me, flourishing is the emergence of a set of desirable, healthy qualities from one's Being in the world, simply living every day. One of several recurrent themes in the text cited just above is that of "flow." Flow is a condition in which an actor becomes deeply engaged in some activity and experiences a sense of fulfillment and deep satisfaction. By pointing to this particular field within a major social science, I argue that flourishing is not some mere philosophical curiosity nor idle dreaming. Distinctions, such as "positive psychology," that name a field aiming to understand how to produce flourishing are evidence per se of a collective awareness that this quality is generally missing in mainstream cultural life. (The idea of engagement, or involvement, will reenter the discussion of everyday products and artifacts in later chapters.) I have already argued that the particular form of technology that has emerged in our modern era produces opposite effects: alienation from the world and self, and loss of ethical competence.

In the title of this chapter I describe sustainability as radical. In terms of exceeding the norms of sustainable development, it certainly is radical. Its ontology is strange. It is far different from sustainable development. It raises political issues. But another meaning of radical without such political overtones fits this definition of sustainability. The etymology of "radical" is closely tied to the meaning of "root." In this sense sustainability is radical but related to the sense that we have become separated from our human and natural roots and need to find our way back.

ARE ALL SPECIES EQUAL?

In defining sustainability as the possibility that *humans and other life* will flourish on the planet forever, I have introduced a number of philosophical and moral questions. And because of the philosophical and moral nature of humans, there is room for different interpretations and beliefs. It is important to understand the context out of which this definition arises. Central to the notion of sustainability is that the human species is merely a single species among the millions that populate the Earth and form a complex ecosystem that supports the biological survival of all. (I claim this last sentence to be true as a fact, not as a statement of the value of any particular species.) This argument does not presuppose that all species live forever either. It is consistent with a dynamic, evolving world where species emerge and disappear. Other than the human species, the evolutionary process seems immune to any species' superiority and right to exist at the expense of any other. But clearly some do dominate others and maintain themselves while others wither and disappear.

Only the human species, with its unique cognitive and linguistic capability, has invented the notion of rights or superiority. Again this is a fact and must be reckoned within any discussion of biological survival. The very existence of a conversation about survival or flourishing derives from human speakers and their concerns about such survival or flourishing. This conversation, by the very nature of language, is subjective, focused on the speakers as distinct entities. And being subjective, the conversation is likely to make comparisons to other living entities and to assess how they impact the humans' survival. But being subjective and immersed in the linguistic context of being, the human speakers tend to lose sight of the fact that they are also part of the living system and depend on it.

If we overlook this dual place for us in the world, we are likely to make errors in our efforts to protect ourselves from natural phenomena that are threatening, or to produce outcomes we believe are going to produce satisfaction, the good life, and all other normative aspects of human Being. We do and will continue to ask whether we are more valuable than other species. We certainly do this implicitly when we use them in a positive sense in our daily life. And we do this in a negative sense when we seek to destroy or isolate ourselves from those species we deem to have pathological impacts, whether they are viruses or man-eating tigers.

The definition of sustainability presented here does not presuppose any absolute scale of importance, including one where all species are deemed to be equal. But since only humans can express the idea of sustainability, I take it for granted that it is self-referential, and some judgment will be made. How that judgment is to be made and by what criteria is a matter of argument. My own way of dealing with the arguments of those who take the polar positions of anthropocentric and biocentric bases for choice is that neither can be proven to be correct and that the pragmatic choice is somewhere in between. I think sustainability as flourishing can come forth even if, for example, we as a dominating species wipe out pathogens.

When it comes to other species that are part of the world but that seemingly serve no instrumental end for humans nor are pathogenic, my response is pragmatic. Believing that the world is a complex system in that it behaves in strange and unpredictable ways, I would assert that prudence is a critical value in making choices that affect the place of species. What is important to our own sustainability is that the whole system flourish. It cannot when our species acts as the often-destructive force it has become. Ecosystems can survive when perturbed, but only by so much. Since we don't really know how much is too much, it again seems prudent to move slowly and observe the results before continuing to plunge blindly forward.

If this pragmatic model is unsatisfying and begs the question of who makes decisions about human encroachment of natural habitats, I would again invoke prudence and precaution and argue we should move very slowly, if at all, to continue to displace species from their habitats. There is plenty of Earth we have already damaged enough to threaten our own culture. This condition leads to a key challenge to the technological modern world: how to maintain the mode of living under this constraint. I am not at all confident it can be done, but that seems to be the most likely way to balance the problematic choice of sustaining flourishing in both the natural world and our human cultures.

I also leave the issue of pathogenic species unresolved. The definition here is not intended to be a philosophical conclusion, following a set of questions about man, nature, or deep ecology. It is rather a vision of the kind of future to which our species can aspire, and that can draw humankind forward day after day toward that vision. It may be that flourishing will involve a conversation about conflicts among living species, but that possibility should not significantly reduce the power of this way of talking, especially when contrasted to the limits of sustainable development as a call to action.

Chapter 6 The Tao of Sustainability

Ours is a culture based on excess, on overproduction; the result is a steady loss of sharpness in our sensory experience. All the conditions of modern life—its material plenitude, its sheer crowdedness—conjoin to dull our sensory faculties. And it is in the light of the condition of our senses or capacities (rather than those of another age) that the task of a critic must be assessed.

What is important now is to recover our senses. We must learn to *see* more, to *hear* more, to *feel* more.
—*Susan Sontag,* Against Interpretation

Flourishing can occur only if we pay close attention to the three critical domains that the forces of modernity have dimmed:

- Our sense of ourselves as human beings: the human domain.
- Our sense of our place in the [natural] world: the natural domain.
- Our sense of doing the right thing: the ethical domain.

These three domains form a set of overlapping fields that underlie any activity designed to produce sustainability (Figure 7).

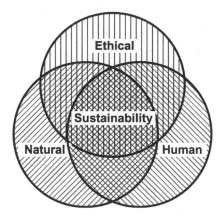

Figure 7. The Tao of sustainability

Sustainability can emerge only if we address all three domains simultaneously. Preserving nature will not suffice if we lose our human distinctiveness in the process, and vice versa. And without taking responsibility for our actions, attaining sustainability would be highly improbable if not impossible. Sustainability is an emergent property of a complex system; we can observe it only if all the relationships on which it depends are functioning correctly.

The first two areas of concern are obvious components of flourishing. Sustainability has emerged in public discourse largely because ecological upsets have become explicitly threatening, and this awareness has been followed by attention being paid to subsequent effects on the social and economic spheres. Many of the threats have come unexpectedly, often in spite of our efforts to avoid them. We will have to address the natural domain directly with new forms of production and strong constraints over the consumptive patterns that now characterize all affluent and rapidly developing economies. Reducing consumption by some factor X, where X ranges from 4 to 50 depending on the writer's calculus, is necessary in the short run but cannot work forever and may even fool us into thinking that we have our arms around the "real" problem.

The second domain relates to the human dimension of flourishing. For human beings, flourishing means that everyone on the planet must be free and able to lead dignified, authentic lives. Being free means more than simply being able to make choices in the marketplace or even at the polling booth. It means that these choices must be unconstrained and domination-free. The results of the choices should lead to authentic satisfaction and the quenching of the momentary thirst for whatever motivated the choice. My intention of presenting a framework for sustainability in this way is to make the human dimension explicit. It is only indirectly and imperfectly captured in the everyday sense of sustainable development. Focusing on the human is not the same as the emphasis on the "social" as expressed in the usual definition of sustainable development. Although taking care of nature is imperative and has been the primary motivating force for action, it is just as critical to include action toward the human dimension of sustainability. Sustainability is an existential problem, not an environmental or social one. In fact, in the course of working on this book I have become all the more convinced of the primacy of restoring the human dimension. I believe that we cannot and will not begin to take care of the world until we become whole ourselves.

The third domain is not so apparent. In the United States and other modern democracies, we live under a rule of law. Ethical issues are important in almost all aspects of daily life. Historians argue that the most important legacies from the Greco-Roman roots of our civilization are the moral and ethical teachings from that past. What, then, is missing? One critical aspect related to this historical cultural sense of ethics is responsibility, the idea of being accountable for one's actions, especially the act of avoiding harm knowingly. Modern technological life has diminished the ability to know the consequences of actions taken by individuals or by collective social entities, because those consequences are often displaced in time and space, and as such have made responsibility problematic. One result is the emergence of unintended consequences, which have become a characteristic feature of modernity.[1] If we do not take this domain into account in designing a new, sustainable world, our efforts are ultimately likely to exhibit the same kind of unforeseen outcomes that diminish or negate our original intentions. Ethics is a human construction and, as such, belongs inherently within the human category. I have, however, assigned it a domain of its own because ethical responsibility is critical in creating sustainability. Ethics belongs to one of the three root domains of care: taking care of others. The other areas in the Tao are congruent with the other two domains: taking care of self and nature.

> [I]t becomes increasingly evident that neither famine, nor earthquakes, nor microbes, nor cancer, but man, is the greatest danger to man . . .
> —*Carl Jung*, The Psychology of C. G. Jung

These three aspects of sustainability form a new framework for the redesign of tools, physical infrastructure, and social institutions that can restore our consciousness, thereby enabling us to continue our deliberate transformation of our way of living from its unsustainable path to one that allows the vision of flourishing to bloom. Awakened consciousness can increase the likelihood that our designs will work the way we intend them to and also help us identify the causes of our problems.

I use *causes* in the plural sense, following Aristotle's identification of four separate categories of cause. One of Aristotle's most famous writings connected (manmade) things and rationality—the way we understand objects.[2] His analysis pointed to four categories (or causes). The first referred to that out of which the thing was formed (the material cause), and the second to its form, such as an urn or a bowl (formal cause). The third spoke of the maker or the process by which the thing came into being (efficient cause), and the last told of the meaningful purpose or end to which the thing was put—the sake of its existence (final cause). These four elements of reason bestow meaning and were invoked as the ground on which objects made sense, as distinct from the general background of the world in which they appeared.

Our present mentality exposes only his "efficient cause," that is, the one that connects a surface phenomenon (effect) to its proximate cause. Such causes are the essence of the reductionism of modern science and are the basis for the dominant forms of modern technology. In Aristotle's terms, the causes related to sustainability may have more to do with the "final cause," that is, the end toward which one acts or uses some form of technological artifact.

Our recent history is seasoned with events critical to our consciousness of deep-seated problems that threaten our future—in other words, that lessen the possibility that constitutes sustainability. The events of 9/11 are in part a sign of technology gone wrong. The terrorist hijackers turned airplanes from a socially positive final cause to one with a terrible goal. But from the hijackers' point of view the technology was extremely "efficient." Chernobyl, another such example, forced changes in the institutional structure of the Soviet Union. Climate change is another that has yet to be seriously addressed and remains a powerful example of our collective blindness to the erosion of responsibility that technology can create. I am not making a Luddite argument against technology here; I am only pointing out that its pervasive use has deepseated, pathological, humanistic, and naturalistic consequences.

Even as I have warned that reducing unsustainability is not the same as creating sustainability, it still makes great sense to remove the proximate causes of whatever is creating unsustainability but recognizing, at the same time, that they are but quick fixes. In our culture attacking the symptoms is the underlying rationale for virtually all responses to the growing set of societal problems, yet even here it is important to design the solutions to avoid doing even more damage. Shopping, as President George W. Bush implored us to do after 9/11, does not seem to be the right way to find flourishing in our selves, in our society, or in nature. In many cases we do know how to combat unsustainability but will not do so because of the resulting apparent threat to one's turf or economic well-being. In the latter case, perhaps this is only because we use the wrong measures. Some claim that gross domestic product (GDP) and other economic measures no longer track flourishing and are instead a grossly misleading signpost.[3] There are no smiles in a unit of GDP, and more and more GDP does not seem to bring forth signs of flourishing. In a recent study of "happiness," determined by a combination of objective and subjective data, the wealthiest countries making up the G8 group fared very poorly, scoring way down in the list.[4]

Fortunately, there is another road to sustainability. But it comes in a very different conception of individual and social action. Our modern way of Being is not only technological as a way of taking up with the world but also is based on a particular assumption about how humans behave. The prevailing view of *Homo economicus* sees each of us as a computer with a set of preferences that always tell us what action to take so that we get the most out of the resources we have and of the choices available to us at the moment. The computer is programmed based on knowledge coming from our past experience, including the theories we have learned. This model of human behavior does not explain where our preferences come from; they just show up more or less shaped somehow by our inherent human nature.

This way of Being constantly fabricates the present out of the past. The past has been captured in our knowledge, which then is used by the computer in our mind to determine what we will do in the present to act to maximize our preferences. When we are unable to do that because we lack something—say, enough money to buy a Porsche—we say we have a problem and go about solving that problem. If the problem seems overly large, we may just abandon the project and move on to something else. The key feature about this mode of Being is that our present is constrained by our past. The answer to every problem we face is contained somewhere in the computer program in our mind and in the data our senses input into it. We take the world for granted, including our preferences. Occasionally, we may suddenly become conscious that acting to satisfy our needs and wants—another way of saying preferences—is not really satisfying. If we care enough to fix the problem, we may go to somebody else to add more knowledge to our computer. Gurus and consultants fit this mold. Or we may go to a different kind of professional, like a doctor or lawyer, and ask him or her for more direct help. Life is predominately about solving problems. There is little possibility in this way of life; computers always come up with the same answer given the same set of inputs.

The alternative is to grab on to sustainability as possibility and begin to *design a world that brings forth flourishing into our everyday activities*. The creative act of designing brings forth something from nothing. It is how artists, writers, and musicians show their virtuosity. It underlies the practice of architects and industrial designers who leave us with inspiring, moving artifacts. It makes great teachers and leaders like those I mentioned earlier. None of them bring their future visions into being by following their present GPS systems. They have all learned to make metaphorical jumps that allow them to transcend the limits of commonplace rationality. How they act is never "reasonable." In the cases of people such as Gandhi, most would say it is just the opposite; no rational human being would attempt to fight against the realities of the world they inhabited. Those who dare to turn off their cognitive computers can discover creative powers to change the world. Sustainability needs such men and women.

Chapter 7 Change, Transformation, and Design

You must be the change you wish to see in the world.
—*Mohandas K. Gandhi*

I have argued that the addictive mode of modern living, with its unconscious repetition of harmful patterns, is one—if not the most significant—cause of unsustainability. To change our behavior as individuals and as a society, we must find ways to break out of that pattern. But as any alcoholic or other addicted person knows, kicking addiction is very difficult. One must first acknowledge that his or her behavior is leading that individual away from the desired end state. Then one must always accept that he or she is indeed an addict. Only then is there any possibility of change. And because the roots of the addiction are usually deeply embedded in cognitive structures, this admission must be repeated over and over again to avoid lapsing back into the unconscious patterns. But one can escape, with help, from the clutches of whatever is in the driver's seat. Escape means that one cannot return to the old ways of satisfaction. In general, this is possible because whatever had captured the body only took over a part of it. Addicts are often able to function competently in selected domains of daily life. Indeed, many become very good at hiding their problems from their colleagues and friends.

Escaping from the stranglehold of modernity is much harder for several reasons. I have been using the term *modernity* to characterize the dominant social paradigm of the West and most other industrialized nations. Its central features include the Cartesian model of objective reality, (economic) rationality, an optimistic view about technology and technological change, individualism, and freedom as choice. Although sociologists and critics may argue about whether specific aspects of our culture are modern or postmodern, the dominant cultural values and beliefs are those of modernity. Its presence is buried deep in the recesses of our minds, as the modern world is all we have ever known. It has shaped what we hold as real and true, and therefore it must be heeded as we contemplate and act.

To escape means that we must rid ourselves of our current view of reality and find a new one. Unlike alcohol, which may not affect the ability to act in areas other than those controlled by the addiction, modernity pervades everything and is everywhere. There is no area of living that is not affected by its belief structure and its tools. We cannot simply give up or lock up one part; we are cultural beings and, from the moment of our birth, follow patterns embedded in our bodies by the very act of living. Only those such as the Amish, for example, who literally take themselves out of the mainstream, can avoid being dominated by the modern culture. The rest of us have no choice but to take it all. That is, unless we stop and create a new reality and set of cultural structures by *design*. Most cultural change happens without a plan. What starts as unintended may become the prevalent mode of behavior over time. Alternately, it is possible to alter the course of cultural change deliberately by designed interventions. The designer then would need a model of change as a guide.

TRANSFORMATION PROCESSES

Producing sustainability takes much more than simple problem-solving and incremental improvements in the present socioeconomic system. That is the way of symptomatic solutions, and, by now, it should be apparent that much more is needed. In the shifting-the-burden archetype (see Figure 3), this means getting out of the upper loop and into the bottom pathway. Sustainability will come only by deliberately addressing the systemic conditions that underlie cultural behavior in the United States, the West, and every modern or modernizing society in the world. Change at the systemic level goes by many names: paradigm shift, transformation, revolution, and so on. All refer to a change in the structural factors that govern individual and collective behavior. To many, the notion of paradigm shift means some abrupt change that arises when practitioners can no longer solve their everyday problems and eventually look to different models to explain their worlds. Philosopher Thomas Kuhn popularized this notion in the context of new, revolutionary ideas in science, but the same process is generally applicable to all forms of institutional change.[1]

I prefer the more neutral word *transformation* to the starker notion of revolution, but, no matter what word is selected, sustainability demands a discontinuous leap from the existing basis of cultural action. Transformation is a very powerful concept, because it denotes a process in which the reality in front of us changes its form: a half-empty glass becomes a half-full glass. It can take some time, as in the opening of a rose or the transformation of Dr. Jekyll to Mr. Hyde, or it can happen in a flash, as when one changes his or her mind about something. Social transformation has occurred historically and is the subject of many theories of change.

Modernity in the form of the liberal democratic political economies of the West has a distinctive, built-in sense of progress. The Enlightenment itself was founded on the idea that knowledge and truth were liberating in terms of escape from the domination of dogma and the harshness of nature. There is a teleological sense in this cultural frame. As time passes, the world will become better and better and move toward some unfolding ideal or at least an optimum state. We will, simply by the playing out of life, move "toward the end of history," a situation where life will be as good as it gets. Progress and transformation are not the same, however. Transformation implies an abrupt, discontinuous change, whereas progress in modernity's teleology is thought to evolve smoothly and more or less continuously.

This notion of steady progress toward the better and better rests on the important notion that the continuous growth of positive knowledge and its applications will become ever more liberating. Positive knowledge is knowledge produced by application of empirical methods (science) to worldly phenomena. It is positive in the sense that we can make affirmative statements about those phenomena. Questions about the validity of the first premise arise in postmodern discourses, with their assumption that positive knowledge is never completely objective and that it always involves some sort of (institutional) power in the shadows. The second key assumption is that technology will continuously evolve such that each new manifestation of freshly acquired and applied knowledge will be better (and more efficient) than that which it replaces. The unintended consequences of technological systems (including institutions such as "free" markets) may now outweigh the outcomes for which they were designed.

In our time we have seen another model of transformation crumble and fall. This is the dialectic model of transformation formulated by Hegel and then by Marx. In the dialectic, the seeds of change are immanent in the present mode of cultural action. Marx argued that human societies had undergone a number of transformational changes over the history of human settlements, each one initiated by contradictions or unstable conditions that led to the emergence of new modes. In the dialectic model, change is bound to come but can be moved along by revolutionary actions. Schumpeter's idea of creative destruction as the process by which current ideas and institutions are destroyed and replaced by newer and more efficient ones has many similar features.[2] The force of change in his model is human creativity. I believe that the seeds of destruction are clearly evident in modernity, but the new positive social world, the antithesis in Hegel's term, shows little signs of its immanence. The absence of such a teleological germ is ominous, as the process, then, is one-sided. Only the unstable "thesis" exists, and so a satisfactory and progressive synthesis cannot happen. If social critic Francis Fukuyama is correct that liberal democracy rather than Marx's socialism is the end of history, then the inherent unsustainability of this final stage may indeed bring the world to an end, but certainly not in the way Fukuyama saw.[3]

Another, very different, model of change is found in the evolutionary theories of human consciousness developed by Ken Wilber, David Bohm, Clare Graves and Don Beck, and Willis Harman and others in the Western world, as well as by many Eastern thinkers. In one way or another, these theories presume that humanity continues to expand in consciousness and understanding of the world. New dimensions of Being unfold as our species, like the teleological model of modernity, moves closer and closer to perfection.

Harman developed a model of expanding consciousness that he claimed would lead to a fundamental change in the structure of Western societies.[4] He postulated a transition through three metaphysical perspectives, starting with "materialistic monism" (more or less objective reality), to which he gave the shorthand description of "matter giving rise to mind." The second stage, "dualism," involves "matter plus mind," and the third, "transcendental monism," puts mind first, "giving rise to matter." The outcome of the shift would be a new opening for health, spirit, and creativity.

Similarly, Graves and his followers developed the notion of "spiral dynamics," in which humans and societies move upward along a spiral pathway from six successive, basic "subsistence" levels with ego-centered foci to two "being" levels, where a different kind of self will strive to live in a way to restore balance and harmony in nature and humankind.[5] Graves's end states are consistent with sustainability as flourishing, and for this reason such a model is appealing. But the grounding for Graves's work and subsequent developments in spiral dynamics is weak, and, moreover, we are still far down on the spiral with little idea about how long it will take to move up. Perhaps these thinkers are correct in their belief that all we have to do is wait until our integral and common consciousness overtakes our culturally limited view and then, as Shelley wrote, all will be right with the world. But nature and the human being are gravely threatened today, and we cannot afford to wait for these time-consuming processes to play out.

The next model is the rationalist belief that the force of sound and reasonable argument can change minds and behavior, but, as I have mentioned, this objective model of reality and rationality contains power and domination in disguise hiding inside of the modernist paradigm. Postmodernity has emerged as an alternative, not necessarily a progressive, succession to modernity largely on the argument that this very fundamental premise to rationality is incorrect and that power always distorts the presumption of absence of coercion. Biologist Humberto Maturana put it well when he said about objective reality that "in this explanatory path, a claim of knowledge is a demand for obedience."

In defense of the basic idea of rationality as a liberating context to human interaction, German philosopher Jürgen Habermas developed an alternate model that he thought could rid the world of the domination of arbitrariness and power.[6] Starting with the notion that human speech was universal and that the one capability that every human shared with all others was basic competence in speech, Habermas postulated a form of rational argumentation and consequent action that would not be fundamentally dominating. Habermas believes that, if we would adapt his model of rationality, we could restore, if it was ever present, the Enlightenment ideal of liberation from dogma and power. I believe his ideas are completely consistent and even constitutive of sustainability, but much has to be changed before the world is ready for a Habermasian model of rationality.

The next possibility is that of education in the sense that the word's origin connotes: a leading to. This interpretation of education is fundamentally transformative as it presumes that the education process will change behavior. Education in this sense is not merely adding theory and facts to the body; it means changing the bodily structures that underpin action. British sociologist Anthony Giddens distinguished between what he called practical and discursive consciousness.[7] Practical consciousness is a property of the body that produces actions; discursive consciousness is the source of the arguments we offer if asked why we acted as did. Maturana connects learning and action, saying, "*All doing is knowing and all knowing is doing*" (emphasis in the original).[8] This kind of education/learning is sometimes called "experiential learning." Such experiential learning, often found in programs based on intense exposure to nature, tends to be discounted by "educators" who live within the dominant view of learning as acquiring (theoretical) knowledge and facts. Like Habermas's model, education could be a very good way to change behavior if the system were to be built on a Maturana-like conceptual foundation of experiential learning. But the present system would first have to change dramatically.

The next transformational or learning process to be considered is that of coaching or other forms of behavioral intervention, such as psychotherapy and meditative disciplines. Like education, this process could be very effective but would need coaches and interveners who are masterful in the field of sustainability and who could spot unsustainable actions and their probable causes. A few such coaches might be found today, and we often look for them as leaders in the cause for sustainability. We certainly do need leaders to call attention to unsustainability and to point the way forward, but leaders are rarely good coaches. So this transformational mechanism will also have to wait for a while.

The last process I will mention is the process of paradigm shift that Kuhn described in his classic treatise on scientific revolutions.[9] Kuhn introduced the concept of normal science, that is, what scientists do routinely in their quest for understanding how the world works. Scientists go to work every day without consciously thinking deeply about the underlying beliefs and tools they use to uncover knowledge about the world. They tend to focus on problems that need unscrambling and explanation. As long as their beliefs, procedures, and tools, which constitute the current paradigm in Kuhn's terms, are working, all is well. But when they can no longer solve these everyday, normal problems, they may become frustrated and turn away, trying to seek some other framework that gets them over the barriers standing in their way.

Occasionally, in a reflective moment, one of the frustrated workers in the field comes up with a new, perhaps revolutionary, idea that breaks the logjam and enables all to move on. Kuhn cites several such "revolutions" in his book, including, for example, "the major turning points in scientific development associated with the names of Copernicus, Newton, Lavoisier, and Einstein."[10] In this model, the new beliefs and routines that kick off a paradigm shift are discontinuous with the old. One simply cannot get there from here. There is no logical argument that can be invoked. The source of the new beliefs is frequently mysterious: dreams and metaphors are the inspiration. It is said that French chemist Kekulé dreamed of intertwining snakes on his way to discovering the hexagonal structure of benzene.

Kuhn's "sociological" theory of science has much in common with the views of Giddens and Heidegger. All assume that normal cultural activities are habitual. We simply do what we do until normality no longer works. Then we struggle and struggle until someone offers a new structure on top of which we can go back to work and return to the many institutional modes of activities that constitute society: work, family, economy, government, and so on. Scientists are different from most workers, because science's paradigm is quite explicit. For most everybody else, their behavioral paradigm is fuzzy at best and is usually hidden from view or buried deep in their practical consciousness. Scientists know when they need to stop and seek a fundamental new way to work. But few if any other domains of human action have such clear-cut rules by which they play.

And so crises come, just as they do for scientists, often without warning or with warnings ignored. Solutions are sought in the same old places because the players are unaware of the rules, and reflection brings only a murky picture of the world. Many have heard the story of the drunk who lost the car keys but kept looking for them under the street lamp because that is where the light was. This pattern should now sound familiar, as it is nothing more than shifting-the-burden or addiction: follow the same rules until the system breaks down. But in the case of unsustainability, the system is so large and complex that no Einstein is likely to come forth with a neat new paradigm.

There is another way out, however, and that is to begin to redesign parts of the structure that underlies unsustainable cultural reproduction, but not blindly and certainly not based on the current cultural structure. This is my hope for the future. I believe that there is a way to sustainability, and the way is *design,* based on taking new ideas from every trace of sustainability we can locate. Nature itself is such a source, and we will explore what nature has to offer as we proceed. In some cases, we will simply have to try new ideas and see what happens. Paradigm shifting is eminently practical. New paradigms replace the old only when those seeking success in their lives assess the new to be a more effective way by which to live. And those who find the new to be what they have been waiting for will almost always have to convince a lot of skeptics and entrenched interests that they should join in.

PROBLEM-SOLVING AND DESIGN

> Technology causes problems as well as solves problems. Nobody has
> figured out a way to ensure that, as of tomorrow, technology won't
> create problems.
> —Jared Diamond

Management scientist Russell Ackoff, writing about problem-solving
some years ago, noted that there were several ways of dealing with
problems.[11] He defines a problem as a situation in which the actors
have alternative courses of action available; the choice makes a difference, and the actors are not sure about what path to follow. He then
notes that there are three types of action that can be taken. The first
is to *resolve* the problem, that is, to select a course of action that is
good enough to restore the action to the unproblematic state it was in
before the problem cropped up. He writes, "To attempt to resolve a
conflict [problem] is to accept the conditions that create it and to seek
a compromise, a distribution of gains and/or losses that is acceptable
to the participants."[12] This approach, which he calls "clinical," often
involves the qualitative judgments of the actors. In the long run this
action is not likely to satisfy the actors, as the problem is likely to re-
cur since the underlying conditions still lurk in the background (recall
the fixes-that-fail archetype from Chapter 2). Incidentally, Ackoff
considers most managers to be problem *resolvers*.

The second approach is to *solve* the problem through a course of
action believed to lead to the best possible (optimal) outcome. This
approach, which he calls "research," involves analysis and often application of mathematical models. This way of treating problems
tends to ignore parts of the problem system that cannot be fitted
into the analytic framework. It is also, for different reasons, not
likely to make the problem go away. Problem-solving and resolving
both follow the upper loop in the shifting-the-burden diagram.
They fail to change the underlying conditions that create the problematic situations.

His third way, to *dissolve* the problem, is quite different. Dissolvers
idealize rather than optimize, because the objective is to produce
long-lasting satisfaction or at least get them back on track to attain
their vision. Here the actors take a course that changes the context
(that is, the underlying system creating the problem) such that the

problem disappears. The change can be to the acting entity or to the environment impinging upon the entity or both. This path follows the lower loop in the archetype diagrams. To distinguish the approach that must be taken for this path, Ackoff calls it *design*. I add the emphasis because I believe it is the only one that can take on the challenge of producing sustainability.

> Engineers are not the only professional designers. Everyone designs who devises courses of action aimed at changing existing situations into preferred ones. . . . Design, so construed, is the core of all professional training: it is the principal mark that distinguishes the professions from the sciences.
> —Herbert Simon, Sciences of the Artificial

Design is a special word in my lexicon. It is not the same as what fashion or product designers do. It is not the same as problem-solving, except in Ackoff's notion of dissolving. In this new lexicon, design is a process in which new action-producing structures are created and substituted for old ones such that routine acts change from the old, ineffective patterns to new ones that produce the desired outcomes. Design is relevant in any domain where routines are not working, that is, bringing forth the world that the actors envision. Design and learning are connected in this sense. Design is an activity that precedes learning. It provides new, alternate action-producing structures that change the mode of behavior from one that has been ineffective to a more effective regime. In the organizational learning field, this kind of changed behavior is sometimes called "double-loop learning."[13] Both "design" and "learning" generally have different meanings in everyday conversation from the way they are used here. These two distinctions are probably not what you expect them to be.

Design comes forth as a process when the everyday, cultural, normal activities of individual and coordinated collectives of actors show persistent breakdowns or interruptions in the flow of action. Every time a break that is reflexively perceived through the actor's sensory filters occurs, the routine and effortless way of action that has been present loses its ease, taken-for-grantedness, or transparency, and the flow is interrupted. One frequently utters an obscenity and says to him- or herself, "I have a problem." In most cases, the actors will have alternate strategies or resources available to throw into the breach and restore the smooth flow. If nothing is available, the flow stops and the actor shifts to a reflective stance, acknowledging the complete stoppage, during which he or she will either abandon the intention or devise a new strategy that will restore the action.

This new mode is what I (and others) call "design." It is a conscious, deliberate effort to change the systemic presuppositions underlying action so that the desired end can be attained. If the design is successful and the consequent actions turn out as desired, this behavioral pattern corresponds to the double-loop learning of organizational theorists and to Ackoff's dissolving. The designer or designers can choose to change any part of the context surrounding the unsatisfactory action, substituting new ways of viewing the world, new strategies, new forms of authority, or new resources for the old. In the next chapter, we will see that each of these four categories plays a special role in the theory of action I have adopted and that they offer four separate, but often interconnected, paths to design.

Design, in this sense, is distinct from the "normal" problem-solving steps taken to deal with frequent interruptions that can be handled by shifting to standby or even innovative means to overcome the problem at hand. Such change in the structure underlying action is called "single-loop learning" by organization theorists like Chris Argyris and Donald Schön.[14] Ackoff, as I mentioned earlier, called this mode "solving" or "resolving." Throwing money at a problem is often a first step. When many things seem to be going wrong all at the same time, we are often advised to reorganize. Firms struggling to compete in changing circumstances may try to "rebrand" themselves, creating new beliefs about what they are all about. But such solving leaves in place the context out of which these everyday problems arise, and so they are likely to reappear.

Design is a natural, spontaneous process that emerges during the course of routine action, and, in our complex society with its characteristic division of labor, design is also the province of professionals trained in the process. In familiar arenas of action, the players themselves are likely to be sufficiently competent to shift from routine to design. They may need some training and coaching to help get the process started and overcome glitches, but the ability to shift from one mode of action to the other is a trait all human beings possess. One of the secrets of the successful Japanese total quality management movement is the involvement of workers in attacking problems that arise during routine operations. The developers of this system recognized that those most intimately involved possessed the kind of knowledge needed to design solutions that would, in many cases, dissolve the problems. This situation is an example par excellence of Maturana's view that learning is doing and doing is learning.

When the problems become persistent in spite of the actors' repeated efforts, or are created by structure far distant from the actors' consciousness and competence to deal with them, then it will be necessary to call in professional designers whose competence lies in this domain. The most familiar of such professional designers are those who create new forms of technology, the primary resource of our modern culture. They are forever bringing forth new artifacts "designed" to make life's real and imagined problems go away. But the fruits of these efforts tend to contribute to the unsustainability of modern life; they continue to shift the burden. In any case, these professionals are not doing design in the sense I have discussed. Their work is more like engineering, which involves the applications of theoretical or otherwise codified knowledge in often artful ways. It is not dissolving in the sense of design being used here.

Design appears in several other common social arenas although we rarely, if ever, think of the process as design. Policymaking is a form of design that tends to focus on changing the norms that govern social activities. It creates new institutions complete with sets of rights and wrongs: the "shoulds" we live by. Policymaking also reorders authority and shifts power. Policymaking goes by various names; in firms it is usually called "strategy," but the two are much the same. Both processes produce visions and norms (strategies), allocate power, and provide for resources to be used in the pursuit of whatever the organization sets out to do.

Education is also a design process, with the student as the target. Education embeds new beliefs and normative strategies, and it enables one to expand competence to new areas. Many forms of therapy have the features of design. Therapists help patients to uncover structure that has locked the patients into a pattern that fails to produce desired outcomes, and then they may also assist in replacing the faulty beliefs and norms with new ones that empower the patients. Education and therapy are similar, because both add new, cognitive resources that support effective, satisfying behavior. Education facilitates both problem-solving and the ability to step into new domains arising from vision. Therapy focuses on old problems but also permits movement toward a truly satisfying life that heretofore has been out of reach.

Traditional psychoanalysis leaves part of the design job to the patient, as therapists tend to leave innovation to the patient, content merely to uncover the blocking cognitive structure. During the 1960s humanistic therapists began to take a more active role suggesting possible alternatives. For example, a patient whose life is run by her belief, coming from her memories of childhood punishment, that a parent did not love her, may embark on a new, effective pattern of behavior on hearing from the therapist that perhaps the parent was showing love in the only way that he or she knew how to do.[15]

Design, as I speak of it, is the *only* deliberate way out of the unsustainable dominating and addictive patterns of individual and social behaviors that have become the norms in the United States and in other affluent, consumerist societies. Exercising collective willpower is not effective. Studies of diet regimens to produce lasting weight loss show that willpower alone does not keep dieters from slipping into old patterns and gaining back what weight they had lost.[16] Quick fixes, such as stomach stapling, are discouraged by many doctors, as they do not address the root problems; further, there is the argument that some form of designed intervention that changes the overall culture, in this case the public health context, is essential to cope with widespread addictive patterns of individual behavior.[17]

Nor does the voguish trend simply to speed up the pace of innovation and change provide a way out. Increasing the pace of life merely revs up angular velocity in the upper loop of the addiction diagram and perhaps intensifies the perception of emptiness and the hope that tomorrow will deliver what today lacks. The moments of reflection that are a prerequisite in shifting to a design mode are rare and are put off by the constant bombardment of our senses by the banalities of advertising and popular culture. Our political system has become as banal as the popular culture. Public education has departed far from the Jeffersonian ideal of producing citizens who could think critically about the society that they as free people have the responsibility for shaping. Public education today is focused on producing workers and consumers, not citizens and competent thinkers.[18] All of these trends tend to inhibit the development of reflective competence. This loss may be connected to the erosion of the capability for responsible action. If I believe that my problems and emptiness will be overcome by more consumption and by reliance on someone else's thinking in the form of new products, services, and diversions, why then would I stop and think about them.

Unless the world comes crashing down, we just muck along, finding more and more excuses for the persistence of unsustainability within our own lives and in the world that shapes us. Environmentalism began with a few sentinels and watchdogs deciding that the world was indeed beginning to crash; the sky really was falling, or at least a part of it was disappearing (the ozone layer). Rachel Carson brought the problems of persistent organic pollutants, specifically the pesticide DDT, to the attention of powerful actors who designed new (regulatory) structure that changed the way chemicals were manufactured and employed. Regulations can be a form of design if they change ideas about what is the "right" thing to do and force the evolution of new patterns of behavior.

Failure to attend to society's needs and dreams often has historically led to redesign through revolution. But revolutions frequently don't work well; in addition to the positive outcomes that the rebels—the designers—envisioned, revolutions can also introduce as many unintended consequences. Obviously, I believe strongly that the time for a quiet revolution has come. My own days are fewer at this stage of my life, but my children and grandchildren will have to live in a world I believe will not work for them. Now is the time to get started on bringing forth sustainability by design. The challenge is truly awesome and daunting, as the structure that propels the world on its present path is deeply entrenched and is kept in place by ever more powerful forces.

Chapter 8 Culture Change: Locating the Levers of Transformation

If culture, then, is a study of perfection, of harmonious, general perfection, and perfection which consists in becoming something rather than in having something, in an inward condition of the mind and spirit, not in an outward set of circumstances,—it is clear that culture . . . has a very important function to fulfil for mankind.
—*Matthew Arnold,* Culture and Anarchy

Every design exercise is built on a foundation of theory, whether that theory is explicit or not. Even the artist has a model of the world behind the words, picture, music, or solid object that represents and reveals the artist's handiwork. The ballerina sculpts herself in the dance playing out a vision of her world. The models that have been both hidden and hinted at in this book need to be made explicit before proceeding further.

Two models are at work within these pages, one nested in the other. The first is a model of collective action, attempting to capture the outward manifestations of a culture and also some "mechanism" to explain what a careful observer sees.

The second focuses on the individual and what it is to be human. The structuration theory of Giddens is my choice for the collective model.[1] One needs such a model in thinking about sustainability and in designing new cultural structure that has the potential to reverse the current trajectory pointing toward collapse. Sustainability is a cultural phenomenon. It emerges from a culture viewed as a system. Even so, its appearance rests on the collective behavior of the individuals within that culture. Sustainability may first appear as patches in an otherwise unsustainable world, but ultimately its persistent presence must rest on a set of shared cultural foundations and new behavioral patterns. We do not have the luxury of retaining the current set of beliefs and values of modernity while counting on technology to get us out of our mess. If we are deliberately to design a new cultural foundation, it is essential to start with some model to guide the design process.

Culture as used herein refers to those routine behaviors of a group of individuals that can be interpreted as intentional and reproduced over time and space. Cultures have spatial bounds, although they may be fuzzy, and, further, cultures exist during finite time periods. I have been talking largely about a specific culture in this book: the modern, Western culture exemplified by the United States. Describing culture is largely the work of sociologists and anthropologists. I have drawn heavily on a few for inspiration in this work. But descriptions are only snapshots or, better, movies of a culture. To begin to redesign culture, we need more than a description; we need an explanation of how it ticks.

We use this simple expression all the time, but what do we mean by "what makes something tick"? Most often we make an assumption that some sort of set of rules or laws can be found such that we can relate the behavior of the system, a culture in this case, to its structure: the relations that govern the working of that structure and its responses to inputs or perturbations from the outside. We want to explain why people act the way they do and how changes in cultural, normal patterns of behavior come about. More simply, we might say that we want to understand the rules of the game of cultural life. By understanding these rules that govern social practice, we would then have clues as to where to start in the job of redesigning them to produce sustainability. How can we, then, find or invent new rules?

This critical step is much harder than it might appear. We cannot simply, as Nike's marketing slogan suggests, "Just do it." The prevalent way to create new rules today is through the tools of science. Science reveals to us ways the world works in abstract, generalizable ways that we can manipulate and apply to create the artifacts and social objects (institutions) we rely upon. But standard positivist science looks at the world through soda straws and can at best see only a minute part of a complex system.

How can we, then, discover the rules that we have created by ourselves, such as positivism itself or the notion of the ego? And which rules do we need to change? Let me address the second question first. Since it is routine, everyday behavior that we aim to change, we must find a model of such social activities. The standard economic model is a poor choice, because it has only a very limited set of levers with which to play: the rules of individual preferences. The economic model first developed by Adam Smith attributes the collective societal economy to the aggregation of individual preferences. But neither Smith nor later economists tell us anything about where those preferences come from, except to say that they arise from somewhere outside the realm of economics. This model has serious limitations as the basis for rules of general cultural activities, because it focuses only on transactions within a marketplace. But many of the meaningful activities in our lives, particularly those that even today seem to be the ones that are most fulfilling, take place outside the marketplace in our relationships with nature and with other human beings.

Before proceeding I must make an exculpatory statement. I have argued that basic beliefs and rules, including theories, of modern cultures are the principal culprits in producing unsustainability and must be changed before sustainability can appear. But I am about to involve a theory following one that Giddens derived by applying those very beliefs and rules. I do not hold this theory to be the "truth" in a positivist sense; rather it is "true" in a pragmatic sense as long as it can produce effective outcomes. This is not to denigrate its author or its power in any way. Among all models or explanations of cultural life, this one seems to me to be the most powerful as a design guide. A theory does not have to be positively true in order to be powerful and useful. It merely needs to work in an unproblematic manner. Such is the nature of Giddens's works in the context to which I bring them. I am not making any claims as to their objective truth by using them here. This same caveat also applies to the theories describing individual behavior I have borrowed.

FOUR PATHWAYS TO CHANGE

Giddens argues that cultural activities, that is, everyday routine societal activities, rest on a structure of rules and resources that are shared by everyone in that society.[2] Theorists also apply the model to smaller organizations like firms or families. The key feature is structure that is shared by all the actors. Giddens divides this structure that produces and reproduces cultural activities into three categories that can help us think analytically about culture and change:

- Structure of signification: the rules by which actors interpret (make sense of) the context (world) in which they are acting.
- Structure of legitimation: the rules that give normative authority to the actions being taken, that is, make them the right thing to do under the circumstances.
- Structure of domination: the resources that empower actors. Power here carries the sense of transformative capacity, not domination in the sense of unequal distribution of such power. There are two sets of resources—allocative resources (the real, tangible tools that are available to the actors, for example, machines, money, groceries, etc.) and authoritative resources (the ordering that determines who has the power to control the actions of others and the way resources are to be used).

These are little more than fancy terms for familiar notions that Giddens has put together in a powerful framework. From the earliest moments of childhood, we all start learning to act by means of these categories without ever speaking of them by name. For example, consider the nature of a conversation between a child and parent that often begins with a question such as, "Mommy, why is the sky blue?" Whatever answer is given creates signification and builds capability to make sense of a new part of the child's world. The ensuing conversation could lead to another question from the child: "Why do I have to wear my raincoat?" Similarly, whatever the answer, it builds the structure of legitimation, which creates a basis for doing the right thing under the particular circumstances, presumably in this case when it is raining (but not when the sun is shining). Then as the child grows older, the questions might become more like, "Mom, can I borrow the car keys?" The answer to this question is all about who has the power to authorize the use of material resources needed to act or do something. This might be followed by the suggestion to walk or ride a bike. The bike, one's muscles, and the car are resources available to the child to carry out the envisioned act of getting from one place to another.

The structure of signification is a way of pointing to the rules that give meaning to the world around us—how we interpret and filter the sensory phenomena impinging on our bodies. Ordinary objects are just that—so commonplace and familiar that we take them for granted. But it is the embodied rules that turn a set of meaningless signals impinging on nervous systems into a chair or tree or iPod. Members of cultures where these objects are not commonplace cannot recognize them for what we say they are. Consequently, we cannot coordinate our actions with them except through some sort of translator. In everyday language, we call these signification rules *beliefs*.

The structure of legitimation is made up of rules that tell us the right thing to do in the everyday situations that come to our attention through the workings of the belief structure. They are social and personal norms that tell us what we should do at every moment. Some of our norms come through institutions such as religions or governments that codify the rules in laws like the Ten Commandments or the Bill of Rights. Others come from our own life experience and we embody them just as we do our beliefs, storing them somewhere within the inner recesses of our nervous system. These rules govern what we might call our habits, like brushing our teeth twice a day. Without such rules, we would have to continually invent our responses to each encounter with the world all day long.

The last category of this model, structure of domination, is composed of two pieces: tangible resources such as money, things in general, or tools that we can pick up or allocate to perform the task in front of us; and authoritative resources comprising the more conventional power structure. In more familiar terms, the power structure determines who has the authority within a society or company or other organization to make the real-time allocations of action-enabling resources. It is important to understand power and domination as related to the actors' transformative capacity—the ability to produce the world they would claim they intended to. Power and domination here should not be seen in the usual sense of some unequal distribution of power or resources. Earlier I briefly quoted Alfred Schutz, a phenomenologist who focused his work on action: trying to understand why people behave as they do and how action was connected to knowledge and consciousness. One interpreter of Schutz put it this way: "Action, then, can be conceived of as a dialectical relationship between the present and the future. While it is grounded and to a degree constrained by experience and the past, it is still open to alternative possibilities; there are still elements of choice of actions. Perhaps there is not the complete unrestrained freedom of the existentialist, but simultaneously there is not the complete determinism suggested by 'naturalistic' social science. The major point is that the purpose of action is change: it is formulated to negate in some sense that which is existing."[3]

These embedded rules are essential to human satisfaction or, more precisely, to our unending striving for satisfaction. They show up when we sit down to eat, go shopping, choose mates, and so on. When satisfaction fails to show up, we try spare, secondary schemes we have stored up, and, if we continue to fail to be satisfied, we may abandon that quest and seek to satisfy another area of striving. The rules of modern societies have generally failed to produce lasting satisfaction, thus leading to addictive patterns of consumption and to shifting-the-burden behavior in general.

Giddens's theory goes on to argue that the structure that creates routines is continuously embedded in the culture in the course of the action. Action creates structure, which creates action, which creates structure, and so on. Giddens calls this circular process "structuration." In the case of a child, it may take a few repetitions of laying down the rules to embed them, but after a while the action will become routine. At least, that is what a parent hopes. Once actions begin to become routine, repeated action embeds the underlying structure deeper and deeper into the cognitive structures of the actors such that they become taken for granted and fade from view. We simply act without "thinking" in the most basic sense of the word. This same pattern of learning occurs in every cultural setting. New employees are socialized into the culture of the firm; citizens are acculturated into the social structure of the society in which they live. Professional athletes take on the culture of their organization. The New York Yankees and the Boston Red Sox both play the same game, but in very different ways.

Language itself is an example of structuration at work. Language is the medium through which human actors coordinate activities among themselves. Language carries meaning through semantic distinctions and syntactic constructions that have become embedded through repeated usage once we become competent in speaking and listening. And in acting, these meanings become even more embedded in a never-ending cycle. Nouns, when spoken, create an assumption that the object exists, even if it has no materiality. Conversations attempting to question the existence of, say, "need" become problematic because merely by using the word *need* we imply that it exists as a thing. This feature of language is particularly troublesome in this book because I am raising many questions about immaterial elements of modern cultural structure, particularly "things" like need, care, concerns, or even sustainability itself.

As we play out our lives and organizational activities, we embed these drivers of our actions ever more deeply. We become more and more machinelike and less and less conscious of the structure that drives action. As long as the structure continues to enable us to solve our everyday problems and to take us to where we want to go, we go on unreflectively and unquestioningly. Perhaps this is an unflattering and stark depiction of humans and their actions, but it is one that seems to fit with observations. The positive feature of this model is that, like the invisible hand notion, societies can function without stopping to think about everything. The negative side is that, at some point, we begin to lose the ability to reflect and may fail to notice that we are no longer being satisfied, until it is too late or exceedingly difficult to replace the faulty structure. Such is the origin of addiction and the drift into unsustainability.

Giddens's model explains why it is so difficult to change one's ways. The model is dynamic and can accommodate change and evolution, but it is fundamentally conservative, maintaining existing structure through the recursive structuration process. Structure produces cultural behavior and is, in turn, embedded through these activities. Unless something happens to introduce new structure in any of the categories, life simply goes on in the same patterns day in and day out, subject to minor variations caused by the weather, moods, newsworthy events, and so on. The response to the subway bombings in London was resoluteness about maintaining the status quo. Much of the response to 9/11 in the United States has been a series of actions designed to protect the status quo. President Bush's admonition to go shopping right after the tragedy could be interpreted as an effort to forestall any deep questioning and reflection about that very status quo.

Although Giddens developed his model to explain how societies come about and persist, I find it useful also to explain isolated, individual behavior. The routines that characterize individual patterns are governed by the same structure, except that the normative and authoritative parts of structure collapse into the individual's own internalized permission granting rules. The presence of unconscious structures by which we make sense of the world and select the appropriate actions is controlling both to individuals and to cultural collectives. No matter how we may explain why we do things if asked for such an explanation, it is the structure lurking in the background that is the real driver. Our verbal explanations may or may not coincide with the embedded structure. Giddens makes a distinction, noted earlier, between practical and discursive consciousness. The former points to the embedded, tacit structure that creates action; the latter to the domain from which our "reasons" come when queried as to why we did something.

The basic structure of Giddens's societal model fits closely with Heidegger's model for individual human beings that I will build on later. In his major text on structuration theory, Giddens acknowledges his debt to Heidegger.[4] Both are built on a process of accumulation of historical experience as the basis for meaningful action. Both base action on adherence to cultural norms rather than the result of some sort of internal calculus with inputs stemming from representations of the world in the mind.

This same model that explains why cultural patterns are so persistent also offers a path going in the opposite direction, toward designing change. If any part of the structure is changed by intervention or some unplanned event, new patterns will emerge. "An idea whose time has come" is a new thought that finds its way into the cultural structure and displaces the current beliefs. Victor Hugo's famous aphorism makes the point that it is not just the idea by itself that can power the world, but the confluence of the idea and an opening into the culture ("time"). If the earlier critique and analysis of the roots of unsustainability correctly identify the culprits in the modern structure, then at least we know where to aim our design efforts.

When any one of the four elements of structure is changed deliberately or by some chance event, new routines will generally emerge and changes may occur in one or more of the other categories. If we, for example, introduce a new technology, changes in the norms and power structure may follow. Stephen Barley showed that, following the introduction of magnetic resonance imaging in hospitals, technicians gained power, and new procedures for diagnosis replaced older forms.[5] New and innovative technologies virtually always change behavioral norms and standard strategies. Postmodern theorists similarly argue that artifacts such as technological devices have embedded messages or codes that are read out by users. This feature of structuration and related theories suggests that, by the careful design of technological artifacts, it is possible to change beliefs and norms toward some end that is socially desirable—in our case, sustainability. We will return to this important concept in a later chapter.

Many forms of therapy are based on similar models that take for granted that some buried structure is controlling, and seek to uncover it so that it becomes conscious to the actor(s) and thus may be amenable to change. The strategy that unfolds below for designing a sustainable world is much like a form of therapy, at least at the beginning. First, the actor or actors must acknowledge that life is not working in the way "it is supposed to." Then, before proceeding to the design phase, the actors have to reflexively identify which of the rules that they are following are not working. The alcoholic must accept that the "rule" that alcohol makes it all right is not working. And then, if the process is carefully done, the actors and their coaches or other helpers in design can begin to address the particular rules and resources that need change. In the case of sustainability, all four categories of structure will require significant change, and all interact with each other. To try and redesign the whole system all at once would be overwhelming and unlikely to succeed. It seems wiser to look at each major category separately as a start.

SELECTING THE MOST PRACTICAL LEVERS

Another way of visualizing how cultural structure produces and re-produces action is through a depiction rather like an engineer's flow sheet, as shown in Figure 8. In the figure, the four categories of struc-ture (in the rectangular boxes) form a circle, with action flowing clockwise. Giddens did not represent his model in this form, but I have found it very useful as a template both for understanding and for design. The ovals represent worldly phenomena, that is, states we can observe or at least hear about. Although one can speak about them and use them to explain actions, they are all buried in the prac-tical consciousness of any individual actor or group of actors. The tools have a real presence, but as cultural structure they too lie in this unavailable domain. The actors monitor the outcomes and the changed world reflexively and feed what they sense back into the structure, either reinforcing it or, contrarily, producing a stoppage and the possibility of design and learning.

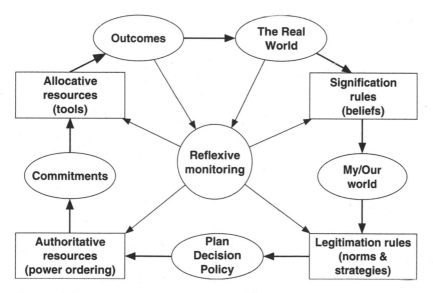

Figure 8. The structuration process (after Giddens)

Action begins at the top within the "real" world. This block represents the world of phenomena. It includes phenomena both inside and outside of the reach of our senses and cognitive powers. It is real in the sense that it is our home and ground for everything we claim to know. It is the place, for example, where global warming and ozone depletion occur, where people are flourishing or not, where life begins and ends. But it is not this "real" world that we act upon. We filter out most of worldly phenomena to produce a smaller world to which our attention is drawn. One might call this "my" or "our" world, but we typically mistake my or our world for the "real world." The smaller bounded world we act within is only a partial chunk coming to our consciousness, delimited through the action of the codes of signification: the beliefs we hold. We create a personal world and focus on some part of it that attracts our attention. For example, I might hear a sound and, after filtering it through my belief structure, determine that it is the alarm clock waking me up. If this scene seems familiar, I turn to a strategy that I have already embodied through the process of reinforcement and react accordingly.

Strategies fall into the category of legitimation, that is, they are plans of action that fit (or are right for) the world I perceive at that moment. In the alarm clock example, I would normally get up, that is, make a choice among a set of legitimate possibilities. As an isolated individual, I skip the next step because I am always my own authority and can move around the circle and come ever closer to actual action by making a commitment to get up. Decisions are easily reversed, but commitment takes me a step closer to the act. Since getting up takes only the coordination of my muscles, I call on my body as a resource and get out of bed. With this observable act as outcome, the world changes, as I am now standing beside my bed, a little bit groggy. To be counted as an outcome, the world must be perceived to have changed in the eyes (or in any other of the senses) of the observer. Then I start the process all over again as I am always the observer of my own acts and so continue to respond to the new world I have made present. Like many, I probably would stumble along to the bathroom to clean up and brush my teeth, and then I would get dressed.

In the case of collective action, the picture shifts slightly, as actions are coordinated among a group. In this case the world to which they turn their collective attention arises from a set of shared beliefs, and the strategies are part of a set that has previously been accepted as normatively correct under these circumstances. If the scene is familiar, the decision to act is likely to be implicit or tacit, as the agreements needed to move together are already buried in the collective consciousness. If more than one possibility is appropriate, someone with authority will determine the course of action and obtain commitments from all involved as well as release the requisite tools into their hands. Then, as in the case for an isolated actor, they will produce an outcome—an observable change in the world.

Throughout the process, the actor or actors monitor the process reflexively, sensing not only themselves but also the whole flow of action. As long as the "picture" fits the image of the world held by the actor, the flow is smooth and seemingly effortless because, if the action is well established in the repertoire, the actors will have become competent and perform without thinking—again, in the everyday way we use the term *thinking*. As a model, I have chosen to portray the process as a set of discrete steps; in life, however, action is continuous without any consciousness of a move from one set of actions to another. Giddens writes that this way of acting is fundamental to human Being; humans are "purposive agents" acting out of reasons which they will describe if asked, but which reasons may or may not be the "correct" grounds.

As long as nothing happens to change any of the structure or to change the world in some unintended way, the actors will reproduce their behavior over and over again every time their attention alights on the same desired outcome. But such tranquility is not the usual context for life. Surprises lurk around every corner. The tools we have don't work as we expect. The boss is ill and nobody is around to authorize our choice of action. The world itself changes, as it always does. A competitor announces a new product that threatens the company. The atmosphere begins to warm up. The car gets a flat tire on the way to work. The computer crashes again. A robot replaces a co-worker on the assembly line. An eminent scientist announces that the newest drug for cancer thought to be the silver bullet has disastrous side effects. Mom corrects the way I use a fork and spoon. In the case of unsustainability, we may awake to discover that the world is not behaving as we expected it to and that all sorts of unintended consequences have arisen from what we thought were simply normal, routine activities.

It is at these moments that opportunities for design enter the consciousness of the actors. We will explore this in more depth in the discussion of Being below, but at this point it is sufficient to note that our seemingly routine everyday life is full of such interruptions. We miss most of them or rush to resolve the immediate problems and fail to recognize possibilities of fundamental change. But if we do stop and reflect deeply enough, then we may be able to shift from problem resolving to design and dissolving.

Four more or less distinctive opportunities for redesign align themselves with the four categories of structure (I will now use shorthand terms for these categories): beliefs, norms, authority/power, and tools. Except for tools (allocative resources), which change continuously through the process of technological innovation, the other three tend to be highly conservative. The structuration process continually embeds the beliefs, norms, and power structure ever more deeply as long as those in power believe the system is more or less working. Given the four-hundred-year-old culture of modernity, many beliefs and norms are now very deeply situated. Economic and political power are narrowly held, and, as anyone knows, those in power want to stay there and will resist change in the structure. The deeper and more entrenched the structural element is, the more difficult it will be to change it. But the possibility of sustainability will offer itself only if significant change does indeed take place in all four categories.

Beliefs are perhaps the most deeply seated and invisible in the everyday way life goes on. People do not stop and reflect on what lies deep in the structure that shapes their daily life. Very few have ever stopped to think about Descartes' model of human being. Norms may be a little more evident but generally lie buried unless and until some sort of breakdown takes place that brings them to the surface. In Maturana's thinking, reality, which is mostly all about beliefs regarding what is out there and what is the right thing to do, enters consciousness only when such breakdowns take place. In the conversations that inevitably follow such breakdowns, humans come to terms with reality, agreeing to whatever they determine it to be as a prerequisite to restarting coordination after the breakdown. Failure to come to terms with reality inhibits or prevents coordination from happening.

In practice, conversations in this sense happen all the time, but explicit reflection about reality is rarely present. The Cartesian model, coupled with a sense that there is always a single right answer to everything, stands in the way of such reflection. Coordination, if it can be called that, continues only via some sort of domination, whether it is by force and sanctions or by economic or other incentives.

In spite of many historic claims that the old ways can be easily overthrown by new beliefs and norms, culture is fundamentally conservative. Voltaire trumpeted the power of a new idea to replace the old. Margaret Mead famously said that one should "never underestimate the power of a small, thoughtful, committed group of people to change the world . . . indeed it's the only thing that ever has." More recently author Malcolm Gladwell has introduced the idea of the "tipping point," whereby the conservative forces that bind a culture are broken by the efforts to introduce something new and the structuration process begins to reinforce the new, rather than the old.[6] Perhaps they are correct, but instances of such changes in history are few. Most attempts end in failure.

These last few paragraphs hint that a direct attack on beliefs or norms is problematic. Our culture has developed over many centuries and is very deeply ingrained. There is a sense in some circles that it has reached a climax in that it represents the end of history: no further change in these deep structures is going to occur. Capitalism has triumphed over socialism.[7] Whatever further change takes place will be manifest in the two other, more observable structural categories: tools and power. Max Weber earlier made a similar claim but with an ironic twist. He believed that the United States had reached the pinnacle of the decline of the West as manifest in the unmitigated chase after wealth as an end in itself. He ended his classic study of the rise of capitalism with these words: "For of the last stage of this cultural development, it might well be truly said: Specialists without spirit, sensualists without heart, this nullity imagines that it has attained a level of civilization never before attained."[8]

One of the five disciplines in Senge's now classic work on organizational change, *The Fifth Discipline,* is the notion of mental models, that is, the system of beliefs and norms that govern individual and group behavior in organizations.[9] In a world that is always changing, mental models get stale and organizations become stagnated and ineffective. These organizations recover their competitive competence only if the mental model can be changed. Senge and others following variants of his book offer many practices to do just this. Given the dominating importance of business—the private sector—in today's world, organizational learning or design in the sense of this book is a critical prerequisite for movement toward sustainability. Business, however, reflects the beliefs and norms of the larger society. Many of the aspects of its mental models cannot be changed without first changing societal cultural structure.

Though difficult, it is still possible to adopt new concepts about the world, that is, to change one's story about how life works. Our current paradigm generally grounds beliefs either in some true reality outside or in the utterances of some transcendent being. Other than scientists exploring new aspects of reality, we are discouraged from questioning the source of our beliefs. Those who depart too far from what constitutes a "normal" set of beliefs are looked upon as out of touch or even crazy. And those who may question the dogma of religious or other authoritative sources are similarly deemed to be heretics, infidels, or simply unbelievers. Political discourse today has tended to move in this direction.

In Giddens's model, this category refers to the ordering of people with authority to allocate the tools and other tangible resources including other humans acting as workers—in other words, this structure corresponds to the "power structure." Applying allocative resources transforms the world from the future perfect to the present, as Schutz wrote. They provide the means to move toward the immediate vision, grand or small, that has triggered humans to act. While it is the tangible resources that actually impact the world, it should be clear that the ultimate result depends on who makes the decisions and on what their values, priorities, or norms are. Putting this argument backward, we could say that the sad state of the world today is the result, in part, of a power structure that ranks sustainability much lower than it does other values. And thus, to achieve sustainability, the power structure should be changed along with the other three categories.

In our culture, where control is considered to be important and valuable, the authoritative structure is also difficult to change. Since many measures of success are based on the quantity of some resource like money and goods, holding on to the ability to command such resources is one of the most dominant values in our culture. It is very difficult to foresee any way to change this situation as long as happiness is measured primarily in terms of whatever set of tangible assets one commands.

This leaves tools or, as I have been calling this category more generally, technology to constitute all the tangible resources or equipment brought into play in the pursuit of cultural activities. Here the outlook is dramatically different. Implementing new technologies is perhaps the most noticeable mechanism for change in modern society. Innovation is seen as the answer to virtually all problems and opportunities. The idea that new technology is always around the corner and will enhance society's ability to master nature and provide ever more ways to produce satisfaction is a cornerstone of the modern, industrial world. It seems rather clear that this, then, is the most opportunistic place to start the redesign process.

The addiction at the roots of unsustainability cannot be addressed simply by voluntary actions by those who have fallen under its spell. Some form of intervention is essential to force a change in the routines. In many cases that intervention comes in the garb of system collapse such that the addictive patterns cannot be followed any longer. But that is hardly a satisfying way to sustainability. The path to be followed below is the design of what might be called "behavior-steering" devices both for collective and for individual behavior.[10] "Device" here means either material artifacts or institutional procedures. The flexibility available in designing tools suggests a strategy. First, replace the ubiquitous commodified devices with tools that are designed to engage us and build our skills in observation and reflection. Second, embed scripts in these tools to guide the way we use them such that we replace old unsustainable beliefs and norms with a new set. Third, substitute new collective processes (organization or institutional tools) in place of those that reinforce the current unsustainable societal set of beliefs and norms.

This choice is a pragmatic one, based on the presumption that it should be more successful than addressing those categories that are more fundamentally conservative and resistant to change. But this is just the first step in the design process. The next and perhaps most critical step is the choice of some model or models to guide the design process. One can already point to many models aimed at reducing unsustainability in the environmental domain. Ecoefficiency is the latest in a succession of approaches that began three or four decades ago. But these models do not contain any positive sense of sustainability, or any explicit attention regarding how to go about restoring the lost sense of nature and the other two domains in the Tao of sustainability.

To produce the action I hope will ensue from this work, you as readers will have to join me and others in creating and coordinating action, and that means we need to share at least a significant part of the new vision of sustainability. Given that we come from a culture with often contradictory beliefs and norms from those I connect to sustainability, sharing may be difficult and will take some withholding of the instantaneous judgments and characterizations we always make upon encountering any new world. After explicating the requisite models of behavior in the text that follows, I ask the readers with opposing ways of explaining action to suspend their disciplinary judgments and accept my choices for what they are—a pragmatic guide to locate and move toward sustainability.

Pragmatism has a critical connection to this work.[11] I have argued that cultural activities played out under the banner of modernity have led to a loss of consciousness in three essential domains: nature, self, and responsibility. Part of that loss can be traced to the dominance of the positivist/Cartesian ideology and its reliance on theory. Facts and values should be completely separated before "rational action" can proceed. Expertise substitutes for common sense and experiential knowledge. Sustainability requires the recovery of the lost consciousness. And this means our culture must regain or relearn skills in reflection and observation, individually and collectively. Pragmatism turns this dominance of theory on its head and substitutes the primacy of experience over theory. Pragmatists such as John Dewey and Charles Pierce based their arguments on a philosophical critique of Cartesianism. I propose a much more down-to-earth formula. In a nutshell, the practical framework that is developed below comprises a set of "devices" for slowly shifting the primary mode of individual understanding and action from positivist/rational to experiential/pragmatic. Basing activities on truths arising from acting-in-the-world will put us closer to the responsible human beings we are and to our place within nature.

Awareness is the critical skill needed to generate these truths. Humans are always conscious in the sense that we continuously process external phenomena. But unless we stop to reflect on these experiences of something happening in the world, no learning takes place and we have nothing left but meaningless memory traces. Pragmatism is basically a philosophy of living that finds "truth" in reflective experiences indicating success or effectiveness. I have put "truth" in parentheses or scare quotes in several places to stress that what I am talking about is a truth that derives its veracity from its role in producing effective action, rather than as some scientific fact or something logically derived from such a fact. Pragmatic truths are never separate from the context of the world of action; indeed, they derive their relevance from that context.

The quality of pragmatic truths depends on the skills of the observers of action, whether an individual is at play or some organized activity is the focus. The rest of this book is directed at the redesign of, first, the everyday equipment each individual uses and, second, institutional and organizational processes that guide cultural activities. One primary objective is the development and application of whatever reflective observational skills are necessary to recover our lost sense of Being, responsibility, and place in the world. Psychologist Sherry Turkle speaks eloquently about the "deskilling" that commodified technology produces.[12] Sustainability as flourishing cannot be found in the theoretical knowledge of detached scientists. Their knowledge is important, but the key to sustainability is the practical truths that each of us discovers in our daily life and that contribute to the collective activities of our cultures.

In keeping with the idea of pragmatism new, more effective routines are equivalent to finding such new "truths" in place of the former embodied structure that no longer produces the envisioned results. Pragmatism can be construed as a system out of which truth will eventually arise. But, given the current state of the world, it eventually may come too late. Fortunately, we can look to several sources for inspiration to kick-start the process.

SOURCES OF INSPIRATION

> Do not quench your inspiration and your imagination; do not become
> the slave of your model.
> —*Vincent van Gogh*

As observers, we have only two choices in seeking inspiration: to look
outward with a focus on the world out there, or to look outward with
a focus on ourselves. When we look outward through a fish-eye lens,
we see nature. *Nature* is another term for *world,* the context in which
we live. In this ontological sense, nature is the complex set of phenomena that we interpret as whatever is out there. It is the whole of
the world we take in as observers. This inclusiveness is different from
the positivistic notion of nature in which our species is usually omit-
ted. Nature shows up when we look outward and bracket our cultural
blindness and presuppositions. How this phenomenon—nature—
becomes interpreted through the prevalent belief structure has a critical impact on cultural paradigms. The dominant view of reality
reflects only one particular interpretation of nature. Nature, as the
broad world outside, is one key possibility for inspiration, but only if
we begin to view it through a new set of lenses.

And what about the other source: looking outward, but at ourselves? But first, what about a third possibility: looking inward? When
we sometimes talk of looking inward, we are really speaking about the
second mode in the last paragraph because we cannot actually look inward. Modern cognitive scientists, attaching electrodes to the brain or
watching areas of the brain light up in the monitor of a positron emis-
sion tomography (PET) machine, would probably argue with this statement. But what they are looking at and what I am talking about are
two distinct sets of phenomena. I'm asking: What makes humans different from other species beyond our "being" as self-conscious organisms possessing highly evolved language and cognitive capabilities?

Can we as human beings look out at other human beings and explain and understand what we see without first having an explanation
of what it is to be human? Descartes' exclamation *Cogito ergo sum*
has powered modernity but fails to give a full account of Being. We
give no forethought to our everyday ways of acting; they are based on
first-order principles that are, in turn, based on the detached human
observer as the source. If we, however, think about the process care-

fully, this mode of thinking and acting has no grounding because it lacks an independent theory of the observer. Further, we can see an interesting and perplexing circularity come forth. In order to write down a theory of the brain, one needs a brain. And further, the observer has to be able to explain him- or herself. What we believe we see and explain are, in fact, second-order phenomena. Explaining rests on the explaining of explaining.

Phenomenology, on which I have drawn extensively throughout this book, arose as an attempt to break out of this circularity and discover the meaning of phenomena—things that we experience, that is, that we perceive as existing outside of our mind. At first phenomenology was mostly about ordinary things like trees or machines, but Heidegger's work moved it into the domain of examining the special thing called "Being": the way humans are in the world. He was interested in determining how we "make sense of our ability to make sense of things."[13] The gist of most phenomenology is that there is more to the world than what meets the eye. Cartesian thinking is fundamentally limited to what does meet the eye, even with tools that can pierce the surface.

I believe there is a relationship between the understanding one gains through a phenomenological lens and sustainability. Sustainability itself is a human construct. I hope I have argued persuasively that, by using only the standard notions of modernity, one cannot hope to understand what it is and why it has become so distant. Further, I have been inspired by those thinkers who say that there is more to Being than the modernist theories suggest. I am drawn to humanists who see a better and more fulfilling life if we can regain the lost sense of what it is to be human. Or, in the words I use, flourishing and Being are tied together in a deeper sense. And finally, I will point to a connection between the ability to see, understand, and care for nature and ourselves and the ability to live in a more authentic mode of existence, as Heidegger would say, or in the Being rather than the having mode, as Erich Fromm would say. Sustainability has been seen primarily as an environmental problem and only secondarily as a social problem. I believe that this is backward. Sustainability is first a human problem and then an environmental problem. If we fail to address the unsustainability of the modern human being, we will not be able to come to grips with other aspects of sustainability.

One might ask at this point what is meant by "sources of inspiration." In the normal Cartesian models of objective reality, this means seeing something new and different in the familiar, since the world is already present in our minds. We can and do do this via the trick of metaphor, using language to cross over from one image to another and, in effect, create new reality. In the alternative, constitutive model of reality we break out of the filters of our historical past and see—that is, interpret—parts of the world we may have missed earlier or reinterpret those that seemed familiar. In either case, inspiration is an enhanced awareness that enables the observer to create new rules and resources and, subsequently, new behaviors. In everyday conversation we would simply say that we have a different story to tell about the world. There is indeed "nothing new under the sun," only new stories about what we have experienced. But if we change our stories about the world, then and only then can our patterns of behavior shift. For sustainability, the most important stories are those about nature and Being.

Chapter 9 A New Story for Nature

After you have exhausted what there is in business, politics, conviviality, and so on—have found that none of these satisfy, or permanently wear—what remains? Nature remains; to bring out from their torpid recesses, the affinities of a man or woman with the open air, the trees, fields, the changes of seasons—the sun by day and the stars of heaven by night.
—*Walt Whitman,* Specimen Days

Since flourishing is etymologically derived from flowering, natural systems seem like a very good place to begin a search for inspiration. Nature, the wellspring of human life, is the source of mystery and enchantment. In discussing the foundations for the definition of sustainability, I noted that flourishing is one of several emergent properties of natural living systems, along with resilience, health, and others. Is there anything about these systems that can explain these properties or cause their appearance? "Cause" here does not mean the usual lawlike relationships that are used to indicate the result of applying a set of rules or empirically relating the outcome of a rule-determined system to the structure of that system. Living systems are "complex," and, as complex systems, their outcomes are indeterminate and cannot be predicted. We can begin to understand these systems only by using terms like organic, holistic, interconnected, and interdependent.

NATURE IS A COMPLEX SYSTEM

Complexity is a critical notion on two counts in relation to sustainability. We have already explored one of these through exposing the systems dynamic behavior of unsustainability: the need to look beyond reductionist solutions that merely shift the burden and, worse, that can become addictive. Complexity in this first sense means simply that the system we wish to manage or even understand is more complicated than we think. I use the word "complicated" here specifically to characterize the case of systems we could, in theory, understand more or less completely if we had all the information about them that we need. Complicated systems can be reduced to sets of interconnected lawlike relationships that describe the causal bases for observed responses to changes arising internally or externally. In this sense, an automobile or nuclear reactor is a complicated system.

Complex does not simply mean more complicated. Complexity in this context is reserved as a description of systems whose behavior cannot be reduced to such lawlike structures. Systems involving living organisms fall into this category. Complex systems exhibit unpredictable behavior under certain circumstances when perturbed, as shown in Figure 9. They may not return to the same state from which they started. Adding humans to complicated systems, such as nuclear power plants, can and usually does produce a complex system.[1] Complex system theory may be confused with chaos theory, which attempts to explain how order can spontaneously appear out of chaotic conditions—for example, how a vortex suddenly appears when water drains from a basin.

Complex systems may behave in more or less predictable ways for long periods but then become unstable and flip into new, unconnected regimes unpredictably. In Figure 9a we see the typical situation in a relatively stable complex system. The collective state of the system, represented by the position of the sphere, is maintained at some position away from the equilibrium point by energy coming

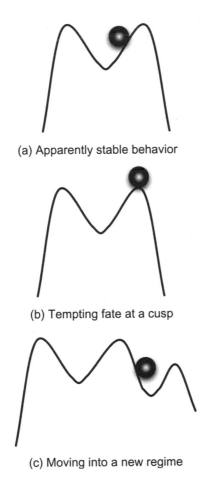

(a) Apparently stable behavior

(b) Tempting fate at a cusp

(c) Moving into a new regime

Figure 9. Complex system behavior patterns

from external sources. In the absence of such flows from the outside the system would move to the equilibrium point. In living systems this corresponds to stasis and death. Without a continuing source of energy, living systems would become static. The state (position within the valley) will change (move up or down) in response to external perturbations. If the perturbations are large enough, the state may move to the cusp (Figure 9b). In this position a slight increase in the perturbing force can push the system over into a new regime (Figure 9c). The familiar eddy that appears in a draining bathtub is an example of a spontaneous flip into a new behavioral regime. Perturbations could also move the system to a catastrophic collapse if a new valley is not connected to the other side of the cusp (Figure 9c).

The carrying capacity of natural systems corresponds to a cusp in such a diagram. If the system is pushed over the top, it cannot recover and return to the original state. This has happened to many of the world's fisheries. It is one of the possible scenarios for global warming, should irreversible melting occur in the polar icecaps. In the interaction between humans and ecological systems, collapse may occur when the intervening forces of human activities overwhelm the negative feedback mechanisms that have kept the system from running up the curve and falling over the cusp. The simplicity of this figure is deceiving; it is difficult in practice to know where the cusp lies and what new perturbation may push it over into a new regime.

Current concern about unsustainability has arisen from observations that both natural and socioeconomic systems are losing resilience, that is, the ability to cope with perturbations created by human activities without the appearance of fundamental, qualitative changes in the functions in these systems. For example, overgrazing can lead to a series of systemic changes, ultimately leading to desertification. At some point the system can no longer return to its original state even if the stress is removed. Social systems also undergo flips, for example, the collapse of the Soviet Union. In general both ecological and socioeconomic systems are nonlinear and exhibit complex and far-from-equilibrium behavior. These systems are not only uncertain but also indeterminate—a key distinction. Not only is it impossible to predict the future except with some finite degree of uncertainty, it is impossible to predict the future with any certainty at all.

> There is no such thing as pure *objective* observation. Your observation, to be interesting, *i. e.* [sic] to be significant, must be *subjective*. The sum of whatever the writer of whatever class has to report is simply some human experience, whether he be poet or philosopher or man of science. The man of most science is the man most alive, whose life is the greatest event.
> —*Henry David Thoreau*, Journals

Observers of ecosystems note that classical systems ecology, based on equilibrium population dynamics, cannot explain many critical features of living systems. The relevance of complexity to sustainability comes from the notion of flourishing so central to the definition of sustainability in this work. Flourishing is an emergent property of complex living systems, as are related properties like resilience, adaptability, or integrity. Emergence is a very important characteristic of complex systems. Emergent properties are features of complex systems that are recognized by observers standing outside of the system. They appear as both behavioral and organizational patterns and are the result of interactions among the constituents of the system but are not tied to them in a known, lawlike fashion. Emergence is the result of relationships among the parts, even if we cannot quantify them.

Some complexity scholars apply the label *emergent property* to concepts like consciousness and even life itself.[2] Similarly, they may call them epiphenomenal in that they have an existence beyond that which can be explained by scientific observation. They are frequently exactly the features that engineers, designers, artists, and social planners seek to produce through their efforts. Familiar concepts like flexibility and almost any other that ends in "-ity" are such notions. In some cases we quantify them (flexibility, for example), but in others (for example, beauty) we must leave any assessment to the beholder. Sustainability as flourishing is more like beauty than like flexibility.

Emergent properties cannot be fully explained by the workings of the parts. Liquidity of fluids is such a property. We cannot explain it merely by understanding the laws that govern the molecules and atoms. In very simple terms, emergence is what we mean when we say the whole is greater than the sum of the parts. The emergent properties are usually what make complex systems interesting. They are the purposes or functions we seek from these systems. For just about anyone except a scientist focused only on acquiring knowledge, what makes these systems meaningful is what they do for us. An art historian may be interested in the mechanics of the artist's technique, but it is the beauty or some other property of the whole that captures the attention of the ordinary viewer. The artist must create the emergence of beauty, which is why paint-by-the-numbers cannot produce masterpieces. Beauty, like liquidity, is an emergent property. So are sustainability and flourishing. I invite the reader to pause for a moment and reflect on the number of such emergent properties that are important in life.

Complex systems are open systems, with energy and information moving in and out of the systems. Evolving living systems emerge from nonlinear responses caused by both exogenous and endogenous changes in the context. They become structured, that is, they exhibit organizational forms arising to maintain gradients of energy starting with solar inputs and ending with the dissipation of highly degraded forms of energy back into the environment. Their structures have evolved (self-organized) to oppose the natural dissipative forces that tend to move systems toward equilibrium and uniformity. Without structure these systems would inexorably move to a state of lifeless, uniform equilibrium. Human cultures create meaningful structures against the meaningless backdrop of the world.

This model of development is fundamentally different from the equilibrium model of neoclassical economics. Leading economists in the field of ecological economics argue that the standard equilibrium models that have won many Nobel prizes are not realistic.[3] Unlike the global ecosystem, which has a fixed supply of materials, economies are closed neither to material nor to energy. Only an open, steady-state system model can begin to portray the complex interaction between the conventional bounds of an economy and the world from which the material and energy enter and leave. Open, complex steady-state living systems exhibit nonlinear behavior. The emergence of new species is such a nonlinear phenomenon.

NATURE IS A COMMUNITY

A thing is right when it tends to preserve the integrity, stability, and beauty of the biotic community. It is wrong when it tends otherwise.
—*Aldo Leopold,* A Sand County Almanac

One does not have to view natural systems as complex to derive other inspirational thoughts. The classical model of ecosystems stresses several concepts that run generally opposite to corresponding cultural notions.[4] Ecosystems are described as highly interconnected, holistic communities with multiple kinds of interactions among the members (species). Isolated, independent organisms (actors) cannot survive for any length of time. Cooperation through mutual or symbiotic relationships is common. Predation is the main route by which animal species obtain the energy that they require, but some form of mutualism is more common in providing other essential features for survival (flourishing), such as habitat. Species limit competition for scarce food supplies in order to maintain some minimum level of individuals. Ecological systems are robust, full of life, resilient, and long-lived, compared to recent epochal stages in recent human history. The closed-loop webs in an ecosystem take little out of their surroundings and put back little as wastes. They naturally recycle almost all materials used in their metabolism. They are parsimonious in using energy and materials.

Ecosystems may also fail to prosper, and that is cause for trouble if one takes this discussion too rigidly. I am weaving a story about nature that can feed new concepts into our cultural paradigm: the story of how the world works. The flourishing robustness and long life of many ecosystems is the main plotline, the one that can provide new metaphors and norms. The negative subplot serves as a precautionary device. One should remain in a pragmatic mood, ready to look for other sources of meaning if the new paradigm fails to produce the desired end states.

Two properties of living ecosystems, interconnectedness and interdependence, are very different from corresponding notions in our current cultural belief system. We practically worship independence and autonomy as social norms. The idea of competitive markets generally implies a predator-prey relationship among producing firms. Ecosystems clearly have predator-prey aspects, but they also display many forms of mutualism and symbiosis. Some systems ecologists claim that mutualism is more important than predation and competition in explaining the evolution and maintenance of ecosystems. Lichens, with their fungal-algal partners, and pollinators such as bees are representatives of mutualism in natural systems. And further, members of one species do not prey on other members of their species except under rare circumstances. By contrast, business strategy as taught in today's MBA programs and as practiced is fundamentally a killer model, where one firm views all others as potential prey.

COMPLEXITY CHANGES THE RULES OF THE GAME

> You can only predict things after they have happened.
> —*Eugene Ionesco*, Rhinoceros

One last subject about complex systems brings us back to the issue of sustainability. The role of the observer is key, because emergent properties exist only as phenomena that we sense and name. We cannot, by definition, infer their existence from known relationships among the parts. The implications of the observer's context and point of view have important consequences to the definition of sustainability I have presented. Emergent properties like beauty depend on the beholder's singular set of values and so are never capable of being reduced to quantitative measures. It will thus not be possible to manage sustainability in the same way we attempt to manage GDP, for example, or for that matter anything that can be measured.

This may appear to some to be a major obstacle to the usefulness of this concept. This "fact," which is so threatening to conventional managers, is instead an opening to the very world that many of these managers aspire to create. We wish to *attain* the flourishing that sustainability makes possible, not to *manage* it. These are two completely different purposeful kinds of action. It would sound strange to speak of managing love. We will certainly need to manage other aspects of individual and collective life, but we can only hope that the results of our managing will indeed produce flourishing. So to argue against this way of defining sustainability as thwarting management is only a category error, confusing two fundamentally different concepts—attaining and managing.

One very positive aspect of this feature is that it opens up sustainability to everyone, not just the experts. Management implies knowledge of the intricate laws that govern the way a system works, and is limited to a select few who have acquired that knowledge by experience or schooling. But everyone is free to look for and seek flourishing in their own and in others' lives. It is possible to subvert such notions as beauty in the sense of George Orwell's *1984*, where power changes the meaning of such emergent properties, including freedom, into their opposites, but this is not likely in the case of flourishing, which springs from life itself and can always be found in nature even if it becomes lost in ourselves.

Complex systems have histories that matter just like the stories that we use to make sense of our cultural world. Their histories shape their present states. They can never be taken out of context without losing this critical characteristic. In the management field such systems are called path-dependent systems. This aspect makes management problematic, because one cannot make judgments about what to do using only the information immediately at hand. Learning what is going on requires observations over time as well as an accumulation of experiential knowledge. Complex systems are frequently composed of nested, smaller complex systems. Arthur Koestler recognized this property in his classic work on the evolution of the human brain, *The Ghost in the Machine,* and coined the term *holon* to refer to the parts of a system that are also systems themselves.[5] One of the challenges to complex system overseers is that each of the nested parts may exhibit different temporal and spatial features.

Natural resource management theory has begun to shift from a foundational model based on conservation and the assumption of equilibrium behavior to a framework based on the complex system model. In this latter system, prudent managers are moving to a form of adaptive management since it becomes impossible to predict exactly what will happen when something perturbs a living system. The key difference is that the assumption of predictability is loosened. Managers and policy analysts cannot assume that actual implementation patterns will follow the results of their generally linear models. More monitoring and flexibility in follow-up actions will be needed. Justification for the precautionary principle is strengthened by this argument: changes in living systems are fundamentally unknowable. The emergence of unsustainability itself makes a good case. Adaptive management and the institutions required to implement it is the primary focus of a later chapter on institutional change.

Taken merely as a description of the natural world, the concepts explored in this chapter have little power to bring forth sustainability. But by drawing on their metaphorical power as a source for replacements for the elements of the beliefs and norms of the current unsustainable cultural structure, they can shift modern societies from addictive patterns and toward flourishing.

Chapter 10 The Importance of Being . . .

For the first time in history the *physical survival of the human race depends on a radical change of the human heart.*
—*Erich Fromm,* To Have or To Be?

Fromm's observation that we have moved from a mode of "Being" to one of "having" is another sign that all is not right with the world. Recalling and questioning Shelley's affirmation of life, we ask, Can this trend be reversed? I believe so, but it will take some thinking about what these two modes of life are all about and about what can be done to recover the lost domain of Being. Transformation toward sustainability carries with it the onus of change at the deepest levels of the structure that creates both individual and social/cultural action. Our beliefs about what it is to be human lie at the very center. Once we settle on a model of our own existence, other basic beliefs about the world—for example, reality or rationality—come forth.

The natural system cannot provide inspiration for every important constituent of a sustainability structure: humans flourish in ways peculiar to our species. We have to look further for inspiration about what constitutes "Being" as opposed to the Cartesian sense of a thinking subject gazing on an objective world. I have been using lowercase *being* to point to things and capital *Being* to refer to the way of being of human beings.

Although many theories of cultural evolution and activities are available as foundations, choices for models describing human beings are much more sparse. Early thinkers sought to discover the "essence" of humans, the inherent properties that gave them the particular appearance they took in the world. Descartes brought about an abrupt shift with his *Cogito*. Since then, the dominant view of the human being is as a mechanistic organism that captures the real world in the mind (knowledge) and operates on that knowledge according to some sort of logical calculus (reason). In this model we are subjects gazing upon an objective world whose existence is timeless and whose meaning inheres in itself. It would be exactly the same whether humans existed or not. A tree would be a tree without humans on Earth. The economist's model of humans assumes that the calculus operates to maximize one's desires, utilities, preferences, or some intrinsic measure of the priority of satisfaction. This model of human being is very powerful and has fueled the evolution of the modern era.

I offer an alternate model, which grounds human action in a cultural and historical context. In this model our humanness is constituted and shaped from birth by immersion in a culture. The Cartesian model leads to concepts like *having* and *need,* while the latter reveals *care* as central to our being. A moment's consideration of these two opposing words should signal the importance to sustainability. Need focuses inwardly while care turns our attention outwardly to the world. Here as in other chapters, I use familiar words but point to specific meanings for these words. Attention to the distinctions among these words is critical to achieving sustainability because behavior is produced by the meanings we ascribe to words rather than the words taken out of context. Caring can be found in many religious traditions but is dominated by *having* or *need* in the mainstream culture.

HAVING

In his remarkable, prescient book *To Have or To Be?*, Fromm wrote almost thirty years ago that "the first crucial step toward [a healthy economy] is that production shall be directed for the sake of 'sane consumption.' "[1] My underlying critique in this book builds similarly on the connection between pathological patterns of consumption (addiction) and unsustainability (an unhealthy economy).

Fromm comes to this notion of sustainability from his psychological/therapist roots by observing the possibility of two modes of human existence—*being* and *having*—and claims that the *having* paradigm now dominating modern cultures has turned pathological. Only a shift to an alternate mode, *being*, can save both the human species and the natural world in which we live. Fromm says that "having and being are two fundamental modes of experience, the respective strengths of which determine the differences between the characters of individuals and the various types of social structures."[2]

Having is a familiar mode of living in which one's sense of self is completely tied up with possessing. *Being* is much more diffuse as a concept. It is the experience of acting and leads to the sense of aliveness and connectedness that only rarely shows up. I know from my own experience that such moments do occur. Fishing is a passion for me, and I go fly-fishing on the ocean bays by our summer cottage on most summer days. The challenge of finding and hooking a striped bass is certainly an important part of what gets me out on the water, but the real draw is the connectedness to the world of nature that I feel. Every day is unique. And on the very rare occasions that I catch and release a really big striper after working for thirty minutes or more to boat the fish, I know that we have become connected. I even wonder if I will see the same fish at the end of my line again.

Fromm notes that Being has become diminished, in part through the modern linguistic practice of using nouns in place of verbs (reification). One says, for example, "I have an idea," instead of saying, "I think." At the extreme, the relationship of humans to each other and to the surrounding world collapses into a pathological equality: "*I am = what I have and what I consume*" (emphasis in the original).[3] Roy de Souza, founder of the Web site Zebo.com, which collects and displays lists of everyday possessions owned mostly by young users, told the *New York Times,* "For the youth, you are what you own." He notes further, "They list these things because it defines them."[4] The potential addictive quality of this equality and its negative implications for sustainability should be obvious. In this latter form, our identity and self-worth become conflated with all the material objects we acquire to provide satisfaction for our needs and solutions to all the "problems" of life. Life becomes Sisyphean; the realization of self is the rock we push uphill to reach the promised land, only to have the material burdens it represents overcome us and push us back to where we started.

Modern consumerism is a form of having. We can also see having in other areas of daily life. Learning and its converse, teaching, have two distinct faces. In having, one gathers in knowledge and holds on to it. Teachers provide such knowledge. Students use notes and references to augment and support what is held in memory. In the Being mode, learning is always contextual and happens in some horizon of understanding. Listening is active, not passive. Having shows up in the ways we converse with others, especially when we are trying to convince somebody to do something. Having shows up as advocacy, which translates to holding on to what we already have and arguing that it is the only way to go. Inquiry and other active collaborative modes of conversation relax having and create space for learning. In general, the having mode turns around and owns me in the sense that it controls my actions in relation to protecting and maintaining the supply of things I have. Relationships between objects in my life and me come to lack aliveness. Love is particularly affected by these two modes. In the having mode, love means possessing a loved one as a thing that contains love. Such "love" strangles and deadens the relationship.

Fromm took this beyond the individual to the behavior of nations, saying, "For as long as nations are composed of people whose main motivations is having and greed, they cannot help waging war. They necessarily covet what another nation has, and attempt to get what they want by war, economic pressure, or threats. . . . Peace as a state of lasting harmonious relations between nations is only possible when the having structure is replaced by the being structure."[5]

BEING

> Man is the only animal for whom his own existence is a problem which he has to solve and from which he cannot escape.
> —*Erich Fromm,* Man for Himself

Although Heidegger never used the word *sustainability,* he, like Fromm, was deeply worried about the state of the world and was motivated in part by a sense that humans were off the track that made them special beings, different from all others. They had lost or were very close to losing the critical feature that made them special. For Heidegger this was Being itself, for in his thinking it was concern for Being that made human beings unique. He saw Being as intimately connected to everyday things used to carry out routine activities. Although his work is groundbreaking in the philosophical sphere, it can also provide practical clues about how the nature of the things we use in our everyday lives—the same allocative resources that Giddens refers to—affect the way we perceive the world and ourselves.

The following discussion is largely based on critical commonalities between the phenomenology of Heidegger and the biology of Maturana. One is the thesis that humans are fundamentally social beings and derive their capabilities and knowledge from interacting with the world through involved coping, rather than detached observing. At any moment, who one is and how he or she will react to events in the world depend on his or her history: the sum total of one's life experience. Human actions reflect the world within which individuals have been acculturated and socialized.

In general, the coupling of human to world drifts along with no apparent direction other than a sense of time—always moving forward toward one's ultimate and inevitable death. I believe it is possible to redesign the action-producing structures of the world so that humans cease drifting and take on a way of living that promotes, not retards, Being and its more explicit form—flourishing.

Maturana, the scientist, seeks scientific explanations for the existence and behavior of living beings. He argues that human beings (and all living species) accumulate the bodily structures that constitute consciousness through interacting with their environment. Consciousness and language may be limited to our species because our structure is more highly evolved than other species, but whatever capability for action exists in all species is the result of learning by doing. In the ontogenesis of an individual (in the case of a human, the development from newborn through adulthood), structure accumulates as the organism continuously adapts to the world that surrounds it. The structure determines the response to signals from the world.

An organism can continue to renew itself (autopoiesis) as long as it can respond to change in the outside world by modifying its structure coherently. Life, either as an individual or in social arrangements, is a conservative process. Life goes on only as far as the organisms are able to respond autopoietically to the world. In an unchanging world, this process would be unproblematic and our habits would never change. But the world is never static; it is always changing, and the individual and social systems must adapt coherently in order to flourish. To "adapt coherently" is a technical way of saying that living systems need to adjust their behavior to maintain autopoiesis and, assuming that the changes are relatively long-lived, to create new structure. Individuals respond only to the world they can perceive through their senses, limiting their ability to respond routinely to unintended consequences of their individual and cultural activities that are not perceived in the normal course of events. For example, the addict is not aware of the impact of his or her habit on the underlying system. A society is not aware of the addictive effects of its habits.

If the new structure cannot support the vital functions of life, the organism will sicken and may even die. In a sense, this theory is quite similar to the notions of complex living systems (Chapter 9). As long as a complex system can coherently change its structure when perturbed, it maintains itself in more or less the same emergent state (resilience), but if the perturbation is such that the existing structure cannot cohere to the intervention, the system will flip to a new state with different properties. We might say in this case that the old system dies and a new one is born, using metaphors from biology. Such renewal is essential to sustainability. Change in the world is inevitable. Populations of humans and other species wax and wane. Over time, species arise and disappear. The inventiveness of humans produces new technical structure. Sustainability rests on the possibility that the system of the present will maintain its structural integrity while the details change.

Heidegger's main quest was to understand the presence of beings— his word for anything that can become distinct in our experience. By becoming present as an experience, we simply say that something is. He set out to explain why and how things show up as meaningful objects to human beings. He saw humans as a very special kind of being whose way of Being incorporates an understanding of what it is to be. No other kind of being has this characteristic. Heidegger even gave the special kind of existence of human beings its own word—*Dasein,* which is often roughly translated as "being there." But this word does not simply refer to a thing but to a way of Being-in-the-world (the *there*). Unlike the dualistic Cartesian mind/body or subject/object separation, "being there" is all about cocreating both, through everyday immersion in the hurly-burly of living, simply doing whatever is normal according to the surrounding culture.

Heidegger probes existence and behavior through the tools of philosophy, using language and, in his case, a particular form of phenomenology. Methodologically, Heidegger and Maturana recognize that understanding is a second-order phenomenon. The observer or explainer—or "understander"—must be able to explain/understand him- or herself in order to make a case that is grounded. Otherwise everything is self-referential. Critics of Heidegger claim that he was never able to escape from this fundamentally circular process. Some have compared the process of understanding what it is to be human to that of peeling a large onion. One can strip off layer after layer but fail to get to the very center, where the ground of being is hidden. The fundamental groundlessness of human understanding is, indeed, a central feature of his philosophy.

It is risky to pick out a few features of a complex and interwoven work such as Heidegger's lifetime devotion to understanding Being, but I will nevertheless try to point to several concepts that I believe relate to flourishing and thence to sustainability. He sought to discover the ontological structure of "Being," that is, characteristics of existence that are peculiar to Homo sapiens. He saw Being as inseparable from the world. Humans are what they are because they are placed (thrown) in the world and are shaped from the very beginning by their social interactions with that world. His philosophy is a radical critique of classic Aristotelian essentialism and the subject/object dichotomy of Descartes. Heidegger refers to "being-in-the-world" as a compound noun. Human beings are aware of their existence and care about understanding that existence. This awareness and care provide Being its special features. Given the circularity of the process of understanding, humans are, however, doomed to remain groundless (or rootless) about being. This rootlessness leads humans to engage in everyday activities aimed at trying to make the world a place where they are secure and can flourish. In everyday life, caring is manifest in the activities one chooses to do.

Being proceeds during a human's existence, shaped by the world but not predestined by it. Depending on which mode an individual applies in dealing with the world—opposing authentic/inauthentic alternatives or an undifferentiated mode—that person has different possibilities. I found a relevant metaphorical definition that defines authenticity as "performing music as nearly as possible the way it was performed at the time it was created." Being comes forth from and is revealed in performance (action). Authentic is more or less what our everyday sense of the word suggests: acting consistently with one's "own" self.

Be careful with definitions here, as the authentic self is definitely not the psychological ego or some inner self waiting to break out. The meaning of authenticity in this sense is the exact opposite of the word in typical usage in which one equates authenticity with seeking the "real self," as if such a self actually exists. In an editorial in the *New York Times* titled "Our Overrated Inner Self," the sociologist Orlando Patterson criticized "authenticity" as leading to self-doubt, distrust, or groupthink. His alternative positive distinction is "sincerity." His claims are based on distinctions developed in *Sincerity and Authenticity,* a series of 1970 lectures by literary critic Lionel Trilling.[6] Recalling Trilling, Patterson wrote, "Sincerity, he said, requires us to act and really be the way that we present ourselves to others. Authenticity involves finding and expressing the true inner self and judging all relationships in terms of it."[7]

Patterson's claims are the same as those I have been developing throughout this book; he has, however, reversed the terms. Sincerity is close to what I am calling authenticity. Authenticity involves an acceptance of the groundlessness of Being, another way of rejecting the idea of "an inner self." Identity is not something inherent; it is an assessment made by others. If actions are authentic (sincere), then these assessments will likely be congruent with one's own explanations of the motivation for the actions being assessed. What Patterson calls "authentic" is closer to the opposite notion of inauthenticity, acting out what is expected by the cultural "they," the essence of political correctness. His article reinforces the basic claim in this book that loss of authenticity, as a proxy for Being, is deeply involved in the unsustainable state of today's world.

Deliberate reflection about the meaning of life is the only possible response to the experience of existential dread without falling into self-deception. Authenticity requires the self-conscious gathering in and acceptance of the conditions of one's own existence, including the inevitability of death. When that choice is made, one can stop "fleeing" from the existential anxiety that inevitably accompanies the recognition of one's finiteness and thereby begin to see and appreciate more of the world that would be otherwise concealed. And with more of the world available comes more possibility.

Earlier I cited the issue raised by McKibben in his book *Enough* regarding how some scientists are seeking ways to prolong life indefinitely by means of technology, and how others are eagerly awaiting this moment. For those who worry that death will come too early, cryopreservation could buy time. This form of technology, it seems to me, would produce the very worst possible result in any progress toward authenticity. In an interview released posthumously, musing on the unrelenting technological domination of the world, Heidegger said, "Only a God can save us."[8] I am more hopeful, as I believe that it is possible to be more deliberate in designing technology that will produce authenticity and not its opposite, thus we can rely on our own capabilities without invoking the always uncertain call on a god for help.

Authentic Being has an ironic sense in that it means accepting that Being is groundless. No matter how intently one tries to understand and explain his or her existence by getting to some foundational idea, the interpretation of the last story revealed in the process depends on the worldview held at that moment. Interpretation is the process by which the phenomena we perceive, including what we listen to and read, are given meaning. The meaning that emerges is always produced by the existing structure—that is, the historical record of life's experience up to that moment. This process is virtually identical to Giddens's structuration model for social action wherein the shared beliefs (interpretive structure) convert the meaningless world into one that provides the context for collective action. But in revealing something new, the meaning-giving structure itself changes (autopoiesis) so that in the next instance the world may take on new meaning. This pattern then repeats indefinitely.

In his early writings Heidegger argued that the traditions of modernity, mainly Cartesianism and scientism, have led inexorably to the disappearance of authenticity and to the dominance of the two other forms of being: inauthenticity and indifference. Inauthentic is the opposite of authentic and means existing, without reflection, according to the norms and fashions of the cultural surround. It becomes an ideology: conformism. Individual beings act completely in accordance with prevalent cultural modes as a rule, albeit a rule that is both misunderstood and denied by those individuals. Inauthenticity shows up when one acts in the context of some external "should" that has not been embodied as one's own rule of behavior. One difference between inauthenticity and authentic ethical behavior is that, in the latter mode, the "should" or "should not" rule has been previously chosen as one's own in a reflective moment.

In the modern world, the public understanding (the dominant cultural norms and beliefs) of Being is that it is, or can be, grounded. When Being is interpreted as grounded, a sense of correctness that guides action comes forth. When this happens, the possibilities open to human actors diminish as they choose only those actions that conform to the conventional sense of what is right and wrong, not in a moral sense, but simply as what is accepted as normal in the culture. This process is consistent with the development of pathological cultural patterns such as those discussed earlier. The hyperindividualism that drives modern consumerist economies is so pervasive that individuals have little choice except to consume as the culture directs them. Ironically, the unceasing search for autonomy has become enslaving.

In the authentic mode, the actor accepts the pervasiveness of the cultural "they" (as in "they" say this or that, or "one" does this or that) as the context for actions, ceases to search for the "real" self hidden inside the body, and chooses to be whatever has shown up historically (at least for the moment). Heidegger makes an important point that the work we choose to do is not a reflection of one's true self; it is a choice among possibilities already present in the culture that has shaped Being. Whatever we do makes sense to us only in the context of the culture. The search for a "self" hidden deep within our bodies is bound to be fruitless. In making this kind of choice, one accepts the groundlessness of Being in the sense that there is no transcendent foundation for life as humans.

One source on the Web defined inauthentic as an intention to deceive, and another as a spurious work of art. In the first case, the concern is not so much deceiving others as it is fooling ourselves that all is right in the world. The second suggests that something may have become lost since Homo sapiens appeared on Earth. Whether one believes in the Creation as told in the Bible or in a theory of evolution, the same question persists. Have we lost something that was once part of our Being? Although sustainability is a vision for the future, the idea also invokes a sense of a lost past—a time when we lived closer to our authentic selves, even as the surrounding world may have been harsher and not so convenient.

The undifferentiated mode is just that; it describes humans who basically drift along without choosing to be authentic or inauthentic. Most humans settle for the inauthentic or undifferentiated modes of being. In indifference, individuals simply drift along in the tide of convention (conformity) without the unconscious denial that they are captured by the cultural "they" or the "one." As in the inauthentic mode, they have little or no possibility in their lives, in spite of the modernist paradigmatic belief that they can locate their real self and follow it to happiness or to whatever personal end state is desired. With a constant focus on finding or satisfying one's self, individuals become narcissistic, and the culture follows. The connection between these latter modes of Being and Fromm's "having" mode is direct. While these two thinkers have come to the same observation from two very different horizons, the results are uncannily similar.

What's important is that Heidegger does not place any value judgment on these modes. He is interested only in the ontology of Being. But sustainability is strongly normative and relates to flourishing (the "good life"). Within this context, the authentic mode of Being takes on special significance.

Authenticity and sustainability are closely linked. Living authentically means that one is conscious of the rootlessness of life—a consciousness that produces a mirror image: the opportunity to change one's identity and consequent actions. It enhances awareness of the human role as a discloser, seeing the world as it is without the cultural blinders that disguise it. The anxiety of authenticity that might be considered negative in the everyday psychological sense of modernity takes on a positive aspect, alerting actors to the real state of their worlds. But perhaps most important, authenticity means the ability to respond to the world in nonroutine ways, designed specifically to break out of unsustainable routines. In a nutshell, authenticity opens up the space of possibility, the cardinal feature of sustainability.

> Language is the house of Being. In its home human beings dwell. Those who think and those who create with words are the guardians of this home.
> —*Martin Heidegger, "Letter on Humanism"*

A second common thread running between Maturana and Heidegger is their claim that language is the medium of human knowledge and Being. Maturana points out that language arose out of the social interactions of humans as a means to coordinate actions, not as a tool for explanations as the Cartesian model would suggest. By languaging (Maturana's word), that is, living in and through language, humans bring forth (constitute) a world. Language is a trait peculiar to humans. Maturana is careful to distinguish between linguistic behavior, which he attributes to many species, and language, which is distinctively human. Reflection, the way we know how and what we know, takes place in language. Language is the means by which we coordinate our social interactions. Linguistic behavior is peculiar to distinct social groups in that the specific words they use to coordinate action regarding similar objects may be different (*voiture* in France, *car* in America), but the role that language plays is the same for both.

An identical object takes on different meanings to individuals whose history and accumulated structure is different. Communications are interpreted differently according to the history as well. Maturana takes pains to show that the meaning of a message is not in the message itself but is provided by the structure of the receiving individual.[9] However, because we observe that we do coordinate actions effortlessly and effectively among different individuals, it is easy to assume that language is the bearer of meaning. Both are clear that this is a mistake and that meaning comes from the individual and the history of that individual in the social, worldly milieu into which he or she has been thrown.

The objects we use are meaningful for the user via language used to interact with them operationally. Another way of interpreting this is to say that the artifacts we use embody scripts that mediate the way we use them. By scripting an artifact to produce long-lasting satisfaction or environmentally thoughtful behavior, it may be possible to break the addictive and environmentally damaging patterns producing unsustainability.

> Man does not have a nature, but a history. Man is no thing, but a drama. His life is something that has to be chosen, made up as he goes along, and a human consists in that choice and invention. Each human being is the novelist of himself, and though he may choose between an original writer and a plagiarist, he cannot help choosing. He is condemned to be free.
> —*Ortega y Gasset,* History as a System

In the course of working on this book I realized that a common theme emerged regarding the models I have come to incorporate in my thinking. In Chapter 8 I considered Giddens's model of how societies and other collectives work. I then examined natural systems through the lens of complexity and explored what it is to be a human being. All of the models have one thing in common: they view living systems as historical in nature. This is not the usual meaning of history, which is a story about, and often trying to explain, the past. Here history means that the present action-producing structure of a living system is determined by the accumulated past experience of both the individuals and the social collective. History has an etymological and practical tie to the idea of story.

In the language of the economist, changes in meaning such as are expressed through values or preferences are held to be exogenous, that is, they arise from some outside, disconnected, even transcendent source. Any such change cannot be handled by conventional economic theory, which relies on the assumption that such values do not change during the period being analyzed. Virtually all decision models resting on conventional notions of rationality assume that there is a one-to-one correspondence between the present state of the world, the action to be taken, and the future state. If one's knowledge is sufficiently certain, the outcome of an action can be predicted within some probabilistic limit.

In a historicist's world, this correspondence disappears. Human actions follow one's meaningful interpretations of the immediate world, and these interpretations always depend on one's historical horizons. The same material world has profoundly different meanings to two individuals coming from distinct cultures and, thus, from distinct life histories. A wave of a hand can mean either hello or goodbye. Similarly, two people from the same culture often ascribe different meanings to the same object because each individual has a unique history. In the Cartesian sense of objects existing independently from the observer's interpretations, the historical route to such meaning is hidden.

BEING IS A DOORWAY TO SUSTAINABILITY

Against this philosophical discussion, the question for sustainability is, "Is there a practical lesson to be learned from all of this?" I am convinced that there is. Summing up this discussion, according to Fromm, Maturana, or Heidegger, humans exist in different practical modes, that is, in the way they live out their everyday lives. The fullness of the revealed world and its possibilities for Being depend on the mode. Authentic living means a life less directed by the cultural "other" (the societal structure) and more directed through freer choice by the self. With authenticity modern humans can possibly break free from the grip that technology has upon them, at least long enough to begin caring for themselves, other humans, and the world of nature. Without such care, sustainability will always be unavailable.

Being authentic is never, however, a permanent state. One does not simply declare that "I will no longer drift along with the cultural crowd once and for all." Authentic choices are made from time to time when the culturally given meaning of world recedes and one can visualize other possible choices. Moments such as this come when one is at rest or in a reflective moment where the world shows itself, and the question of what it is to be human comes forth. In such moments one may be able to access the caring quality of Being that lies under our everyday, practical activities or the loving quality that Maturana claims is an essential feature of human beings.[10]

And it is such moments when one can make flourishing an issue and seek to bring it forth when one returns to the busyness of daily living. The triad of Being, nature, and ethics fuses together; sustainability may emerge, even if just for the moment. Without such breaks in the routines of living, it is difficult or even impossible to take on sustainability—the possibility of flourishing—as one's own job to produce. Those who would redesign our unsustainable world must learn how to produce such moments of satisfied restfulness and reflection. Our way of Being in relation to technology was not always as it is today. Even if technology indeed has an iron grip on humanity, we should be able to redesign the specific forms of technology we use to reveal the world rather than hide it from us, and to open us up to authenticity. We need to learn how to design our equipment and our cultural institutions so that moments such as these are available to everyone and so that the commitments to authenticity and caring can be more easily realized in the midst of everyday activities.

With the objective of increasing the possibility of flourishing, this last assertion can be restated as a question: "Is there a way to design our tools (equipment) such that they promote our appreciation of the care structure of Being (see Chapter 13) rather than hide it from us?" Equipment here is just a name for all the goods and services we consume. Can we break the magic spell that our equipment and the technological way of framing the world have cast upon us? Designers are learning that their artifacts do not merely manifest usefulness. They speak to us and offer suggestions or direct us toward actions beyond the mere satisfaction of our momentary concerns. If these designs are done artfully, our individual daily actions can become more aligned with sustainability. Culture would then follow.

Chapter 11 Consumption and Need

I just need enough to tide me over until I need more.
—Bill Hoest, The Lockhorns

One of the basic premises in this book is that technology, in spite of its negative side, will continue to be the primary means for virtually all cultural activities. For satisfaction humans will continue to rely on things made by others. This book's critique of technology is not a Luddite call to destroy the evil machines that enslave humankind. Although I believe that technology has eroded the Being mode of living, I also hold that the culprits are the nature of the particular technology and our attitude toward it. By designing our tools and resources with Being in mind, it should be possible to produce a more favorable balance between authenticity and inauthenticity. My vision of sustainability and the means to approach it are eminently practical and not utopian. I do not see the future as one of Huxley's *Brave New World*, in which drug-induced bliss is always at hand. The key to sustainability will be a balance between devices and commodified consumption such as the philosopher Albert Borgmann has described, and products and services that can transparently restore the human capability for caring and coping in all dimensions of living.

CONSUMPTION AND UNSUSTAINABILITY

This common word, consumption, has many meanings in everyday usage. One refers to the taking in of food; another to the wasting away (or using up) of the body (tuberculosis); and another to the action of an external object (consumed by fire). Many of the meanings have an economic sense and refer to the using up of resources either in their material forms or as measured by a monetary equivalent. Other than the less commonsense meaning of wasting away, all these definitions focus on the process of using up and on the materiality of consumption. In talking about sustainability it is important to understand consumption beyond the reified, material way the term is used in economics.

Economists use the term in several ways but most frequently point to expenditures for goods and services by final demanders, such as households, governments, schools, and other civil institutions. Goods and services used in manufacturing or delivery of services to these sectors are accounted for separately. The distinctiveness of goods and services is quite arbitrary. Goods are the output of traditional manufacturing, mining, and agricultural sectors. The materiality of the outputs is evident in the form of substances like iron and steel, and in the form of functional products. Services apply to the outputs of presumably nonmaterial economic activities such as banking or communications, food, hospitality, and similar sectors. The materiality of the output is seemingly absent in the case of telephone services, although it takes a large technological infrastructure to produce such outputs as a telephone call. Goods and services have one key aspect in common: both serve to satisfy something that a consumer wants or, in economic terms, demands.

Consumption in this sense has two important aspects that relate to sustainability. First, although conventionally measured in monetary terms, consumption is primarily manifest through material goods. The consequences of the production, use, and disposal of these goods are the proximate cause of damage to the environment and to its present state of unsustainability. The second is that economists also make a naïve connection between the level of consumption and human well-being—more or less equating the two in quantitative terms.

The importance of the quantitative nature of consumption in the affluent world has been long recognized as a major contributor to unsustainability. Arguments calling for reduction in the quantity of consumption continue, often based on the widely quoted IPAT ($I = P \times A \times T$) relationship: an identity between impact (I) and the product of population (P), consumption per capita (captured in the affluence term A), and impact per unit of consumption captured by the technology term (T).[1] The difficulty of influencing either population or economic growth in the short run leaves technology as the only relief valve. Earlier calls to reduce material and energy consumption by a factor of four now argue for as much as a factor of fifty. Sustainable development strategies in general are focused on this factor.

Ecoefficiency—more value for less impact—is the term most generally used by industry as a means to continue to supply the demand for goods and services but with significantly fewer repercussions on the environment and on the natural resource capacity of the Earth. Specific strategies include industrial ecology[2] and a number of derivative practices: dematerialization, material loop closing, ecodesign, biomimicry, design for sustainability, The Natural Step, Natural Capitalism, and many more general concepts and specific frameworks.[3] The importance of following such practices cannot be understated, as these guidelines and frameworks represent, perhaps, the most immediately effective means to slow down and hopefully reverse environmental unsustainability. None of these approaches will, however, create sustainability as I have defined it. Although often referred to as "sustainability" frameworks, all such strategies are limited to the job of reducing unsustainability.

Consumption as a phenomenon needs to be carefully examined beyond the economist's perspective if this discussion is to make sense, and if we will be able to think carefully about the nature of the goods and services we consume in the ordinary sense of the word. The commonplace idea of consumption always refers to something happening with things. It is interesting to me that economics focuses on the things that are consumed rather than on the people that consume them. This viewpoint is just the opposite of the perspective of this book. We are most certainly interested in the things consumed, as they are the proximate cause of the pathological effects on humans and the natural world, but if anything is to be done about this situation it is critical to understand these things and how they relate to human Being.

Consumption as using up is not the primary process maintaining Being, except in the fundamental process of incorporating things into our body, such as eating or taking medicine—even viewing a picture or listening to music—whereby a substance (or a sight, or a sound) actually disappears inside of our body. Most of what goes for consumption in economic jargon is related to the equipment, artifacts, tools, products, services, resources, and so on that are used in the process of providing some sort of satisfaction. Economists refer to these objects by counting up all the money we spend in the marketplace in certain categories, but they leave out some critical categories as well, in cases in which no market transaction takes place. Many of the most important domains of human activities lie outside of what economists include in their accounts.

To explain why humans "consume," psychologists and others call upon the concept of "need." Need, as a noun, is very difficult to explain, as it has no material existence nor can it ever be observed in action. Its verbal form, as in "I need X," refers to a statement about one's beliefs about some mental state. "X" can be all sorts of things, both material and emotional: money, cell phones, cars, food, love, happiness, and so on. Need is better considered as an explanation for something else. Need is always associated with something that is missing. Need makes no sense without an "X." When one says that another is needy, this means that the other lives as if he or she lacks many things all the time.

Economists do not often use the word "need." Their term is "preference" or "utility," referring to the ordering in one's mind of a desire to acquire something, provided that he or she has the means to get it. Which of the things available to me right now would I choose first, second, third, and so on under the constraint that I have only limited resources available? Economic thinking is more about "wants" than needs. Utilities refer to specific objects like cars or Big Macs, or to more generic things like love or happiness. This feature of economic thinking has contributed to the equating of intangibles like love with material objects that can be the subject of accountable economic transactions.

But it is exactly things like happiness or love—and not the objects we acquire toward these ends—that seem to be more fundamental to our Being. Consumption implies a lifelong striving to satisfy such needs. Consumption might better be called the activities involved in such satisfaction. But if we stop and think for just a moment, we realize that this is virtually all we do in our waking hours. Or, to be more philosophical for a moment, consumption is just another way of referring to the tangible activities involved in living. Consumption entails the acquisition and use of material objects: the equipment we use every day. I prefer to use Heidegger's word, "equipment," because it has an obvious utilitarian sense, one that is missing in the notions of either "goods" or "products."

Modern forms of consumption have become addictive, and they produce serious unintended consequences. Instead of getting nearer to the ends we seek, they are ever more distant. Our physiological and psychological health suffers. If the quantitative measure of consumption is correlated with well-being, then it is difficult to explain why male suicide rates have about doubled worldwide during the same period in which per capita GDP (the standard measure of consumption) has also doubled.[4] Suicide rates would seem to be a better indicator than polls of general satisfaction. To counter the wealth effect, that is, that wealthier people consume proportionally less of their income than do poor people, I also looked at some recent data from China, where income levels are still low compared to the affluent countries of the OECD. From 1994 to 2005 Gallup poll results indicate that the ratio of negative to positive assessments of satisfaction increased at the same time that per capita income increased by a factor of about 2.5.[5] Many social indicators in the United States show perverse trends against continuing economic growth.

This model of consumption places no limits on demand or want. Human demand is assumed to be insatiable, constrained only by the ability to pay for or otherwise acquire the means to quench the desire. This model is firmly fixed in the modern view of human behavior. The concept itself, however, may be only a "side effect" of the addictive pattern of modernity. If we are locked into the upper loop of the general pattern of addictive behavior, observers who fail to consider the existence of an alternative path to success and satisfaction would reasonably infer that human needs (as the means of satisfaction) are insatiable. The alcoholic's desire for a drink is insatiable, not because of any inherent "need" for liquor, but because a proper solution is out of sight. As long as the voice of modernity keeps telling us, "We are needy at the core," we will continue to act accordingly until the addiction is broken.

In a world with limits, this model of consumption underlies unsustainability. Nature is treated as a scarce resource in economic terms; that is, when something becomes increasingly expensive, due perhaps to its absolute scarcity, people will move to less costly substitutes. The fact that critical natural resources may be depleted is of no consequence. Technology and innovation will always show up just in time and offer substitutes. This interpretation of consumption and its causes is a key factor in producing unsustainability.

EXAMINING "NEED"

> What we need in order to survive, and what we need in order to flourish
> are two different things.
> —*Michael Ignatieff,* The Needs of Strangers

Let us consider the notion that we spend every day seeking to fulfill or satisfy some lifelong set of aspects of living. Is there just one member of this set: happiness—or felicity, as the Fathers of the Enlightenment called it? Or are there many such ends of our striving? Consumption in the everyday economics sense quietly ignores this concept. Economists measure consumption as the monetary value of purchases by households and a few other economic sectors. The drivers for consumption are the preferences or utilities of the consumers, constrained by the resources they have at hand. It is interesting that economists speak of demand as the potential for consumption, conflating desire and ability. Need as a distinction is hard to find here. The closest equivalent concept is want. The two are very different. Want has a voluntary aspect. It is about something I could do without yet I desire it anyway.

Need has a different connotation. A search of etymological sources associates need with conditions requiring relief (satisfaction) or things or conditions that are necessary but lacking. Further in the background are the notions of essential or indispensable—but essential or indispensable to what? To answer this question, I turn first to psychology and then again to the ontology of Being. The psychologist Abraham Maslow developed a hierarchy of needs that relate different kinds or categories of needs to different aspects of Being. His original hierarchy contains five stages of needs (indicated by an asterisk), which were expanded in a later revised edition (1998) of his classic text on psychology, *Motivation and Personality*.[6] Briefly, Maslow's steps are:

1. Basic physiological:* food, shelter, clothing, sleep, etc.
2. Safety:* Home and family and other security measures; a child's security blanket.
3. Love and belongingness:* membership in groups, clubs, or civic organizations; peer camaraderie.
4. Esteem:* self esteem gained through successes, peer recognition.
5. Knowing: curiosity, education, or exploration.
6. Aesthetic: order, beauty, or art. Maslow spoke of the urge to straighten a crooked picture on the wall.
7. Self-Actualization:* Maslow's own words serve best to characterize this category: "A musician must make music, the artist must paint, a poet must write, if he is to be ultimately at peace with himself. What a man can be, he must be. This need we may call self-actualization."[7] While other needs may be met fully, self-actualization is seen as "growing," that is, as a continuing driving force.
8. Transcendence: connecting with something beyond the ego.

Maslow claimed that people moved upward through these stages, fulfilling one level before they progressed to the next. Satisfaction, in his terms, is a state in which the need at one level has been met. The significance of Maslow's scheme is that need is not undifferentiated, as the marginal preference model of standard economic theory suggests.

Manfred Max-Neef, a Chilean economist, proposed a different taxonomic system of needs:[8]

• Subsistence
• Protection
• Affection
• Understanding

- Participation
- Leisure
- Creation
- Identity
- Freedom

His elements, although named differently, show many similarities to Maslow's and are arranged in much the same order as the Maslow hierarchy, but Max-Neef makes the key point that all needs must be satisfied all the time to make a person whole. He dismisses the notion of hierarchy or succession. With a focus on underdeveloped societies, Max-Neef speaks of poverties in the plural, as deficiencies in multiple categories, to make his critique of standard economic theories of development very stark.

Max-Neef introduces the concept of satisfiers: the means by which needs are addressed. He includes both tools and institutional processes (interactions) as satisfiers. His interest is primarily in development in the political economic sense: how can institutions be designed to serve human-scale needs? I would say that he is fundamentally interested in what I am calling sustainability. His work arose in the context of undeveloped and developing economies, but it is also a useful foundation for thinking about the developed world.

For me, the key point in Max-Neef's treatment of need is his discussion of satisfiers. These are the objects and processes by which needs are satisfied. Anything that goes by the name of product or service fits this distinction, from a hamburger at McDonald's (subsistence) to a trip to a ski resort (leisure). Max-Neef focuses mainly on institutional processes and activities as examples of satisfiers. His work rests on a critique of modern cultures, arguing that they operate through means that do not produce satisfaction and, further, may destroy what satisfaction may come from other means. He describes five types of satisfiers: two positive and three negative.

- Singular
- Synergic
- Inhibiting
- Pseudo
- Violators or destroyers

"Singular" means to produce satisfaction in just one category of need. Borgmann would call these means "devices." Giving someone a present might satisfy the need for affection, but nothing else. Going to a football game satisfies leisure needs. A second, more powerful set of means satisfies more than one category of need simultaneously. Max-Neef calls these "synergic," corresponding roughly to what Borgmann calls focal experiences. Although aimed primarily at one domain, they also supply satisfaction in others. The examples Max-Neef includes reflect his critique of highly developed societies. Breast-feeding is primarily aimed at subsistence, but it also satisfies needs for protection, affection, and identity. Preventive medicine aims primarily at protection, but it provides satisfaction for understanding, participation, and subsistence. Borgmann's frequent example of home cooking satisfies the need for subsistence as well as for affection, participation, and identity.

The next three categories of satisfiers have negative overtones. "Inhibiting" satisfiers interfere with obtaining satisfaction in some other categories in the process of addressing a specific need. For example, unlimited permissiveness in a family may satisfy the need for freedom but may inhibit satisfaction in protection, affection, identity, and participation. Taylorist production systems offer workers satisfaction in the subsistence domain but inhibit understanding, participation, creation, identity, and freedom.

As the name suggests, the next class, "pseudo-satisfiers," fails to create more than momentary sensations of fulfillment. Fashion and status symbols superficially satisfy the need for identity. Charitable food programs fail to satisfy needs for subsistence fully. His point here is much like the saying "Give someone a fish and you feed them for a day; teach them to fish and you feed them for life." "Violators or destroyers," which are means directed toward some need, make the satisfaction of needs in other areas problematic or even impossible, and also may act only as pseudo-satisfiers in the primary area. War is, in theory, a means of protection, but it destroys the ability to provide for the needs for subsistence, affection, understanding, participation, and freedom.

In Chapter 12 I develop a set of categories superficially akin to those of either Maslow or Max-Neef but based on the phenomenological model of Being instead of on economic (Max-Neef) or psychological

(Maslow) roots. Max-Neef's concept of different types of satisfiers remains relevant for this alternate set and can be a powerful input to the design of equipment and of the institutions that provide such tools for everyday living. The notion that some forms of equipment can inhibit or negatively impact satisfaction in other areas is generally missing from standard market models used both for design and for market research. Immediate satisfaction of some particular "need" is the Holy Grail. Little or no consideration is given to the other possibilities. Even if designers and marketers continue to stand on standard models, by using Max-Neef's typology of satisfiers they would focus their efforts on the development and marketing of artifacts that are truly more satisfying in the Being, rather than the having, mode.

Satisfaction is a key distinction in the path to sustainability. The dominance of need as the target of economic activity produces only temporary satisfaction. The objects we acquire and employ function in the upper loop of the addiction diagram. They provide immediate relief but fail to address the basic "problem" of life: the unending quest to understand what it is to be human. Life is generally inauthentic. Our activities reflect only what is the right thing to do according to the cultural "they."

This ironically fundamentally unsatisfying pattern can be reversed if *care* replaces *need* in the design of our equipment, places, and institutions. Our continuous engagement with life can then produce a different kind of satisfaction: a state of completion or perfection. The consequences for consumption and addiction should be clear. One can stop, rest, and reflect without the nagging voice of need always in the background. I do not mean we should strive for the Buddhist notion of Nirvana, an enlightened state of mind reached only after one frees oneself of all desires and worldly things. Being is just the opposite, coming only through involved engagement with the world. Satisfaction comes with reflexive awareness that one's concerns—the worldly manifestation of care—are being authentically addressed. It does not mean that these concerns go away; it means only that, for the moment, whatever has been the focus of one's involved coping has been addressed. Life is only and all about care and coping.

Chapter 12 To Care Is Human

But the care of the Earth is our most ancient and most worthy and, after all, our most pleasing responsibility. To cherish what remains of it, and to foster its renewal, is our only hope.
—*Wendell Berry*, The Art of the Commonplace

The products and services we employ in carrying out everyday, routine activities can provide meaning in our lives far beyond the fleeting satisfaction of needs implied by the standard economic model of human behavior. The first step in exploring this possibility is to replace the elusive concept of needs with the notion of "care," a concept central to Being. Care connects one to the world of nature, other humans, and self rather than isolating the actor via the narcissistic, inner-directed source of action related to need. To get to the core of what care means, I begin with an examination of the bases of the meaning of the things we use routinely every day.

Being, for humans, springs from concern about Being as an issue. Among all creatures we are the only species that can and does ask questions about our existence, and this is another way of illuminating the notion of care. Care is the deepest structure on which Being rests. This means caring for oneself, other human beings, and everything else in appropriate ways that reflect the being of those other entities as themselves, not as utilitarian objects.

To understand this portrayal of care better, perhaps this thought experiment might help. Imagine a time when the world was much younger and hominids were just emerging. The long period needed by these protohumans to raise their children necessitated some form of social organization and a corresponding means of coordinating action among the members. In seeking such coordination, language began to emerge, enabled by the unique biological features of Homo sapiens. At first, language might have been just a set of guttural sounds without distinct meaning. In the course of social life, however, individuals progressed to making repeated, distinctive sounds while pointing to objects (phenomenon). After a while these objects became known by the sounds. The language ultimately evolved into a form more like ours, with a grammar and vocabulary.

Objects (nouns), spatial relations (prepositions), and actions (verbs) were the result of observations about the world perceived by these early humans. The objects and actions that were meaningful to them in their daily social lives started to exist as distinctions against a larger, diffuse background. This is just another way of saying that language arose around the coordination of actions that humans cared about and with the objects involved. Now stop and ask yourself, "Which came first, the things or some activity that needed names for the objects to facilitate coordination among the actors?"

Meaning, looked at this way, is closely tied to relationships involved in action. Objects in the world are not simply something out of context with an intrinsic, essential meaning; rather, they take on their meaning within a network of relationships between the actor and the world. The Western philosophical tradition has been largely a progression of ideas that lend an essence to objects in the world and portray them as independent from our own existence. The relational aspects solidify into reifications, making it possible to "own" things rather than "be" with things. Language itself distances us from the context out of which phenomena, such as things, take on meaning. Language allows us to take what always derived its meaning within a particular context out of its home and give it some abstract, objectifying, often quantitative sense. Over time, as we use language unreflexively, we lose awareness of the connectedness of the world and the criticality of such relationships to the success of our activities, whether we are at work or at play or involved with any other endeavor.

EQUIPMENT AND MEANING

Things have been the subject of thought since ancient times. One of Aristotle's most famous writings connected (manmade) artifacts to rationality: the way we understand objects. His analysis pointed to the four "causes" I mentioned earlier. Heidegger rejected Aristotle's essentialist argument that the meaning of a thing is embodied in the thing itself, arguing instead, as he does always, that meaning is tied up with Being as the ground out of which beings (things) become distinct. For him, the primary mode of being of objects is as "equipment." Equipment, as the word suggests, comprises objects that derive their distinctiveness through their connection to everyday work—that is, to meaningful action. Equipment, in its most basic mode, is "ready-at-hand" or "available," meaning that it can be picked up effortlessly and used competently without conscious thought in the pursuit of some activity.[1] This notion is closely related to the idea of user-friendliness, designing goods to be used with a minimum of conscious engagement. Although this feature is certainly desirable in most cases, we shall see that the design of objects that induce learning and behavioral change, a key strategy in this book, requires deliberate interruptions in the flow of action.

Heidegger's famous example of a hammer illustrates this point. The meaning of hammer arises only through its involvement in hammering. There is nothing inherent or essential in what we would call a hammer such as those found in a hardware store. If we pick up a rock instead, as might have been the case in prehistoric times, the rock could become a hammer. Equipment is always associated with an "in-order-to-do" something. Further, a particular item of equipment draws its meaning from connections to other equipment; it never stands alone in its functionality or utility. A hammer is meaningful in the context of a workshop (place) along with other equipment, for example, nails in this case.

Equipment, as already mentioned, becomes meaningful only in terms of its worldly context. Equipment is a thing *with-which* we are involved, *in-order-to-do* something (an activity that an observer would notice). The immediate in-order-to-do, in turn, has a meaning *toward-which* some underlying end, a *for-the-sake-of-which*, that is, a more basic concern or care. And all of this always occurs within some practical spatial context or *where-in* (place).[2]

Let us see how this works for a common, everyday piece of equipment, the automobile. Every weekday morning at home (where-in) I get into my car (with-which) in-order-to drive to the office as a step toward my taking orders for-the-sake-of my being a good worker. While driving to work, I turn on my left-hand directional signal in-order-to let cars behind me know I am about to turn, toward-which protecting others for-the-sake-of my caring for other people. On Saturday or Sunday morning, I get into the same car in-order-to drive to my religious center as a step toward praying for-the-sake-of my spiritual concerns.

In Heidegger's model of routine action, the notion of a transcendent ego is absent. One's Being rests on a basic structure of care. Care is ontological and makes possible the apparent intentionality of everyday activities. Care in this sense is not the same as some set of pragmatic or utilitarian drives. Care is, however, manifest through one's everydayness, and can be revealed and characterized just as one's "values" can be implied from observations of discrete actions. The reified equivalent of for-the-sake-of-which is "identity" and that of care is what I will call "concerns" to distinguish the ontological from the practical. Identity is not some inherent aspect of one's nature. One's identity as a parent, for example, comes from the actions that he or she undertakes for-the-sake-of a more or less generic concern, which I will call family in this case. Below I will suggest that concerns are universal within a common culture and can be itemized according to a small list of categories.

It is fairly easy to construct scenarios, like the ones above for the automobile, for virtually everything we do routinely. But this is not what we usually do to explain our actions to others, as our modern Cartesian view always takes things out of their context and endows them with inherent, essential properties, more like Aristotle's model of things than like Heidegger's. A car is a product designed to move us from one place to another without much regard to the context, particularly in failing to address the more fundamental concern: the for-the-sake-of-which. It makes little difference to the designer whether a car is going to work, the doctor, the store, a place of worship, a grandparent's house, the countryside, and so on.

This presentation has meaning both philosophically and practically. Heidegger overturned much of the essentialist ground of classical philosophers and introduced ideas that have fueled postmodernism, deconstructionism, and several other -isms. His philosophy deeply questions the intentionalist model of behavior inherent in the economist's notion of humans as maximizing, autonomous subjects: autonomous in the sense that they possess some innate, transcendent nature, including their desires and needs. Heidegger's philosophy, however, leads to an unending spiral should one seek to uncover the center of Being itself, if there is indeed a center, that is, some foundational human nature. Heidegger claims that such an essentialist center does not exist: living shapes our Being, and what comes to be meaningful is the result of lifelong immersion in a culture. Authentic Being is the mode that acknowledges the groundlessness of being—another way of disclaiming the existence of any absolute center.

So again a reasonable question might well be, "Is there any practical value to this scheme in the sense of sustainability?" My response is, "Definitely, yes!" A powerful pathway to the design of "sustainability" products and services can be found in it. Please excuse the clumsiness of this last phrase, but "sustainable" as an adjective does not convey its meaning according to this text. Products cannot be sustainable in the sense I use. It is possible, but not likely, that both the production and consumption of products can continue for some time in the way they have been, but this is better described as continuing or persisting, but not sustainable. Sustainable X is always more about X than about sustainability, where X could be development, business, buildings, and so on.

Changing the behavior of the user directly through design and, subsequently, the culture indirectly through the structuration process has two openings: the equipment itself, and the spatial context—place. This artifactual pair—equipment and place—can be designed to raise the core care structure to the conscious level and induce reflection and conscious choice, and these steps may, in turn, break addictive, unconscious behaviors. I will focus only on equipment here. And, if the care structure that underlies cultural activities can be reduced to a limited set of domains, somewhat akin to Maslow's or Max-Neef's categories, the number of design targets can be reduced to a manageable handful from an essentially endless set of needs. Care and need are very different. The psychological or economic origins of need suggest a *need-for* something. The phenomenological or existentialist origins of care suggest a *need-to-do* something.

A TAXONOMY OF CONCERNS

> All the world's a stage,
> And all the men and women merely players.
> They have their exits and their entrances,
> And one man in his time plays many parts.
> —*William Shakespeare*, As You Like It

The central and unifying theme in the treatment of Being is "care." Care has the sense of making Being itself an issue. Care has an ontological origin and is not the same as the everyday sense of worry about specific problems one faces. Thinking about care in terms of the "cares of the world" gives a sense more in the ontological vein. Furthermore, what is important for sustainability is that care is also manifest in the everydayness of life through specific concerns such as subsistence or affection.

Flourishing, in human terms, might be considered in two ways. The first, paralleling the ontology of Being, is a sense that all is well in the world. My concerns are being served; I am satisfied. I am the caring that makes human beings what they are. Flourishing, in this sense, relates to authenticity: a genuine understanding of Being. I recognize myself as a self I have chosen on my own, but I also recognize that my self can be found out there in the culture as belonging to many others as well. When one comes to experience flourishing in this sense, it comes with all of the recognizable attributes that Maslow tied to Being (see Table 3). The interweaving and redundancy of attributes in Table 3 reinforce Max-Neef's claim that "needs" should be considered in a systems context, and not as independent domains corresponding to some compartment of human nature.

More closely related to the design and practical thrust of this book, care shows itself in reflective assessments that the immediate concern that has been occupying me has been dealt with satisfactorily and I can move on to something else. It is important to be clear on what is meant by concerns. Concerns manifest themselves as activities we engage in for-the-sake-of something having to do with our Being, that is, virtually all our routine activities. From a designer's perspective, since living involves so many different activities, a practical question arises: "Is it possible to characterize our concerns as falling into a relatively small number of categories?"

I believe the answer is yes, but based only on a practical scheme that arises from observing cultural life today in modern societies. It is important to avoid equating any such set of categories to specific features of human nature, as that would be completely inconsistent with the phenomenological basis of this model. I will lay down such a scheme in a few moments, but I want to repeat a caveat that has shown up before: this set of categories should be taken as pragmatic and not as something absolute and exclusive.

Earlier, I asked you to perform a little thought experiment related to the emergence of language. Now I would like you to continue the same experiment. Imagine our early ancestors engaged in the process of building the social structure that has always been at the center of human settlements. In whatever moments of reflection broke through their everyday involvement with the rigors of their existence, they could have become conscious of only three distinctly different kinds of entities. Stop again and ask yourself what these three could be . . .

Everything they perceived had to fall into one of these three categories: their own being, other human beings, and everything else. Together the three would completely constitute their whole world. As they developed coping routines, these three types of entities must have been the sources of their concerns and must have provided the context for the evolution of the question of what it is to be a human being. Over time an observer might begin to catalogue the activities around these three domains: caring for oneself, for others, and for the world in general (Figure 10). Such a typology is merely an analytic representation of a more diffuse ontological structure in the background but can serve as a framework for further analysis and design. This typology is reflected in the Tao of sustainability diagram shown earlier (see Figure 7). The three domains in that figure correspond roughly to the three primary areas of care:

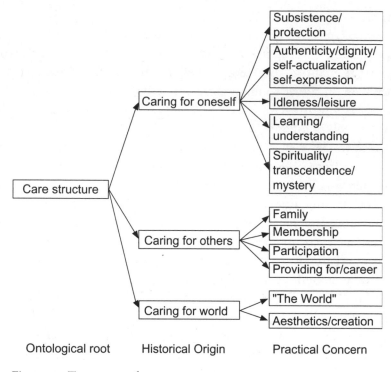

Figure 10. Taxonomy of concerns

- The human, or caring for oneself
- The natural, or caring for the world
- The ethical, or caring for others

   If one steps back from the hurly-burly of everyday living, so full of contingency and chaos, it is possible to observe particular domains in which people persistently strive for satisfaction, that is, take care of their concerns. These domains have emerged over historical time and form categories to an observer looking down on social activities. We can describe a society in terms of these domains or, better, in terms of the observable forms of institutionalized activities that emerge and evolve to produce worlds for individuals in which perfection or completeness (or any other form of satisfaction) can be found in the present rather than in visions of the future. For example, the market system is an institution that has arisen out of a need to provide satisfaction in many of the persistent domains, such as maintaining the body. The body is at the center of much of what we do. One can, in this way of thinking, trace back the origin of major institutional areas to some area of persistent need or want, but the caution here is that *need* or *want* is an ascription given by an observer to explain a routinized set of activities that appears to have a fixed intentional character or condition of satisfaction.

Starting with these three major categories (self, others, world), I explored a wide range of activities characteristic of modern societies and summarized what I found into a small set of topics, shown in the third column in Figure 10. Most apply to societies throughout history. Each element provides the context for the for-the-sake-of-whiches that stand behind all purposeful human activities. The similarity of this diagram to the schemes of Maslow and Max-Neef hints at the possible universality of the categories. Each scheme was derived empirically by observing human behavior, as opposed to some set of theoretical principles. Each element in Figure 10 can be broken down further to indicate characteristic identities, typical equipment, and places wherein related activities occur.

Table 4 elaborates each of the domains of practical concern showing a typical identity, equipment, and place for each of the domains. Providing-for (or career) encompasses such a wide set of variations that it has several entries. Work has become such a central aspect of lives today that this item merits extra attention. The place, identity, and equipment combinations are but a few examples of the myriad possibilities. That so much possibility exists gives life its richness and creates an opening for hopefulness and authenticity.

Some of the more commonly used terms in the previous and following sections need a warning flag: identity, concern, role, and goal. In the model for human behavior I have been developing, these terms should not be taken as permanent features. They are merely handy ascriptions of behavioral patterns that might appear to some observer as fixed in nature. The for-sake-of-whiches are not goals in the sense that they can be attained and thereby completed just like crossing off items on a to-do list. One might, if asked to explain what has been going on, point to an identity or role or goal, but such explanations always refer to the cultural meanings of these terms, not to any internal intentionality. Such reported observations of one's own behavior, by necessity, always occur out of context of the actions to which they

Table 4. Equipment context for universal concerns

Domain of Concern (for-the-sake-of-which)	Identity Revealed	Typical Equipment (with-which)	Place (where-in)
Subsistence	Living creature	Food, water	Dining room
Choice/authenticity	Self	None needed	Body
Idleness/leisure	Hiking	Trail shoes	Woods
Learning/understanding	Student	Workbooks	School
Spirit/transcendence	God-fearer	Prayer book	House of worship
Spirit/transcendence	Natural Being	None needed	Wilderness
Family	Parent	How-to-do manual	Home
Membership	Neighbor	Teapot	Neighborhood
Participation	Citizen	Ballot	Voting place
Career/providing for	Doctor	Stethoscope	Hospital
Career/providing for	Worker	Lathe	Machine shop
Career/providing for	Legislator	Law book	Legislature
World	Advocate	Picket sign	Public square
Aesthetics/creation	Writer	Word processor	Studio

refer. One must always interrupt the action to explain what has been going on. Like equipment, the meaning of human action can be understood only in the context of that action.

Identity is the name ascribed to the collection of meaningful actions that one has learned to perform that fit under some cultural category. As one becomes more and more competent in acting in any domain of concerns, identity, as seen by an observer, appears more and more sharply defined. Identity, as defined in this way, should not be confused with the psychological sense of ego or the true self. Identity is shorthand for naming the characteristic set of actions in any area of concerns connected to a person. It is what either an actor or an observer of the actor would say they are being at any instant. A woman might say she is being a mother while nursing a baby, a parent while scolding her child, a friend while visiting a neighbor, and so on. Identity is an assessment of one's actions, not any inherent property of a "self." Identity comes forth in action in the course of satisfying concerns. As in Shakespeare's familiar passage quoted above, people play many parts (identities, plural) in acting out their lives. Unlike the pathology of multiple personalities in a psychological sense, normal existence requires that one take on different identities matching the concerns being attended to at the moment. Identity shows up in what Heidegger called "workshops." Workshops are not simply a space where work is done, but a metaphor for the entire nexus of place, equipment, and norms that provides the context for action toward satisfying one's concerns.

Similarly, the word *concern* is a substitute for the more cumbersome "for-the-sake-of-which." Concerns are lifelong domains of action, not some immediate problem to solve. One never can fully satisfy concerns in the sense that one has finished the job. Subsistence clearly cannot be neglected, or the body will stop working. Satisfaction comes in assessments of the state of the immediate task, not the concern.

The eleven domains of practical concern in Figure 10 may be construed as defining flourishing beyond its metaphorical sense. Flourishing requires that all concerns be regularly addressed, and some sort of balance maintained. The absence of flourishing might be attributed to such a lack of balance even in our affluent world. Seriously neglecting any one or more of the categories inhibits Being and leaves one less human. Lack of attention to world is very clearly evident in our neglect of the environment. Learning is in trouble in U.S. secondary schools, with a lower percentage of students graduating than in other parts of the modern world. Participation in community activities as observed by sociologist Robert Putnam in his book *Bowling Alone* has fallen to a low level.[3] Putnam referred to this phenomenon as evidence of declining social capital. Other sociologists have made the same point by exposing the hyperindividualism and narcissism of the U.S. culture.[4] One of the key objectives in any sustainability design scheme should be to restore balance among all the elements of care as a practical means of restoring Being and creating flourishing.

SUSTAINABILITY BY DESIGN

The importance of equipment design and place to the satisfaction of our cares follows from the discussion so far. Our actions aim to satisfy not merely some unconnected "need" but, rather, a particular concern tied to one or more of our basic domains of care. Furthermore, the use of equipment designed with sustainability in mind can reveal our caring to us (see Chapter 13). Place, similarly, can reinforce a sense of identity beyond whatever utilitarian purposes for which the corresponding space is intended.[5] In both cases, the design should induce reflection and an awareness of what has been going on. Such meaningful reflection is an essential step in breaking habitual or addictive behavior patterns. One must consciously confront the embodied pattern and acknowledge that it is no longer working. If, at the same time, the reflective moment reveals something fundamental about deeper concerns, the actor may be able to begin to address the underlying concern and replace ineffective behavior.

Returning, then, to the question about the practicality of this scheme, we can now point to two areas in which design can reveal the underlying care structure and open up the possibility of authenticity. The first is the equipment used in routine activities. Next is the place or the architecture of physical milieu in which each domain is customarily attended to. I will not elaborate further on the role of place in this book. The design model developed for designers of mundane, everyday equipment is, however, also appropriate for architects as designers of place.

It has taken a long and winding path to get to these last few paragraphs, but the journey has brought us to a critical point in the story. If one looks at the way we design technology, spaces, and cultural institutions today, a single criterion dominates: utility. This should not come as a surprise since the central theme of our way of evaluating any set of alternatives for choice or design is to determine which produces the most utility, whether for an individual or for a group.

But as is apparent in Table 4, a few of the entries have no "economic" entities attached. It takes no equipment to attend to choice/authenticity. Spirit may simply come forth in a wild place. But wilderness is vanishing simply because it has little economic value relative to almost any utilitarian usage. Engagement with what is still available to us as nature can accentuate identity in a very practical sense. In 1995 Xerox introduced a product line of innovative digital office machines that not only embodied state-of-the-art functionality but also pushed the environmental performance envelope. Inspired by the simple motto "Zero to Landfill," the machine came very close to its goal of being

100 percent recyclable, reusable, or remanufacturable. The story of this remarkable exercise in creativity and culture building began with the immersion of many of the team members in a nature-based training program, ending with a twenty-four-hour solo stay in the New Mexican desert. Their experience was reflected throughout the project not only through a heightened concern for nature but also by a sense of care for the group rarely observed in business settings.[6]

When all of our designs are driven by utilitarian factors, sooner or later the original sources of concern get lost, and human beings and the world both become impoverished. No amount of efficiency can reverse that trend. Alternatively, we can stop designing everything with utility as the only goal and start designing with the underlying concern or concerns as our guide. We do have "needs" to attend to, but they are, as noted earlier, needs-to-do, not needs-for. Sustainability as the possibility of flourishing, can come only when a balance between both kinds of needs replaces the monotonic focus on utility and its modern avatar, wealth.

Chapter 13 Creating Possibility with Products

Design is directed toward human beings. To design is to solve human problems by identifying them and executing the best solution.
—*Ivan Chermayeff*

How can we revolutionize conventional wisdom about technology and technological artifacts? On the one hand we have the centrality of technology in our modern culture with its promise of leading the way to a better and better life. On the other, we have the addictive power of technology that lulls us into unconsciousness. Its grip is so powerful that Heidegger, near the end of his life, was afraid that "only a god can save us." There are few, if any, signs that a dialectic evolution is taking place with some new synthesis of technology and humanity emerging. The response of those who sense the deep-seated threat to their Being and to the world is generally revolutionary, perhaps railing against capitalism or moving to a life of voluntary simplicity outside of the cultural mainstream.[1] Those who see only the problems around the edges (shifting-the-burden) seek incremental albeit important solutions, relying on technology or technocratic solutions. I deem these incremental because they all are built on the same cultural structure that created the situation in the first place. I hope I have dispelled any expectations that this approach can work beyond quick fixes.

What, then, is left to do if one takes on this problematic situation as an essential step in creating and maintaining the possibility of flourishing now and in the future? The solution I offer as a serious option to sidestepping the unpromising paths is to create an ongoing, deep-seated learning process by redesigning the artifacts we use every day, and also the rules that constitute the institutions inside of which we pursue the satisfaction of our existentialist concerns.

I have already pointed to the theory on which this strategy rests: the structuration model of Giddens. The route to widespread societal change via the structuration path is subtle and subversive as opposed to the head-on opposition involved in political change. By introducing new tools and changing the context in which action occurs, structuration works its way subtly by creating new (institutional) rules to conform to new norms and beliefs that are encoded and embedded in the design of the tools.

Viewed in this way, design is normative rather than, or in addition to, functional or utilitarian. The designer, through the design per se, guides the actor toward what ought to be done in using the artifact. Later in this chapter I will point to a two-button toilet as an example of this kind of design. By requiring that a choice be made in the mundane process of flushing a toilet, the designer has superposed an ethical dimension on a nominally instrumental act. The rest of this chapter looks at ways in which design can directly address unconsciousness in two domains of the Tao of sustainability: our own loss of meaning and our ethical responsibilities. If it is possible, as I believe it is, to restore our understanding of care as central to Being, then I believe we, individually and collectively, will begin to address and start to care for the third sector: our place in nature.

TURNING PROBLEMS INTO POSSIBILITY

Although we usually take for granted what our tools do for us, we interact with them in different, distinctive ways.[2] Let me again illustrate this with one of the most familiar of all objects, the automobile. Before

I retired, whenever I left the house in the morning to go to work my car was usually parked in our driveway behind my wife's. The car was *available*, meaning I could use it without thinking or deviating from my normal pattern: I could simply hop in and go to work.[3] I was coping with my concerns in (to an observer) a seemingly effortless manner.

Occasionally I found my car blocked in our narrow driveway by my wife's car. This arrangement always depended on who came home last. When my wife did pull in after me, my car was, for the moment, literally unavailable for use. It had become *conspicuous* to me in the sense that I became aware of its presence and also had to stop and adjust my behavior. I could either arrange to exchange cars or simply move her car out of the way. In the case of the former, my wife's car was available to me in the same way as having a spare tool in my toolbox. My normal pattern was only momentarily interrupted.

On other, less frequent and usually very cold mornings, I would go outside to the car, hop in, turn the key, and await the roar of the engine but instead hear nothing—the battery had died. The car was being *obstinate*, thwarting my best intentions of getting to work. Some cussing followed, together with some thinking about what would happen at work in my temporary absence. I would have to call my local garage and wait until the emergency truck came and recharged the battery. I had to eliminate the cause of the breakdown before moving along. I was much more aware of the car than in the other situation, and I had made a number of mostly pejorative assessments about it. I was also more conscious of and concerned about my professional identity. In spite of the nuisance, I did not give up my goal of getting to the office and eventually always did arrive there.

On another occasion, when I was coming home quite a few years ago, the motor sounded an ominous bang and simply stopped working; every warning light on the dashboard came on. The engine had blown up. I had to stop and come up with an alternative way to get home so I could play my roles as parent and spouse. So I glided to the curb, cleaned out the essential papers, and walked home. There wasn't much else I could do. I was helpless for the moment; fortunately, I was only about a mile away. The car had become *obtrusive* in that it completely broke the flow of my routine trip home. During my walk I thought about why I needed a car in the first place in the context of what I was all about. Could I manifest my identity as a provider and parent without a car? My identity came forth in my thinking even more than in the other situation. In that reflective, tacit conversation with myself, I was reinforcing those identities, taking them as my own. My thoughts were to find an alternative to the car, walking in this case, and to the role of caretaker I was about to take on when I finally got home. Identity seen as an inherent characteristic of one's nature comes forth only when the action is interrupted and the "self" is decontextualized.

Each of these experiences, respectively, brought increasing awareness of what was going on. My consciousness of the automobile and the immediate activity became greater as the availability of the vehicle decreased. In both cases, I could have simply abandoned the action and gone on to something else but chose to stick with the for-the-sake-of-which that was shaping my behavior.

These situations all depict unexpected interruptions, but equipment can show itself in these modes during normal operations as well. Most objects today, especially consumer electronics, require an actor to perform prefatory tasks, more or less rote sequences, ranging from turning the device on and off to more complicated sequences such as programming a digital video recorder. If no more than flipping a switch is required, the equipment is merely conspicuous. I notice only that something about it needs attention before proceeding.

But given the multifunctionality built into so many devices today, more complicated interactions are often required. This preliminary "tuning-up" requirement produces obstinacy, similar to the case of my car with a dead battery. I must engage with it more intimately before it will perform the task I want it to do. The interaction frequently involves some sort of remote control: a universal remote for all the devices in my den, or the thermostat that controls the furnace. The interaction is almost always mysterious, as the workings of the device at hand are usually hidden inside of some real or metaphorical "black box." The actor cannot use the equipment before engaging with it, but the helplessness associated with obtrusiveness—my car with the blown motor—is missing. During this prelude before the main act I may reflect on what I was about to do (the towards-which). But given that all I want from the device is its commodity—sound, computing power, speed, and so forth—I am not likely to reflect more deeply. My underlying concerns remain hidden.

In general, such prefatory requirements do not interfere with the subsequent availability of the equipment. But not always. The prelude may become a nightmare, and the mode then shifts from obstinacy to obtrusiveness, or even deeper. Videocassette recorders (VCRs), now already relics, were notorious for their obtrusiveness. Many people talk about feeling helpless when trying to program one or a similar device. This helplessness could be resolved by finding an alternative resource, often someone else in the room, or by referring to a manual. The actor often also makes some negative self-assessment, saying or thinking that he or she *should* have been able to manage the task at hand. Conversations like this produce inauthenticity. "Should" always refers to some cultural "they" as the source of the scolding inherent in such conversations. On the other hand, success can bring forth a positive, authentic sense of taking care of some concern. If alternate means cannot be found, the project will have to be abandoned. The mode will shift further to *occurrent,* and the original concern will recede and disappear. The equipment becomes just a hunk of stuff out of the context of action. The revealing potential of the encounter with the equipment disappears. This is the mode corresponding to the conventional Cartesian model of the world, with a detached subject gazing on a material object.

Other kinds of equipment require a similar but distinctively different engagement before they are ready for use: for example, tuning a guitar before playing it, or laying a fire before lighting it. The engagement between the actor and the equipment, often requiring manual dexterity, is more elaborate than the simple act of turning on a device or going through a sequence of mechanical steps. Heidegger observed that the origin of our present technological artifacts was to be found in ancient craft-making or *technē.* He saw this as a creative (poetic) act in which the craftsman and artifact were closely bonded. Perhaps the "laying on of hands" creates such engagement and adds meaning lacking in most ordinary technological objects. The actor cannot begin the task until the preparation is complete. During this period, the equipment obtrudes. The actor is, in a sense, helpless, because the curtain on the main act cannot be raised yet, but not helpless in the sense of one stymied by a refractory remote control. The preparation itself requires that the actor be conscious of the immediate world. Every time one tunes an instrument, the situation is different. On the other hand, programming a VCR demands that the actor follow a pre-scribed routine. Any deviation will produce disaster. The actor has no choice at all, precluding any possibility of authenticity.

In later work, which took a more existential tone than earlier work on the hierarchy of needs, Abraham Maslow spoke of "peak experiences."[4] His clinical observations led him to people who had experienced moments in their lives that were qualitatively different from their ordinary day-to-day lives. Compressing many divergent ways of describing this phenomenon into one simple phrase, they all said that they felt alive. Albert Borgmann uses a different term, *focal experiences,* to describe experiences that illuminate several elements of concern simultaneously.[5] His critical references to "devices" and the commodities they deliver is part of his argument that most of what we use to accomplish the tasks of everyday life delivers only some discrete utilitarian function, and fails to expose the context and concerns being addressed. The old-fashioned hearth not only provides the heat (commodity) that a furnace in the basement (device) can, but it also serves as context for family activities and offers a possibility for authenticity. Language gives us a clue to the difference: we might say the hearth provides us warmth, but the furnace only heat. Commodity-producing devices correspond roughly to Max-Neef's singular satisfiers. There is nothing inherently wrong with this form of equipment. It is inadequate, however, to produce the full range of experience needed to support human existential concerns.

This form of engagement (tuning up, preparing) exposes the ontological context—the equipment, place, and identity being enacted. Borgmann uses the preparation and partaking of a family dinner as an example of focal experience. The central actor in this case also becomes engaged far beyond knife sharpening to take in the place, the participants, and so on. A casserole filled with a delectable stew obtrudes; it must be savored before it disappears in the ordinary act of eating. Such focal practices may involve many pieces of equipment as in the dinner example. The context makes the difference since the same knife used to pare an apple for a snack may not invoke the same consciousness as the chef's knife.

In the last few years, starting first in Europe but now growing in the United States, people turned off by the fast-food culture have created the "slow food" movement.[6] Underlying this shift is a desire to restore connections to the people sharing meals, those who prepared the meals, and the food itself. Some point to the need to consider the impact on the rest of the world of what we eat. Referring to the domains of concern in the previous chapter, this practice addresses multiple concerns: subsistence, authenticity, family, participation, world, and aesthetics/creation.

My own example is that of fly-fishing. As I mentioned in an earlier chapter, I am an avid fly-fisherman. I have been one for some fifteen years, ever since my son-in-law convinced me to put away my spinning rods. Before making the first cast, however, one must go through a series of preparatory steps beginning with tying the flies for the day. Then, the right line style (floating, sinking, intermediate) must be selected and put onto a reel. Finally, one strings up the rod and attaches the fly to the leader. From the very first moment of tying a fly in anticipation of the action, I find myself reflecting on many different things. I can almost taste the pleasure the first bite brings, connecting me closer to nature. I sense the peacefulness of the whole process. The primary feeling is that of involvement in the world of nature.

The power of such experiences in producing context came to me in listening to a conversation between one of my grandsons, then about eight years old, and his father during a visit to our summer cottage in Maine. Will was grappling with some sort of technical problem and asked his father for help. His dad said, "Ask your grandfather, he's a scientist." Will's response was, "No, Dad. Grandpa's a fisherman."

Focal experiences are different from complete immersion in some activity such as computer games. Seeking focal experiences on the computer or other electronic devices is difficult, as the computer has become one of the most transparent of tools we use. One example, however, is the Sims set of games, which invites the user to create (design) the characters and guide their relationships. "Design" is the clue to this experience, as opposed to other forms of games. This feature is something that all focal experiences hold in common: the actor has been involved in the design of the activity that follows. Alternatively, we might say that the actor has become involved in the choices of the subsequent action in a mindful way. The sense here is that the actor is present amid a vision of what is to come. In the vernacular we could say that focal experiences always require a form of "getting ready."

PRESENCING

I use the term *presencing* to distinguish the nature of the interruptions whereby equipment becomes either obstinate or obtrusive.[7] Presencing is an experience in which an awareness of the worldly context of the action shows itself to the actor. A presencing moment offers the actor an opportunity to continue or to turn away to do some other task. Choice is the critical aspect of the moment; by making a conscious, reflexive choice, the actor owns the world and all of its contextual elements: concerns, identity, place, and equipment. The action is authentic. The actor owns the subsequent action and, if the interruption is deep enough, also the concern from which the action comes. Authentic behavior is by no means inevitable. The actor can simply ignore the questions raised and return mindlessly to work.

The general presencing scenario is:

1. An actor sets out to do something routine toward satisfying some for-the-sake-of-which that fits the present world (for example, I leave the house for work each weekday at 7:30 in the morning).
2. Something happens to interrupt that routine, whether by accident or design.
3. The context becomes present. The extent to which the context emerges depends on the severity of the disturbance. Conspicuousness brings out properties of the equipment (the car is blocked by another). Obstinacy raises consciousness of the interconnectedness of equipment (the car is part of everything I use in pursuing my professional identity) and the immediate intention (towards-which): getting to my office. Obtrusiveness does all the above and brings forth an encounter with the identity being acted out (for-the-sake-of-which).
4. The actor stops and reflects. In this moment of heightened presence (consciousness), the actor has an opening to the concerns being served. The actor may be able to find a spare tool and move right along without much of a break in the flow. Such a break will produce an awareness only of the context-sensitive properties of the equipment. In more serious breakdowns, the actor may stop and call on a familiar way out of the "problem," like summoning an emergency service. Here, the connectedness of the equipment and the immediate goals may become present. In the most serious kind

of breakdown, obtrusiveness, the actor remains engaged but becomes helpless for the time being, and may reflect on the place of the faulty equipment in the larger scheme of things: other equipment, identity, concerns. In each of these cases the actor remains engaged in the pursuit of some concern. Consciousness of identity—what concerns are being taken care of—becomes increasingly available as the interruption deepens. Continuing to pursue the same "toward-which" can be seen as a choice to own the act authentically. The opportunity may be overlooked, however, and the action simply continues without any heightened awareness. Or the actor may exhibit frustration, abandon the present task, and turn to another concern.

An obtrusive experience frequently produces anxiety. In Heidegger's phenomenology, anxiety is connected with authenticity, as this mood appears whenever the actor faces up to and chooses to address the concerns that have become present. The deepest mood of anxiety shows up when a human is confronted with the choice of accepting or rejecting his or her inevitable mortality. This existential kind of choice is completely different from the utilitarian choice of which object to possess next. It leads to Being, not having, and is a key to flourishing.

In the lesser case of obstinacy, the actor may be faced, depending on the design of the equipment, with ethical (normative or "should") choices, as simple as which button to push. Let me illustrate this with a piece of equipment we all encounter every day in our modern setting—the toilet. In northern Europe and, increasingly, in other places in the world, many toilets have a flushing mechanism with two buttons or two levers. One of the buttons or levers is larger than the other to lend a distinction that is hard to miss. The difference between the two is the volume of flush produced when one or the other is actuated. When it is time to flush the toilet, the mere presence of two buttons creates a temporary interruption or disturbance in the flow of action (obstinacy). The user must make a choice before proceeding. The choice depends on what was just eliminated from the body and on an understanding of the environmental consequences of flushing.

In the reflective, conscious moment that follows such a break in the action (presencing), the question of rightness and wrongness of the action looms before the subject, lending an ethical context to the task at hand. At least for the first few times, the presencing will remind the actor that there is no "away." It may be that, after many encounters with such a toilet, one becomes so familiar with the operation that it becomes effortless and, in essence, mindless. If so, then the ethical nature of the task has become completely intertwined with the more practical aspects of the process.

This process of transforming what at first are nonroutine actions into the normal way of behaving is one of the primary objectives of this overall design strategy. When the actions become routine, the associated beliefs and norms become embodied. As more and more individuals follow the same new routine, the beliefs and norms will begin to enter the collective, social consciousness. At some point, the whole group will begin to act in concert. Malcolm Gladwell speaks of this as the "tipping point."[8]

In both cases the unavailability of the equipment interrupts the action and the actor must stop and reflect on what is happening before moving on. Of course, it is possible that the actor will simply return to the former routines that had become habitual. But if, as in the case of the two-button toilet, the design guides the action in the direction toward sustainability, what had been a mindless pattern with consequences producing unsustainability is transformed to a positive routine. When the presencing is deep enough to cause reflection on the identity and care category behind the action at hand, again it is possible that the actor will recognize and choose the identity as his or her own, transforming what had been indifference to authenticity and addictive emptiness to satisfaction. The "need" to continue to consume can slowly disappear as the "real" source of satisfaction becomes explicit.

Addictive behavior is a clear example of inauthenticity: patterns of behavior in which the actor has virtually no choice. Simply telling an alcoholic that alcohol is not working and is causing other problems in his or her life rarely is an effective intervention. It takes ongoing intervention until new action-producing structures become embodied. Alcoholics Anonymous and other organizations based on the same principles use the company of peers to bring the addiction into the room or, to use a less familiar verbal form, to *presence* the condition. Presencing is a critical step in overcoming addiction or in changing any habit or routine. If one is not aware of the habitual nature of some action, it simply occurs without signaling its presence—but it is always in the room.

Both individual and collective behavioral change are essential to the achievement of sustainability. Flourishing rests on balancing all the practical concerns on which Being depends. Indeed, one way to think about flourishing is as a state where all the domains of concerns are being taken care of consistently and continuously. Whereas almost all sustainable development strategies depend on technological solutions such as ecoefficiency or marginal shifts of consumption through pricing mechanisms, none address the importance of changing behavior to recover the three lost domains of the Tao of sustainability.

Behavior can be changed only after such presencing moments. Without interruptions in the flow, actors will continue to keep on doing things the same way that they have done before. This does not mean that every moment and every day will be exactly like the past. In the model of Being and behavior on which this text is based, actors follow rules that have become embedded during their life. Each moment builds on the accumulated body of rules or norms. Like explicit rules in a game, for example, these rules prescribe (must rules), proscribe (must not rules), or offer options (may rules). The existence of "may" rules lends the appearance of free will to the actions of individuals. Some forms of insanity might be said to arise from the absence or suppression of "may" rules in one's body. Patterns of behavior are then so constrained that the actor has no choice but to follow the same course over and over again, even if the concerns behind the action continue to be unsatisfied.

What follows from the presencing process is not only an embodied strategic act coming out of past historical learning. The concern that underlies action, but is usually hidden, may also present itself to the actor reflexively. As the actor begins to recognize that care is involved, rather than some utilitarian motivation, he or she may experience a sense of Being that is normally absent. Thinking back to philosopher Hans Jonas's earlier critique of modern technology (see Chapter 3), in which he argued that it tends to remove the actor from both the intended and unintended consequences of the act, designing equipment to produce presencing can be said to dissolve his critique and restore ethical responsibility as normal.

Chapter 14 Presencing by Design

Design is the term we use to describe both the process and the result of giving tangible form to human ideas. Design doesn't just contribute to the quality of life; design, in many ways, now constitutes the quality of life.
—*Peter Lawrence*

Some years ago the toy company Mattel brought out a new line of talking toys. In 1960, the company introduced "Chatty Cathy," a doll that would speak single sentences and make requests such as "Please brush my hair" each time a string protruding from the doll's back was pulled and then released. This was in the days before such toys had batteries and electronic guts. No matter what a child was doing with the doll, the voice making a statement or carrying a request stopped the action and the doll became very much present. The child could do as requested or ignore the voice, but the interaction of child and doll, under these circumstances, was a two-way process and not shaped by the child's actions alone. Now fast-forward to the present and ask yourself what might happen if the objects you used as equipment had such a voice built into them. This is not so strange, as many such examples do exist. Some high-end cars speak to the driver, for example, to warn that the seat belts are unbuckled. Recently I watched a television advertisement that showed a startled BMW driver listening to a message from the car that its next service was due. Closer to home, my computer talks to me whenever I neglect an alert that needs attention.

Imagine if, every time you got into your car and went to turn on the engine, a voice would advise you that for every X miles you drive that day you would release Y pounds of carbon dioxide into the atmosphere. Or, when you step on the lever that lifts the trash container lid so you can throw away some garbage, a voice asks whether you have separated all the compostable materials. The effect of these small voices is the same as that which Chatty Cathy produces. The equipment you were about to use for some routine, "unthinking" action has suddenly shown itself to you. The equipment shifts its mode of being from available to unavailable (conspicuous, obstinate, or obtrusive).

Most interruptions to the routine flow of action come uninvited. Product designers strive to avoid such stoppages by making equipment reliable and "user-friendly." When some activity is interrupted or thwarted by a malfunction or a non-equipment-related interruption (for example, when the doorbell or someone's cell phone rings), the response might be one of annoyance, or worse. The introduction of mandatory seat belt interlocking systems in the United States several decades ago brought an angry outcry from many who believed that the interruption in the process of starting their vehicles was an invasion of both privacy and freedom. Many had the interlocks inactivated, and a few years later Congress repealed the law. Today, a light on the dashboard has replaced the interlock.

Despite their largely negative connotations, these interruptions in the flow of action can be designed to be positive and can contribute to sustainability by reminding the actor of his or her responsibility for the outcomes and by revealing the care structure that lies in the background of the task at hand. In the last chapter I introduced the two-button toilet as such an example. Something very interesting is going on here. It is as if the toilet is speaking to the user, asking a question something akin to, "What are you doing?" The first few times that this happens the user has virtually no choice but to stop and consider what to do. In our culture, questions virtually always interrupt the flow of action. Stop for a moment and think of the possibilities for breaking the transparent, utilitarian, functional, addictive patterns of everyday life and focusing attention on the care that underlies the action. . . . (Could you have completely ignored this last request before reading any further?)

ACCESSING CARE THROUGH CONVERSATIONS WITH PRODUCTS

Access to authentic living, potentially deeply satisfying at the level of concern, comes on the tail of presencing: the bringing forth of the worldly context and structure of whatever action is going on at the moment. But does presencing require a breakdown in which the equipment fails to work, like a car with a dead battery? If it did, people would soon find alternate ways and other devices that were more reliable. Fortunately there is another way to produce a presencing moment in the midst of the hurly-burly of routine action: ask the actor a question or make some other request. Requests, including questions (a request to provide some information), are a form of speech acts with an important attribute. It is virtually impossible to ignore a question, as I noted above. Questions stop the action similarly to the effect of equipment failures. If I were to ask someone in the middle of a task what they were doing, they would normally stop, take stock of the situation, and answer. Then, having responded to the question, they might choose to return to the task.

Does this mean that some person needs to be in the room, acting like a guardian angel? Such an arrangement would be completely impractical. Again, fortunately, the answer is no. The equipment itself can make a request. Earlier I mentioned the two-button toilet. The action stops while the user responds to an unvoiced request from the toilet to make the right choice: large or small button. The toilet has "asked" the user to reflect on which form of elimination was involved and then guides the user toward the right choice. "Right" in this case is to save water by using the smaller button after urination.

Product designers call the unvoiced dialogue I describe here a "script," and this term belongs to the larger category of product semantics.[1] Products or equipment talk to us through their design. The meaning of an artifact comes from "conversations" one holds with it.

Except for the examples discussed earlier in which the artifact actually talks, the conversation is tacit. The idea that things create meaning through language is consistent with the phenomenological theme of this book. Heidegger has said that language is the house of Being. It is through language that we make sense of the world and act in it meaningfully.

From earliest childhood, once words start to come, a child builds meaning via questions: "What is that?" or "Why do I have to do that?" In Maturana's biology, meaning and action always rest on the current structure of the body. The meaning of what we hear is determined by the structure, not by the content, of the message.[2] But the present structure represents the accumulation (history) of all our past activities, particularly those that have become routine, successful coordinated actions with other people and with things. We accept that words have meanings that trigger a response when we hear or see them. We can get along in the world of people and things only because the meanings we have collected correspond with those of others.

But is an object any different from a spoken sentence? It is just another phenomenon coming through the senses to the body to be processed somewhere inside. We treat things the same way that we do isolated sentences when asked to talk about them. There is no difference between our explaining what a particular sentence meant and our explaining what some object is all about. Explanations about objects often sound strange because people interact with them in many more ways than they do with sentences. A painting can evoke many different conversations, while the word "stop" has the same meaning for everybody.

Interaction among people is mediated through linguistic signals, whether they come as spoken or written words or familiar forms of body language. We accept the notion of body language as telling us something meaningful. Why, then, not talk about cell phone or frying pan language? We often say this or that object speaks to me. We know how to use frying pans first by watching our parents use them to cook our dinners and then by our own use of them. Is there any difference in the embodied language of the frying pan and the words of a favorite poem or play script one has memorized? We can recite the poem effortlessly and use the frying pan without mishap. Meaning in both cases is the result of a process of structuration. We learn by doing, that is, through reflexive monitoring of actions, and the more we do the same thing, the more deeply the structures become embedded.

French sociologist of science Bruno Latour has developed an extensive body of work exploring the way humans interact with nonhumans.[3] He uses the word "nonhumans" in place of "objects" as an attempt to avoid the presuppositions deeply ingrained in the predominant Cartesian model of reality. He argues that both humans and nonhumans are actors in the vast network of material entities that constitute the life-world. My attribution of language in the form of speech acts to such nonhumans is consistent with his notion of scripts. In contrast to traditional objective materialists, Latour and others have illuminated a substantially larger role for artifacts (nonhumans) in mediating the activities of human actors and in shaping the story of reality.

The secret of designing objects to produce presencing is through scripting, that is, through the designer's art in making the object "speak" in a distinctive and planned way. This notion is not new to designers. Product semantics has been mostly directed to make objects speak in a marketing voice. "Buy me because I am soft and cuddly!" "Buy me because I will make you young and beautiful!" Nike, Procter & Gamble, Coca-Cola, and many others have spent fortunes building their brands around such tacit messages. Advertising complements the tacit message in the product design with real words reinforcing the products' own inscribed message.

Latour and another researcher, Madeleine Akrich, have elaborated on the concept of scripts.[4] Inscription is the designer's process of embedding a script in the artifact. Prescription, allowances, and proscription are the actions the artifact demands (must), allows (may), or prohibits (must not). Subscription is the message as interpreted by the actor. Description is the message ascribed to the object by an observer or analyst. The example they use to illustrate these terms is the heavy key holder used by many hotels to deter guests from going off with their room key. An analyst might describe such keys as saying, "Please don't forget to return the keys." The inscription is the translation of the message into properties of the artifact; in this case the heaviness that presences the keys, saying, "I am much too heavy to carry around."

Presencing takes place in use. Inscribed messages are different depending on the context and situation. The following list contains different kinds of conversations relevant to presencing and other modalities of equipment. Each one is a form of speech act, which is italicized.[5]

1. "Stop and buy me! I promise to do X for you." This is the general form of *offers* (*promises*) made in the marketplace. The equipment is *occurrent,*[6] meaning that it is out of the actual context of future action, although the actor may have a picture of how and where it will be used. The shopper is accessing some internal set of criteria. In this mode, the actor is in the Cartesian mode as a detached subject gazing upon a context-free object. Product designers and market specialists can apply theories derived from conventional science, often psychology, in their efforts to make their offers more attractive on some utility scale than others. The failure to understand that an actor operates in a very different mode of Being once the object has been acquired and put to use may account in part for failures to produce authentic satisfaction. The ubiquitous presence of advertisements lends "reality" to the objectiveness of just about everything, since one can find ads somewhere for just about everything. Advertisements reinforce the having mode of living.

   Ecolabels are increasingly popular as a means to induce buyers to make choices that carry less environmental impact. It is important to distinguish this strategy from the presencing framework being developed here. Buying activities are always out of the context of action within one of the domains of concern and will not produce fundamental behavior change. The effect may even be perverse, leading to shifting-of-the-burden. Ecolabels say only that "I am better than that other product," but ask no questions about the behavior that will ensue when the purchases are put into play.

2. "You own me so use me. You already know all about me." Here the conversation has two parts. The first is an *invitation,* followed by an *assertion* corresponding to the availability of the object. The invitation directs the actor to the object, but without any conditions. There are no future consequences if the object is ignored. This conversation corresponds to primary, normal functionality. Every useful object speaks this way to an actor about to pick it up and employ it. We know what a chair is without consciously

thinking about it. But the assertion applies only to actors who are already familiar with the object. An alien without legs would not understand what a chair is because the meaning is not manifest in the materiality of the object. For simple objects, like a hammer, this is the only (normal) conversation involved in the interaction between actor and equipment.

3. "Stop. Fit me to the situation at hand." Here the equipment is making a *command,* coupled with a *request* to do something to it prior to putting it in play. Most objects today, especially consumer electronics, ask an actor to perform prefatory tasks, more or less rote sequences, ranging from turning the device on or off to more complicated sequences such as programming a VCR. In general, such requests do not interfere with the subsequent availability of the equipment. But not always—VCRs were notorious for their obstinacy.

4. "Stop! You have an ethical choice coming up very soon." This *command* creates obstinacy and forces the actor to consider the rightness of the subsequent action. This mode differs from the previous one, as the request is couched in stronger language. We enter into this kind of conversation all the time without thinking about it. Our response has already become embodied. Octagonal road signs, even without the word "stop" printed on them, interrupt the flow of traffic. Speed bumps say much the same. The two-button toilet relies on this conversation to work. But this conversation also requires that some cultural norms be present to inform the actor. An indigenous native of the Australian outback, if magically transported to a Dutch bathroom, would not have a clue which lever to pull, perhaps not knowing even how to use the toilet at all. Equipment becomes meaningful, that is to say, what one does with these artifacts, only through socialization and culturally bound learning. The device alone cannot provide the normative context of what is right or wrong, only a reflective opportunity for choice in the matter. If successful, this conversation produces responsibility connected to the actor's choice of the right thing to do. Ignoring this command has potential future consequences. Running a stop sign invites an accident or citation. Hitting a speed bump at full speed challenges the integrity of the vehicle.

5. "What are you doing this for?" This *question* arises in a mode of obtrusiveness after the action has already stopped, and it presences the identity of the actor: I am doing this for-the-sake-of my being a teacher, or father, or something else. Complete breakdowns such as that of my car's engine failure raise this question. Playing a stringed instrument, which typically involves first tuning the instrument, also raises this question. Fly-fishing involves tying and selecting the right fly, and checking the knots and equipment. The worst thing that can happen to a fisherman is to lose the big one because a knot has slipped. Similarly, I think of myself as a pretty good cook and love to cook for family and friends. Even for a modest dinner at home with my wife, I have a picture of the meal in front of me, and often I believe I can smell and taste the meal before I cook it. Focal experiences occur in the context of this question. Engagement with the equipment and the context is deeper than in the situation just above. The difference between this conversation and the one involved with a mechanical set of preparatory steps is that the context of engagement expands beyond the actor and object to the entire constellation of equipment and people involved. The concerns that surface often include others or the world.

In practice, the boundaries between these different conversations and the modes of presencing are not as sharp as these descriptions might suggest. Most articles we use every day do not engage us through conversations beyond, perhaps, turning them on and off. For example, most space heaters are simply placed on the floor and switched on. Sven Adolph, an industrial designer at Cranbrook Academy of Art, has designed a space heater that departs from conventional forms for such a device. The heater (Figure 11) is placed in the center of a room, with the cylindrical shell adjusted to radiate toward the people in the room. The engagement of the actor goes beyond merely turning it on, a task involving only the actor and the object. By adjusting the shell, the actor is taking care of more than simply providing heat (subsistence). Here the process of readying the equipment requires awareness of the entire space and the occupants. Other concerns of the actor (for example, family) surface and offer a chance to reflect on and take ownership of the identity or identities that show up, lending authenticity. He or she

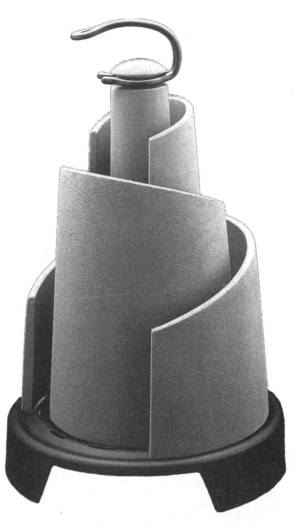

Figure 11. Space heater (Design by Sven Adolph). Ceramic Space Heater © Momentum Design, Zurich www.momentum.ch

is Being: showing concern, not merely providing heat to a room. Once the equipment has been adjusted and turned on, it recedes and reverts to the transparency of availability.

It is important to note that the message can get garbled at several places along the way. The designer may fail to inscribe the intended message. The theory being used may not produce the desired results. Heavy keys might not deter anybody. The user may subscribe, again, differently from the intended message. Context, once again, is everything. This has significant implications for design and for designers. Inscription cannot be done in the vacuum of a studio; design must be tried out in the world with actors who will be using the products.

SUSTAINABILITY DESIGN PROCESSES

Design theorists and practitioners are rethinking the way they design equipment—useful artifacts.[7] The previous discussion should raise questions about traditional engineering/technical approaches to design. Engineers and technically trained "designers" operate largely in their own world, separated from the world of the users of their products. Directions for new products come from market research that is largely based on psychological models of need. Such "research" will surface only cultural norms and inauthentic responses. Subsequent new products and services will embed unsustainable practices more deeply. Further, the technical approach fails to appreciate the linguistic processes at play when human actors interact with equipment. And for most product designers, the idea that interruptions in the flow of action might be positive would be anathema.

"Participatory design" is now a recognized process in product development. As a method, its roots lie some thirty years in the past in Scandinavia, when workers were brought into the design of workplace structures. The designers recognized that it was critical to have the users involved in the process to provide some semblance of actual practice. Further, they recognized that the workers possessed knowledge that was tacit and that could not be reduced to some set of scientific rules. If product development were opened up in this way in general practice, I would expect that innovative concepts far from the initial thoughts about some new technological artifact would show up. I would also expect, although I have no scientific grounds for this statement, that whatever finally reaches the market would find a warm welcome because the final form would reflect the concerns, not merely the needs, of the potential consumers.

Today such ideas are more common although still relatively rare in the United States. In a discussion of participatory design, system design theorists Joan Greenbaum and Morten Kyng identify four issues for design:

1. The need for designers to take work practice seriously: to see that work is done as an evolved solution to a complex work situation that the designer only partially understands.
2. The fact that we are dealing with human actors, rather than with cut-and-dried human factors. Systems need to deal with users' concerns, treating them as people, rather than as performers of functions in a defined work role.
3. The idea that work tasks must be seen within their context and are therefore situated actions, whose meaning and effectiveness cannot be evaluated in isolation from the context.
4. The recognition that work is fundamentally social, involving extensive cooperation and communication.[8]

These points are closely related to characteristics of a "wicked problem." In a classic paper by urban planners Horst Rittel and Melvin Webber of University of California–Berkeley, directed at those who "design" solutions to institutional policy problems, the authors defined wicked problems as those that could not be solved by the mere application of technical/scientific methods.[9] Paraphrasing a few of the authors' ten defining statements: the design objectives cannot be formulated out of the context of the action; the results will be known only after the fact in practice; every "need" hides another "need"; and the planner (designer) has some responsibility for the results. The planner/designer must "understand" the problem. Understanding comes only by involvement in action as opposed to "knowledge" as constituting the body of the technical foundations of the trade.

Given that it is obviously impractical for every designer to become involved in the products in the same way that potential users will become involved, the next best choice would be to bring such users into the process. This is the essence of participatory design. Many forms and processes can be found in practice, from product design to policy planning to organizational design/change. Organizational change agents use "action research" as a form of design in which the researchers and actors seeking a solution "study" a problem interactively. Differences in the identity of actor and designer may become quite fuzzy.

To finish this brief discussion of sustainability design, I point to one process suggested by a Canadian academic working in industrial product design. Table 5 summarizes a framework for a sustainable (I would

Table 5. Sustainable design versus conventional practice

Current Practice	Sustainable Design
Industrial design	Design of functional objects
Product design	Creation of material culture
Specialization	Improvisation
Conventional	Uncertain, uncomfortable
Professional	Dilettante, amateur
Specific	Holistic, integrative
Instrumental	Intrinsic
Problem-solving	Experimenting
Solutions	Possibilities
A priori design	Contingent design

say sustainability) design process developed by Stuart Walker.[10] I include his scheme as illustrative of how product designers are thinking about sustainability. Walker avoids the usual pejorative attached to his use of the words "dilettante" and "amateur" by pointing to their roots, delight and love, respectively. His aim is at the designer, criticizing conventional attitudes in the field. It is clear to me that most of the items in the right-hand column require the user's presence.

Since I am not a professional product designer, I cannot offer any more details on how to inscribe any of these scripts or conversations in objects. But I am encouraged by the increasing evidence that academics and practitioners are exploring this route toward making our everyday things more enriching and engaging. I am convinced that some balance between the disburdening features of devices that deliver commodities (singular satisfiers) and devices that induce presencing can be achieved without significantly slowing down innovation and the promise of new things. Maslow's observation of peak experiences and their impact on people's aliveness and Being strongly suggests that, given a chance, new products that increase engagement can hold their own in the marketplace. This strategy is not only subversive but also ironic: using consumption-creating market forces to reduce the drive to consume ever more stuff.

The challenge to designers of this approach to sustainability is substantial. The foundations are strange and countercultural within the profession. The designer must walk a fine line in creating the proper language in the scripts. Producing presencing requires a delicate touch. One wants to create obstinacy or obtrusiveness, but not too much. It will be important to balance the inscribed ethics lesson with the added annoyance. Authentic satisfaction rests on an engagement where the context comes forth. When equipment becomes overly obtrusive or occurrent, the opposite may happen. Perhaps artificial intelligence and fuzzy logic might enable designers of complicated devices to build in scripts that interact creatively with the user the way a fly rod does with me. Transforming the inauthentic experience of working with so many devices today into an enriching, revealing experience would begin to restore care as the essential feature of Being and put us on the road to sustainability.

Participatory design procedures primarily have been created for and directed at the designers without recognizing the potential opportunity for inducing presencing in the users who might also be involved. Users—that is, consumers—can discover and confront their concerns during the design process in the same sense as those revealed by encounters with the equipment in use. Designers should always recognize that the artifacts they create inevitably become less transparent and available to the user in practice, as contrasted with the designers' out-of-context vision of how the artifacts will work. If the process is well structured, all the participants will have to articulate explicitly what concerns they expect the device or system to address. Participatory design processes, which perhaps are not as powerful in changing behavior as presencing encounters with the things per se because they are limited in time and occur outside the context of normal action, nonetheless can guide and change behavior. "Fashion design" is not the same as the process being discussed here and merely substitutes an altered form of the same thing that was already in play.

With this concluding discussion of the design process, we have pointed to three similar but distinctive ways to induce presencing and get out of addictive or shifting-the-burden habits. The first is to inscribe "instructions" in the design itself that stop the action and guide the users to examine the authenticity of the action, reveal the domains of concern being addressed, and perhaps also remind them of their responsibility in the matter. The second is to design the product to require that the users become intimately involved in the preparation for routine use, that is, tuning up. As we have seen, tuning up is a form of presencing. And finally, participatory design can also be a presencing activity.

Chapter 15 Creating Possibility Through Institutional Design

The care of human life and happiness, and not their destruction, is the
first and only object of good government.
—*Thomas Jefferson*

Heidegger focused on equipment and space in his work, taking the social context as a given. Authenticity depends on the degree to which one chooses among the possibilities offered up by the social milieu. He saw the technological character of the modern milieu as so dominating as to reduce such choice virtually to zero. In the end he was very pessimistic about the possibilities of flourishing, although he never spoke of it in those words. For him, recovering Being was paramount. Given the modernist social milieu, I would have to agree with his diagnosis.

But what if that cultural milieu could be changed? What if people could cope better within their identities as parents, citizens, workers, doctors, students, and so on? Like philosopher Thomas Kuhn's concept of revolutions (paradigm shifts) in science that may occur when current practices and theories cannot overcome problematic barriers that stymie practitioners' efforts toward understanding, a revolution in Being is possible, but only if those who are coping with everyday concerns come to realize that both the equipment and cultural rules that shape identity and guide social behavior are not working. The presencing process will not work to change culture unless the "right" rules are in place. The addictive nature of life today attests to the absence of such awareness. Is there a "place" beyond the physical surroundings that creates the context for one's identity in the same sense as an artifactual workplace operates to satisfy the concerns that constitute identity? If there is, then, it should be possible to redesign this "place" to produce outcomes consistent with sustainability.

Such a place does exist in the notion of institution. Unlike a laboratory, kitchen, or forest glade, an institution in this sense is not a real place. Institutions are ascriptions of social structure underlying collections of successful routine outcomes in distinctive areas of social activities. Institutions can be considered simply as those "more enduring features of social life." [1] These more enduring features map the set of concerns and identities that constitute Being into recognizable spheres of activity. Their persistence can be attributed to their function of providing the social structure in which human cares are served, and identities are acted out.

Historically, unorganized care preceded the institutions within which we now categorize sets of related activities. Aesthetics/creation (see Figure 10) could be observed in the paintings of early cave dwellers, long before there were artists' guilds or museums or galleries. Such institutions arose only after humans created distinctive names for the activities springing from care in one or another domain. Just as the equipment (tempera) and place (studio) were designed to serve aesthetic concerns, so too were the institutions that emerged. To the extent that consciousness of concerns has continued to evolve reflexively in social life, institutions have coevolved historically to serve them. We speak of the institutions of baseball, marriage, business, the Church, and so on. What makes institutions distinct is the identity being expressed through the activities carried out under the institution's auspices. Marriage is the arena for acting as a spouse. Organized religion is the arena for acting out one's identity as a believer in a transcendent God. Business is an institution where one acts in several identities, shifting from one to another during the workday: providing for, subsistence, learning, and more. Society is a meta-institution in which all identities are enacted.

The focus of the preceding chapters was on seeking cultural change by the "subversive" process of introducing sustainability beliefs and norms as coded messages in everyday artifacts, and using these same artifacts to induce reflective breaks that reawaken one's essential concerns for self, others, and the world. This chapter takes a different tack and provides strategies for changing cultural structure directly by replacing unsustainable practices with new ones that are aligned with sustainability per se, and that also serve to reinforce the implicit new beliefs, norms, and authorities in the cultural consciousness through the structuration process, just as the routine use of artifacts reinforces the coded messages in an individual's practical consciousness through repeated use. *Practices* are the institutional equivalent to equipment used by individual actors. Institutional design, after equipment and place, is the third opportunity for sustainability design.

The coherence of a society arises from the coordination of actions within the key institutions of that society. Every separate cultural institution maintains its distinctiveness through the particular societal activities that are legitimately associated with it. Each institution has its own set of rules and resources as manifest in the structure of meaning and authority and in the resources peculiar to it. Government uses very different tools to operate than do educational or religious institutions. Government has its own set of roles to play: making laws, providing police protection, keeping vital records, and so on.

All institutions in a coherent society share some common beliefs and norms. Indeed, if they did not, we might say that no society existed at all, or that the society was dysfunctional. Over time, the commonly held norms and beliefs arise within separate institutions and diffuse into others and into the whole social fabric. Which institutions are to be the sources of these beliefs and norms depends on their relative power. In a rapidly changing and turbulent world—as many observers characterize the current scene—many institutions vie to become the dominant legitimate authority for the beliefs and norms of society.

The domains of individual satisfaction are not the same as those of broad societal aspirations or norms. The ends of justice, autonomy, freedom, equity, and so forth form a broad emergent framework for assessing the state of a society. Such norms permeate the structure that constitutes and produces action in smaller organized units such as work settings, family, or church. The challenge to those who would design social structures at any scale—policymakers, planners, organizational designers—is creating such structures that will satisfy the individual intentions of the actors while producing the broader social goals at the same time.

Taking on institutions directly and attempting to change them is an exceedingly difficult challenge. Institutions are fundamentally conservative; the structuration process tends to reinforce the past in the present. In much the same way that individual actors make sense of the world through acting out their daily routines, institutions make sense to those actors living inside of and constituting them by following habitual patterns. Beliefs, norms, and power become strongly entrenched over time. Unless the system comes to a halt and breaks down, the flow of routine life and cultural patterns keeps on going, similar to the case for individuals. The institutional world, like the world of an individual, is full of equipment readily available to those actors laboring within it. Individuals move their activities from one institutional arena to another during the day and also along their life's temporal journey. One goes from home (part of the artifactual context of family) in the morning to the office (the place where one lives in the institution of business), to the theater in the evening, and so on. Each of these institutional arenas is distinct, built on different structure and satisfying different domains of human concerns.

Institutions change when something happens to interrupt the flow and wake up individuals to the situation. If those in power stop and reflect as a consequence and adopt/design new rules and resources, routine institutional patterns of behavior will change over time. I have previously argued that this direct road to change is problematic because institutional/cultural patterns are so deeply ingrained. Individuals are reluctant to give up positions of dominating power. Even if the action is stopped and a design activity initiated, the models available to the designers generally will come from the same tired, old paradigm that has created the breakdowns. The earlier focus on equipment—the tools in institutional structure—is based on the presumption that it is easier to change individual behavior by introducing new presencing equipment and places than by changing institutional rules directly through education, incentives, or coercion.

Inscribed scripts in artifacts designed for sustainability add new norms and beliefs to the existing "body" structure and slowly change patterns of behavior through the doing-is-learning mechanism. The model for institutional change is identical. To overcome the challenge of entrenched interests and their beliefs and norms, new processes would carry "scripts" based on the beliefs and norms in the sustainability paradigm presented just below. In the circular structuration process, these scripts will become subscribed to (enacted) by the actors and replace parts of the existing structure. But because the skills of collective observation and learning are just as dulled as those of the individual actors, an equivalent process of awareness-raising and learning is necessary.

LOCATING THE KEY CULTURAL FACTORS

Unlike equipment that can be designed explicitly to carry new scripts and encoded norms, social action is driven primarily by its preexisting structure. Presencing was proposed earlier as a means to rebuild individual learning skills. In a moment I will introduce the strategy of adaptive governance, which can lead to the same kinds of enhanced observational and reflective skills in a collective sense, but cannot by itself change cultural structure. If the process works as advertised, "adaptive governors" will eventually learn what set of beliefs and norms are most effective in bringing forth the desired properties of the system. The key to this sentence is the word "eventually." The time available for adaptation is limited by the pace of the movement of the system toward a cusp such as illustrated earlier in Figure 9. Since I believe that some urgency is critical, this chapter offers an alternate set of cultural beliefs and norms as a starting position and a substitute for the lengthy process of learning by doing. This list is offered only as a way of starting; nothing can ultimately replace the pragmatic, continuous learning framework that I claim is essential to sustainability.

But first let me expose the beliefs and norms that drive modernity today. Using the metaphor of a collective mindset for the "Northern

Table 6. Characteristics of an unsustainable culture

Cognitive	Worldview	Contemporary Norms	Psychological
Reductionist	Atomistic	Efficiency	Repression
Proximity	Mechanistic	Quantitative	Denial
Simplicity	Anthropocentric	Disenchantment	Projection
Determinacy	Rationalistic	Narcissism	Rationalization
Discrepancy	Individualistic	Techno-optimism	Insulation

elite," my colleague in the business and environment field, University of Michigan professor Tom Gladwin, has classified some twenty unsustainable characteristics that underlie social and individual activities in modern industrial societies (see Table 6).[2] The column headings in the original paper, and a few of the entries, are slightly different from the more abstract ones I have used. His own definitions are full of irony and are worth repeating here. The four headings are, respectively, in his words:

- Biomind: "a cognitively bounded biological mind, inherited from our ancient ancestors, maladapted to modern challenges of systemic complexity";
- Worldview mind: "an obsolete worldview mind guided by tacit and outmoded assumptions about how the world works, based on religious, philosophical, and early scientific traditions";
- Contempmind: "an addicted contemporary mind that has been powerfully programmed to believe in various myths and ideological doctrines that appear to serve the interests of a few at the expense of the many"; and
- Psychomind: "a delusional psychodynamic mind that deploys subconscious defense mechanisms to ward off any realistic and moral anxieties posed by awareness of ecological and social deterioration."

Some of the items on Gladwin's list, like "reductionist," refer to our cognitive structure and the way we perceive the world. Others, like "individualistic," reflect the cultural evolution that started with the Enlightenment. Some, like "efficiency," refer to contemporary values. Another, our obsession with the quantitative, has generated the conventional mantra in business, "If it can't be measured, it can't be managed."

Gladwin, in the last column of the table, points to a set of psychological characteristics related to the ways we defend our psyches from anxiety. In the case of unsustainability, the anxiety is social and universal springing from a sense that we, as individuals, lack the competence to produce happiness, or, in other words, the satisfaction we seek is always just beyond our means to produce it. Denial is the element I discussed earlier as the most illustrative of our current dilemma; others include "repression" and "rationalization."

Narcissistic behavior, as noted earlier, is a natural outcome of living in the having mode. I looked up the definition of narcissism (Narcissistic personality disorder) in the standard mental disorders handbook used in the medical profession.[3] What I found was full of irony:

> The symptoms of narcissistic personality disorder revolve around a pattern of grandiosity, need for admiration, and sense of entitlement. Often individuals feel overly important and will exaggerate achievements and will accept, and often demand, praise and admiration despite worthy achievements. They may be overwhelmed with fantasies involving unlimited success, power, love, or beauty and feel that they can only be understood by others who are, like them, superior in some aspect of life.
>
> There is a sense of entitlement, of being more deserving than others based solely on their superiority. These symptoms, however, are a result of an underlying sense of inferiority and are often seen as overcompensation. Because of this, they are often envious and even angry of others who have more, receive more respect or attention, or otherwise steal away the spotlight.
>
> *Treatment for this disorder is very rarely sought.* There is a limited amount of insight into the symptoms, and the negative consequences are often blamed on society. In this sense, treatment options are limited. *Some research has found long-term insight oriented therapy to be effective, but getting the individual to commit to this treatment is a major obstacle.*
>
> *Prognosis is limited and based mainly on the individual's ability to recognize their underlying inferiority and decreased sense of self worth.* With insight and long-term therapy, the symptoms can be reduced in both number and intensity. [The added emphasis is mine.]

One has only to substitute inauthenticity for inferiority to begin to appreciate the connections between the modern way of living and the impoverishment of the human condition. That treatment for this pathology is so rarely sought is testimony to the stranglehold that addictive patterns have on societies and on our personae. The limited prognosis is potential cause for further social depression and pathology.

Psychological motivation is not part of sociologist Anthony Giddens's structuration model. He does not invoke the notion of a mind in a psychological sense and refers instead to embodied structure in a more diffuse sense. I have included this last column here because it adds to my argument that much of what we take for granted about the way we are and act is not an immutable part of human nature. Another way of looking at the psychological items in Table 6 is as indicators of sustainability or unsustainability. They are names given to distinctive types of behavior assumed to be tied to the psyche. If the mode of being shifts from the present, diminished form to the fullness implied by flourishing, we might expect these generalized psychological states to become correspondingly transformed. One of Abraham Maslow's theories is that our psychological health is largely shaped by our life experience rather than being the inevitable outcome of our wiring that determines our instinctual, innate responses to the world.[4] Fromm also has argued that personality, the manifestation of "human nature," is shaped by culture, not the other way around.[5]

Before proceeding further, please try another thought experiment in which you, the observer, are standing outside of a world that is operating under these current beliefs and norms. I challenge you to find or even intuit flourishing in this set of notions. It is much easier to find explanations for the failures of modernity and the emergence of the unintended consequences I call unsustainability. If these drivers of action and cultural behavior are presumed to be fixed and unchangeable, then we can continue to act only in a "modern" way: keep applying the quick fix. But if these are contingent and subject to change, then it should be possible first to propose and then to select the key elements of a new paradigm. I believe the latter: each and every one of the elements in Table 6 is mutable. So here is a challenge: "Where can one locate an alternate set of values, beliefs, and characteristics to replace those in Table 6?" What are the sources of inspiration?

I have already discussed what seem to be the most relevant sources for sustainability: nature and Being. Based on these sources of inspiration, I have redrawn the earlier table substituting concepts

Table 7. Characteristics of a sustainability culture

Cognitive	Worldview	Contemporary Norms	Psychological
Interconnected (n)	Holistic (n)	Equity/justice (b)	Remembrance (b)
Distance (b)	Organic (n)	Qualitative (n)	Avowal (b)
Complexity (n)	Bio-centric (b)	Enchantment (n, b)	International (b)
Indeterminacy (n)	Intuitive (b)	Other-directedness (b)	Accurateness (b)
Graduality (b)	Communitarian (b, n)	Techno-skepticism (n)	Sensitization (b)

that, via association with the sustainable character of nature or Being, might underpin a sustainable culture.[6] The letters in parentheses in Table 7 point to the source of inspiration for these new elements: "n" to nature as the source, and "b" to Being. Interconnected, complexity, indeterminacy, holistic, organic, and communitarian spring from observable characteristics of natural systems. Techno-skepticism derives secondarily from indeterminacy and the ancient notion of prudence in societal matters. Similarly, qualitative is tied to a new appreciation of flourishing as an emergent (qualitative) property. The current dominance of quantitative thinking springs, in part, from the Newtonian, Baconian concepts of science, and, in part, from a mechanistic view of a world that can be understood as a set of deterministic, ultimately mathematical, rules relating the behavior of one part to others. This view is reinforced by the hegemony of modern economics, which stresses quantitative measures as indicators of human well-being.

Enchantment, or spirituality, springs from both nature and being. Nature, the wellspring of human life, is the source of mystery and enchantment. Mystery, and the acceptance that there are aspects of the world we simply don't understand within the bounds of rationality, spring from our awareness of the fullness of the world. And, as Maslow claims, transcendence (another way of speaking about mystery or spirit) and Being are intimately coupled. Communitarian reflects the social foundation of Being and also the holism of an ecosystem. All of the new psychological entries derive from Being. Once we have reached the Being level, the world opens up and one attains "a more efficient perception of the world and more comfortable relations with it."[7] Equity and justice as replacements for efficiency also can be derived from being and nature, and similarly as replacements for other-directedness in place of narcissism. Community and interdependence suggest these and other norms. Again, in Maslow's scheme the deficiency needs that focus one inwardly give way to a turning outward.

The widespread notion in neoclassical economics that greed and self-interest drive all actions has been questioned in the work of James Fowler at the University of California, San Diego.[8] Fowler developed a game to see if the players would voluntarily spend their own money to reduce maldistribution. He found "that subjects reduce and augment others' incomes, at a personal cost, even when there is no cooperative behaviour to be reinforced. Furthermore, the size and frequency of income alterations are strongly influenced by inequality. . . . The results suggest that egalitarian motives affect income-altering behaviours, and may therefore be an important factor underlying the evolution of strong reciprocity and, hence, cooperation in humans." Perhaps a more human side is hidden away deep inside of us, waiting to come forth if only the unsustainability cultural expectations become replaced by the sustainability set.

The remaining four elements are also associated with Being. The anthropocentric stance of objective reality gives way to a biocentric worldview when we come to realize that we are deeply embedded within, and are a part of, the world that we normally think about as detached and out there. This last sentence makes an ontological, not moral, statement. The acknowledgment that we are part of the world does not place values on species and inanimate objects per se. At some point, as noted earlier, a sustainability paradigm may have to come to grips with this issue, but at this point it is sufficient merely to change the lens and adjust the focus later.

Gladwin's use of intuitive in place of rationalistic is consistent with the constitutive basis of reality and elevates experiential learning from its neglected place today. Finally, the last two, distance and graduality, come from nature and Being. Both represent a widening horizon for interpretation and action. Whereas today, where we tend to act only when the world looms suddenly before us, the enhanced perceptions of Being can signal the need for action earlier and further away from the immediate scene.

Gladwin's taxonomy is not complete; other important beliefs and norms are absent. Competition, for example, is the ne plus ultra of modern political economies and theories of the business firm. And while competition is certainly powerful and can produce many desired outcomes, taken too far it can and does produce social pathologies and unsustainability. Cooperation and mutualism are two counter-vailing possibilities for design coming from nature. Globalization is another powerful norm today, but it runs counter to the essentially smaller-scale and local character of most ecological systems. Diversity is yet another feature of sustainable ecosystems. Diversity provides resilience and adaptive capability. In social systems, diversity increases the stock of knowledge and wisdom, and reduces the likelihood of a reality that is constructed by power or groupthink.

As I said at the beginning of this chapter, the selection of paradigmatic structural details is always arguable. Others will want to add and subtract items of their choice. So please do not take the specific suggestions for the sustainability beliefs and norms as the "right" ones. I believe they do make good sense, but at this point they are only conditional and have to be borne out in practice. I encourage you to carry out an exercise such as I have outlined here. Seek your own source of inspiration and tease out the important underlying structure of sustainability.

COMPLEXITY POSES CONTINUING INSTITUTIONAL CHALLENGES

Complexity as I am using the term here is as yet a strange notion to most people. Complexity remains mysterious even though we observe such behavior all around us. Most academics are unversed in its concepts and practices. The tendency to call on experts and specialists is deeply rooted in our modern culture and will be very difficult to counter. Sustainability, however, depends on coupling complexity with management and engineering, taken to represent all fields of applied science.

Some of our most familiar terms need to be replaced in the vocabulary of engineering, design, and management. Instead of speaking of knowing, we need to talk about understanding. Knowing carries with it a sense of certainty that is unjustified for complex systems. And further, our everyday way of knowing comes through reductionist, analytic methods. Understanding carries a more holistic sense and suggests recognition of the particular context of whatever it is that we understand. Analytic skills should be matched by capabilities to synthesize. Experiential knowledge, as opposed to analytic knowledge, is a form of understanding, as it is always produced in action.

Another important linguistic pairing is possibility versus probability. Future states in complex systems should be referred to as possibilities, not as probabilities, because behavior is unpredictable, especially when the system is near a point of bifurcation, that is, a shift into a new regime.[9] Probabilities assume that we can know enough about a future state of a system to be able to predict it within some degree of certainty. Institutional designers, whether legislators, organizational consultants, or policymakers of all sorts, should consider the outcomes of their schemes as only possibilities. This was the theme of one of the most famous articles about policy implementation: Yale University political scientist Charles Lindblom's "The Science of 'Muddling Through.' "[10] Although Lindblom argued on practical grounds, saying that history shows that incrementalism works where analytic policy tools do not, his framing is entirely consistent with complexity models of organizations and societies.

As a final note in this discussion, let me stress the importance of monitoring and feedback in all institutional change processes. Since futures are only possibilities, it is essential to watch carefully what happens after some design has been put into play. Even during the design phases, interaction with all the stakeholders should bring a degree of learning that is absent from expert-driven processes, hence the argument for participation by those that will be affected. The assumption that the system will work more or less as planned generally leads to underdeveloped and underfunded monitoring provisions.

Chapter 16 Implementing Adaptive Governance

From disorder (a chaos)
order grows
—grows fruitfully.
The chaos feeds it. Chaos
feeds the tree.
—*William Carlos Williams,* The Descent

This chapter draws heavily on works on adaptive management of environmental systems as outlined by the creator of this concept, systems ecologist C. S. (Buzz) Holling, and his many collaborators.[1] Management as a deterministic notion has been rethought and redefined by these scholars in the light of complexity. Managers typically presuppose that a system can be directed to a desired end point by pulling levers and turning cranks according to a deterministic model of the system. One critical outcome of the work of Holling and others is that complex systems require a fundamentally different approach to management than do merely complicated systems, based on the presumption that people can never totally understand the functioning of a complex system. Furthermore, whereas early emphasis was on the natural systems, scholars and practitioners have turned more recently to view the interactions of society and nature as an interconnected, complex system. Starting in around 2000, many authors began to refer to "adaptive governance" of social-ecological systems, and I will use this term in place of the earlier phrase, adaptive management.[2]

One principal difference between adaptive governance and traditional systems management is the objective. Management tends to focus on some quantitative outcome, such as sustainable yield—the amount of biomass that can be harvested each period without reducing future yields or, in business terminology, quarterly profit. Furthermore, systems management tends to focus on a single output. Adaptive governance, alternatively, seeks to maintain some emergent system property such as resilience. Since sustainability as flourishing is, in this text, such a systems property, the adaptive governance framework seems to be an appropriate choice. Given that emergence is a property of the whole system, reductionist approaches are inadequate.

This complex system model for building the foundation of sustainability may appear to be riskier and more unsatisfying than models coming out of the comfortable equilibrium school of neoclassical economics or classical ecology. It is rare that managers seek new regimes, often explicitly avoiding such discontinuous changes. Most efforts are directed at tweaking the present system to produce more of something. Jumps from one state to another do not, however, have to be negative. Given that the current cultural system is not producing sustainability, change ultimately must depart from the current regime. The idea of creative destruction has inspired economists, business planners, and resource managers for some fifty years, since economist and political scientist Joseph Schumpeter first offered this theory of economic innovation and change.[3] The same idea persists today in explanations of disruptive changes in firms.[4]

Ecosystems exhibit several emergent properties related to sustainability, such as robustness, resilience, and integrity. Each one of these has a qualitative and metaphorical relationship to the idea of sustainability as flourishing. In some ways sustainability is a metaphor of a metaphor, translating the qualities of flourishing that are, in turn, found in resiliency and integrity (wholeness or wholesomeness), into a vision of life on Earth for humanity. It is a short step, then, to try to design and construct flourishing human systems and to maintain the ecological world to produce these properties.

The indeterminacy of complex system behavior should not deter efforts toward improving the world. We can model our thoughts and projections on computers and learn to sort out the better ideas. Robert Costanza, an ecological economist currently teaching at the University of Vermont, and some of his colleagues offered an optimistic forecast some years ago, saying, "Complex-system analysis offers great potential for generating insights into the behavior of linked ecological economic systems. These insights will be needed to change the behavior of human populations toward a sustainable pattern, one that works in synergy with the life-supporting ecosystems on which it depends."[5]

For some time, Holling has argued that adaptive cycles are a fundamental property of living systems and, further, that these systems can adapt to disruptive changes in a manner such that each succession maintains properties deemed to be healthy.[6] Holling has defined sustainability as "the ability to create, test, and *maintain* adaptive capacity." He further defines development as "the process of creating, testing, and *maintaining opportunity*" (emphases added). In his argument he uses normative terms, such as resilience, wealth, and opportunity, to characterize a particular form of succession where each one retains many of the positive properties of the preceding one and perhaps even adds more desirable traits. Putting all this together, Holling's notion of managed adaptive cycles might seem more or less the same as sustainable development. But this is not the same sort of sustainable development that the "standard" Brundtland definition is built upon (see Chapter 2). His notion is closer to the qualitative concept of flourishing, the metaphorical vision of sustainability.

The concepts and practices of adaptive governance are evolving quickly today. No consensus on any standardized methodology exists or is likely to emerge given that the source of this notion is the complexity model of nature. But there is a reasonably clear set of general principles that is becoming distinct.

1. Match governance to appropriate temporal and spatial scales.
2. Make design flexible to facilitate adaptation to changing conditions.
3. Involve diverse publics in the design process. Networks, as well as the actors in them, should map onto the nested levels of the social-ecological system. The nested external set of designers should resemble the nested structure of the system.
4. Use computer simulation to build shared, albeit synthetic, understanding of the system to be managed.
5. Experiment with the design in small-scale settings, if possible.
6. Plan for adequate monitoring. Learning by observing the behavior of the systems is essential, but it is critical that such learning not be equated with certainty.
7. Replace technological prediction with wisdom and prudence.
8. Have patience; the process takes time. The time needed to establish the social network and build trust among the actors is often seriously underestimated.

If a single feature of adaptive governance stands out, it is the criticality of building understanding about the system. In practice this generally means a constant search for and recognition of areas of uncertainty and ignorance, coupled to planned interventions designed to produce learning as well as keep the system functioning and healthy. This duality of purpose distinguishes adaptive governance from conventional rational schemes. But the process does not end with a successful experiment; adaptive governance requires continuing and persistent attention to the learning process. Institutions and institutional processes are critical since the learning acquired through the adaptive process cannot be completely reduced to context-free rules. This concept of governance is completely at odds with the technocratic basis for virtually all mainstream theories of management in play today, and would certainly constrain the popularity of formulaic, how-to best-selling books that come and go. The faddish nature of the management books today suggests that they fail to understand and capture the complexity inherent in any significant social organization.

Scientific knowledge is only a part of this process. Resource managers have come to recognize that traditional knowledge, the understanding of natural systems possessed by people living close to and relying on nature for their livelihood, is closely related to adaptive governance.[7] Over time, these cultures have come to embody practices that have been found to work but not in the sense of some discursive theory. Such traditional practices related to flourishing have become lost in modern cultures. In today's world traditional cultures are often seen through some romantic lens or are viewed pejoratively as primitive, lacking the sophistication of modernity. In many ways, this book seeks to reverse this process and recover the most fundamentally traditional feature of human beings, that of flourishing. Adaptive governance, like the other items in this section, cannot by itself accomplish this objective, but it can introduce beliefs and norms that can move the system toward the historic and natural roots of sustainability.

There is an important caveat. Adaptive management has arisen out of experience with ecosystems involved in natural resource management. Can the learning that has occurred simply be transferred to larger social-ecological systems, assuming that they are just larger ecosystems containing humans? In one article a group of distinguished social scientists asks, "Why are systems of people and nature not [simply] just ecosystems?"[8] Ecosystems are the product of evolutionary processes that reflect changes in structure and behavior responding to perturbations caused by natural phenomena and human interventions. Human systems evolve very differently due to the peculiar properties of our species. We can reflect on the world, develop abstractions through scientific inquiry, anticipate and visualize futures, and deliberately design material (technological) and institutional structures to guide our world toward a chosen future. Other species can do some of this, but to a much lesser degree. Squirrels gather nuts for the winter, and beavers build dams, but nothing in nature comes close to human capabilities in these areas.

Our future-looking vision is not free from history and so to some degree humans couple the backward-looking, path-dependent evolutionary processes of nature with our vision and designs. Adaptive governance should capture and understand both the historical (backward-looking) feature of human consciousness and behavior as well as the visioning, forward-looking mode. It is clear from the experience of ecological systems managers that tacit or local knowledge is involved, as well as generalized abstractions.

Implementing adaptive governance requires fundamental change in the norms and processes used in making collective decisions. The modernist model of rationality and standard positive scientific epistemology is of little use in explaining and managing complex systems. Much of what is on the environmentalist agenda today cannot be treated entirely by scientific management. The Earth's atmosphere is simply too complicated to describe within acceptable error bounds (and it also may exhibit chaotic patterns characteristic of complexity). Thus we enter into constant bickering about the degree and pace of global warming and climate change.

Several implications stand out and form the basis for the rest of this chapter. One is that, because science can no longer be privileged as the route to management, governance processes at all levels should be broadened to admit other forms of knowledge. The call for broader participation that has so often accompanied radical thinking from time immemorial now has acquired a "rational" basis beyond its justification on moral or political grounds. Further, our present system of education is designed to create an elite set of leaders who draw their inspiration and guidance from the many theories of natural and social science. Economics rules the policy roost, but economists rely primarily on theoretical models of individual and social behavior. The governance of complex systems cannot follow this path. We need to take a more critical and detached stance toward conventional positivist theory as a guide from the start. In theory's place we must substitute observation, learning, and new forms of design. But this requires a radical change in the basic pedagogy and structure of all our educational institutions. One of the primary themes that I follow in the redesign of institutions and social decision-making processes is the criticality of participation, reflecting the epistemological weaknesses of conventional science and the egalitarian context for sustainability.

Complexity and the basic inability to know the rules in the conventional sense call for precaution. The idea of complexity grounds precaution as an operating principle rather than as a means of minimizing regret or other form of risk balancing. The notion of risk itself is fundamentally different in a complex system. In standard decision science, risk assumes that there is some deterministic outcome, but that we cannot predict that outcome with absolute certainty. Uncertainty arises from the incompleteness of the theories and models as well as the inherent randomness of many phenomena. Uncertainty of outcome is also a property of complex systems, but it is another kind of notion; we should better call our inability to predict outcomes "unknowability" or some comparable term to distinguish it from the normal sense of risk and probability. In place of standard decision-theoretic processes and governance structures based on this science, including economics, new processes avoiding the hubris and domination of objective reality are needed. Some examples follow.

PRECAUTIONARY PRINCIPLE

> Precaution is better than cure.
> —*Goethe*

As we increasingly appreciate that we live in a complex world, as discussed in Chapter 10, the concept of precaution takes on a new and important role in social decision-making. The idea of prudence in societal governance can be traced back to the Greek notion of *phronesis* (Latin form, *prudentia*). Phronesis, as practical knowledge, was one of the primary forms of knowledge along with theory (*epistēmē*) and technical knowledge (*technē*). Aristotle took pains to distinguish among these forms of knowledge and emphasized the importance of practical knowledge in governing the affairs of society.[9] But for him the notion of practical knowledge was very different from the modern view of practical knowledge as technical control, which in essence collapses the notions of all three ancient forms of knowledge. Prudence was derived from experience and reflection on that experience in light of the unfolding of societal activities and their impact on humans. Reliance on prudence is very close to the central foundation of pragmatism.

The modern paradigm holds scientific knowledge as primary and privileged in matters of governance. Decision-makers are directed to select the proper path only after all of the "facts" have been established by "sound science." This call can still be heard loud and clear today in many critical areas bearing on sustainability. Action toward relieving the stresses caused by releases of greenhouse gases has been stymied for a long time by those who insist that the facts are not yet in. Because the level of uncertainty is high as to what the projected outcomes might be, these individuals argue that no action can be justified. As a result of arguing further that doing the wrong/precautionary thing might cost society a penalty in terms of economic growth, a wait-and-see attitude dominates. This same argument has been used over and over in the past to argue against placing restrictions on the introduction of new chemicals or drugs.

In Europe and in a global context, however, concerns over the unintended consequences of technology have led to the codification of the precautionary principle. The World Charter for Nature, adopted by the UN General Assembly in 1982, was the first international instance. It showed up again in the 1987 Montreal Protocol and in the 1992 Rio Declaration on Environment and Development. In February 2000 the European Commission adopted a communication on the precautionary principle. A group of academics and participants from largely North American NGOs, meeting at the Wingspread Center in Wisconsin in January 1998, published the following statement on the precautionary principle: "When an activity raises threats of harm to human health or the environment, precautionary measures should be taken even if some cause and effect relationships are not fully established scientifically. In this context the proponent of an activity, rather than the public, should bear the burden of proof. The process of applying the precautionary principle must be open, informed and democratic and must include potentially affected parties. It must also involve an examination of the full range of alternatives, including no action."[10] This was the first instance of a public position on this principle in the United States. More recently, the European Commission adopted a comprehensive policy on chemical substances in June 2006. The framework for this policy on the Registration, Evaluation, and Authorisation of Chemicals (REACH) rests solidly on the precautionary principle. One key feature is to reverse the burden of proof, requiring that, in the future, companies that engage in commerce demonstrate that any chemical they offer to the market is safe. Previously the burden was on some government agency to prove that use would cause harm.

This past activity has occurred largely within the standard scientific model and follows from the recognition that some future outcomes cannot be predicted with certainty. In those cases where some kind of significant, high impact outcome is possible, this principle argues that no action should be taken to implement the technology until the uncertainty of harm can be reduced to some acceptable limit.

The legitimacy of these past instances of precaution or prudence is usually couched in moralistic terms. Most arguments boil down to a claim that the utilitarian calculus of cost/benefit is inappropriate where small probabilities of high impact events can occur. Precaution suggests that it is better to assume that they will occur, and make decisions on that basis. If the benefits still outweigh the costs, then, this calculus would support taking positive action. Other arguments rest on minimizing regret or some other a posteriori social judgment.

Shifting from the positivist but uncertain model to a complexity-based model for the system being examined changes the ground rules. Outcomes are no longer merely uncertain but are unpredictable. As the sweep of technology becomes more pervasive and ties together the world in a tighter and tighter web, complexity seems a better model to explain the behavior of large sociotechnical systems such as the whole U.S. economic system. The tighter the interconnection of elements of a complex system, the more rigid the system becomes and the greater the possibility of discontinuous regime change.[11]

The problems that decision-makers now face become not just complicated and difficult, but messy and wicked, to use a few of the terms I have already introduced.[12] While Rittel and Webber, who coined the phrase "wicked problems" (see Chapter 14), did not use the language of complex systems, they were clearly inspired by what we now call complexity. Their term was "open societal systems." Rittel and Webber defined a wicked problem by these ten statements:

1. There is no definitive formulation of a wicked problem.
2. Wicked problems have no stopping rule.
3. Solutions to wicked problems are not true-or-false but good-or-bad.
4. There is no immediate and no ultimate test of a solution to a wicked problem.
5. Every implemented solution to a wicked problem has consequences.
6. Wicked problems do not have a well-described set of potential solutions.
7. Every wicked problem is essentially unique.
8. Every wicked problem can be considered a symptom of another problem.

9. The causes of a wicked problem can be explained in numerous ways.

10. The planner (designer) has no right to be wrong.

The last item in the list says that a decision-maker (planner or designer or manager, and so on) cannot invoke the failure of a hypothesis based on a deterministic model as the cause of unintended outcomes. Whatever outcome ensues must come back to the decision and those involved in making it. This is not the same as saying that the designer/planner should be held responsible for the consequences in some punitive or monetary sense. It does mean, however, that it may be advisable to replace the present tort system with a different way of compensating for any harm caused by unintended consequences. It also suggests that participation by those concerned about both positive and negative outcomes seems prudent.

Precaution is now not just some moral stand, but is called for by the basic functioning of the system. Not to be cautious is to exhibit hubris, an attitude that we do know or can ultimately know everything about the world around us. The implications of such a shift in attitude are profound and call for very different procedures for decision-making in cases where the system includes the general public. It is no longer possible merely to balance the cost and benefits of some predicted outcome. This will be true for every situation that can significantly impact the environment as well as the basic fabric of society.

PARTICIPATORY DESIGN

> Tell me and I'll forget. Show me, and I may not remember. Involve me, and I'll understand.
> —*Native American proverb*

In the technological world, design is generally the special province of experts of all sorts, from engineers to lawyers. In the participatory way of finding new artifactual and institutional devices that work, the design task falls on a much larger group of players who have diverse stakes in the outcome. The sharing of the process raises a new challenge, that of the placing and sharing of responsibility for the outcomes, both intended and unintended. In the reductionist world, unintended consequences are always someone else's problems to solve. In the world of complexity, no such easy alibi can be invoked. All who tinker with the system have a responsibility for all the outcomes (see items 3, 5, and 10 in the list above).

Decisions made collectively are fundamentally different from simple decisions made for oneself, even if one's own decisions and subsequent acts affect others, as is generally the case. One's own, individual decisions following and explaining an action are available only after the fact. It is our custom to provide such an explanation if asked, but there is no compelling mechanism that implies truth in the ensuing statements. The act itself changes the horizon for explanation of events in the world, and so any statement about the past, even a few moments earlier, is always colored by the present.

Collective decisions, which by their very nature always impact others beyond those making the decision, are fundamentally different. Explanations always matter. The details of the process leading to a decision is a central part of explanation and provides whatever legitimacy is needed to enlist the consent of those affected. Authoritative (and authoritarian) processes dominate decisions in critical institutions in most modern nations. Governmental and business institutions follow "rational" decision-making processes, based on the results of applying models from the natural and social sciences. This tradition follows from the ideals of the Enlightenment that "truth" will lead to freedom from dogmatic and arbitrary rulings.

The legitimacy of these procedures has been called into question by critics of scientific methods as a valid way of producing "truth" and further is eroded by complexity models of socioeconomic systems. Kuhn's classic work (see Chapter 7) showed that science moves in fits and starts from one paradigm to another, in which truths of one era are superseded by a new story of how the world works. Anticipating and reflecting complexity, sociologists of science coined the phrase *post-normal science* to indicate that the classic scientific method is not up to the task of producing "truth" in very messy systems like modern societies.[13] In their model of the new science, values cannot be left in the background when it comes to the design of social and technological structures within complex systems. Given that no one can claim the privilege of knowing the truth in a complex system, decisions involving the public should be made under conditions where values and assumptions are made explicit.

The idea of a priori assessment of technologies with broad social consequences is not new, but most past models have been highly technocratic and have failed to incorporate significant public inputs. Starting in the early 1990s, largely following work in the Netherlands, the concept of constructive technology assessment (CTA) takes a different perspective, arguing that a wide variety of actors should be involved in the process.[14] "Constructive" points to a continuous critical examination and modification of the proposals as the process exposes possibilities of both unwanted and more desirable outcomes. The basic message is that the ways a technical system will work in practice cannot be determined a priori by modeling the system outside of its practical, specific context. And, although it is obviously impossible to duplicate the future practical world, the design context can be made more realistic by involving a variety of actors that have some stake in the outcomes.

Constructive technology assessment was developed primarily for large public technological projects, but the process is just as relevant for product development processes in business. Products that have been developed by a substantially technical process with additional inputs from conventional market research lack the contextual appreciation necessary to anticipate actual outcomes in practice. Presencing is a subtle phenomenon, even if it is startling to the actor. The process of inscribing scripts is not reducible to a mechanistic set of rules. If the designer is truly interested in addressing concerns, rather than needs, and in producing presencing, users should be intimately involved in participating in the design process.

The epistemological shortcomings of science, coupled with the "wickedness" of key problems facing decision-makers, suggest that the process should be expanded to include participants other than the experts and executives conventionally involved. The public should be involved to legitimate the outcome of the process whenever the decision involves some sort of public goods, as is virtually always the case in public policy. The broader the impact of the technology or policy instruments being designed, the more diverse the public(s) that participates should be. The diversity will lend local knowledge to the process and counter the tendency to adopt highly technocratic processes in just those cases where expertise has the least to offer.

SMALL-SCALE SOCIAL EXPERIMENTS

To avoid serious unintended consequences, small-scale social experiments could be run to test new ideas and designs to determine their robustness.[15] Observing and monitoring is essential and should be integral to the experimental design. Again, this practice differs from our current process, which rarely includes funds for ex post testing on the false belief that the outcome will be just as the models predict. The authors of the article cited above describe two such experiments in the Netherlands. One involved the development and introduction of an advanced bicycle for commuting. The objective was to replace the automobile as the commuting vehicle. Although the project did not achieve its goals, the participants learned a great deal about mobility in general and how the complex overall transportation system worked. The learning that occurred within the project participants was, however, not effectively diffused beyond the team. For small-scale experiments to result in broad societal change, new communication mechanisms will have to be put into play, and the experiments will have to be better integrated into the policymaking machinery.

NONPUNITIVE, NONPERSONAL AWARDS OF DAMAGES

The United States has often been described as a lawyer's paradise. Tort reform has been a prominent topic in many recent election campaigns. The legal system in the United States recognizes that individuals can and do suffer harm created by others. The remedy for such harm (tort) is the imposition of damages provided that another actor can be shown to have caused the harm. In many cases proof can be established by invoking some theory or set of relationships that connects the causal actor to the harmful outcomes.

As technologies behave more and more in accordance with Hans Jonas's (see Chapter 3) claim that modern technologies separate the actor from the act in time and space, proving causal relationship within the degree of certainty required by legal standards has become very difficult, particularly in cases where the environment is involved. Complex systems add another confounding factor. Complexity means that some outcomes of system behavior cannot be related to the properties of the system, including the actors and their behaviors, in a determinate way. If the notion of complexity becomes accepted as a legitimate belief in place of or alongside the modern, positive notion of the world of phenomena, the fundamental basis of proving harm and assessing damages consequently becomes deeply flawed.

Accidents in complex systems cannot be predicted and perhaps cannot be avoided. This was the premise of an important text by Yale University sociologist and organizational theorist Charles Perrow titled *Normal Accidents*.[16] Perrow, without speaking of complexity theory directly, argued that, as sociotechnical systems became large and highly interconnected, they could exhibit patterns that were not predicted or were believed to be of such low probabilities that they could be ignored in the processes of design and system operations. He used nuclear power plants as such an example. His book, published after Three Mile Island but before Chernobyl (or the space shuttle *Challenger* disaster), was eerily prescient. Perrow argues that accidents are normal in such complex systems, that is, they are going to happen at some point even if no one can be shown to be blameworthy as the agent or agents that "caused" the event. Complex systems theory leads to the same conclusion. Even after exhibiting behavior conforming to the designers' or managers' expectations for long periods, complex systems can become rigid and flip into a new and discontinuous pattern of behavior, often associated with catastrophe, collapse, or disaster. Meteorological and atmospheric phenomena, such as hurricanes, tsunamis, or global warming/climate change, should remind us that it is not only in constructed systems that such "accidents" happen.

Accepting that some accidents will be normal and the result of a system failure rather than attributable to some causal agent to whom blame or responsibility can be assigned seems to fit the reality, but it carries some risk. The present system tends to make individuals along a chain of organizational responsibility careful. But in this case care is different from the caution involved relative to prudence. Faced with the possibility of being held responsible and liable for monetary damages or worse, individuals act out of self-interest, a process that only more deeply embeds the beliefs and normative structures about objective reality as being the only way of finding "truth" in the world, and that also creates rigidity in the system. Adaptive governance requires managers who are willing to take risks and try new approaches.

If this system were changed to provide public funds for those harmful outcomes that could be attributed to normal accidents or complexity, the process would be more coherent with the characteristics of the underlying reality. Given the centrality of rationality as one primary criterion of decision-making and legitimation, such a process would actually be more "rational" than the arguably irrationality of the present legal framework. But such a change would introduce moral hazards at the same time.[17] Any time some form of contract, whether private or social, reduces the personal responsibility of an actor to behave responsibly, the probability of misbehavior and consequent harm to others rises. Again, this model of human behavior assumes that individuals "cause" accidents to happen. New means of determining what kinds of decisions about what kind of systems should be treated as wicked problems will be needed. If the public is to pay damages for harm, then the "public" should have a strong role in deciding whether to implement such systems in the first place.

Implementing any of these practices—precautionary principle, participatory design, small-scale social experiments, or nonpunitive, nonpersonal awards of damages—would require significant leadership and political action. All are so countercultural that none could be easily slipped into practice with the ease that sustainability products, such as the two-button toilet, can come to the market. There are a few signs that some of these concepts are taking hold, particularly in Europe. The success of these small efforts should begin to change basic beliefs and norms, and even the power structure. As this happens, encoded elements of a sustainability paradigm, exemplified in Table 7, will begin to replace the old cultural pillars. And as the structuration process works its evolutionary way, the whole system should become more and more open to sustainability, providing fertile soil for the visions of the designers to take root.

Chapter 17 The Special Role of Business

The business of business is business.
—*Alfred T. Sloan*

The institution called "business" has a very special role in modern societies with respect to sustainability. Business is the largest and most powerful global institution in terms of financial power, exceeding the historically dominant role of governments. It is the largest employer and, with assistance from academia and governments, the major source of technological innovation. Business is now a global institution matching the scale of the largest set of unsustainable symptoms. Business, more than any other major institution, is focused on innovation and change.

Business is indirectly the "agent" of much of the damage to the environment. I use quotation marks to make clear that *agent* as used here does not mean that there is some deterministic relationship between the activities of business and effects on the environment. I claimed earlier that technology in its many forms is the proximate cause of most environmental damage. This means that, if one created a set of linked causal loops in the systems dynamic sense, a technological device would be found next to the damage. Cars and power plants produce most of the greenhouse gas emissions and therefore can be said to be the proximate cause of global climate change. The same set of causal loops would also show many other contributors: consumers, government policies, investors, and so on. But since business uses technology and provides it for everyone else, it can be (and often is) said to be the critical actor in the chain. The "polluter pays principle," explicitly codified in European environmental policy and also found in U.S. regulations, recognizes this role. Failure to grasp the whole system, however, is one of the reasons that unsustainability continues to plague us.

For these reasons, business should be a key target—perhaps *the* key target—for institutional change regarding sustainability. But first, one must understand what businesses do. This seems like a very simple question, especially since business is so dominant in the social and cultural landscape. But it turns out that finding such a definition or description is not simple. I searched through a number of classic texts and extensively on the Web, but I found that most descriptions were circular, much like Sloan's quote in the opening epigraph.

Many refer to the creation of profit as the purpose along the lines of economist and Nobel laureate Milton Friedman's famous statement, "The social responsibility of business is to increase its profits."[1] Peter Drucker associated profit with business similarly, saying, "Making money for a company is like oxygen for a person; if you don't have enough of it you are out of the game." Drucker, perhaps the most widely read and quoted management thinker in history, also said, "The purpose of business is to create and keep a customer."

None of these statements, nor myriad others, reflect the place of business within society at large, that is, they do not tell us what business does in a cultural sense. To understand business in the broader context, I turn once again to Anthony Giddens and his model of the constitution of society. Business influences the cultural structuration process in all four elements. Its primary role is to provide the equipment and physical structures that everyone uses every day (allocative resources). To the extent that these products, including cultural products like music and film, carry encoded beliefs and norms, they will impact the existing societal norms. This is the intersection between business and culture, where design for presencing and behavior steering will play itself out. The process is no different than that at play in the transition to an information society. As information technology of all sorts becomes more and more embedded in everyday practice, the whole cultural set of beliefs and norms changes. And so has it been since the industrial revolution and the appearance of mass-produced commodities in commerce. The nature of products and the means to manufacture them is reflected back on all other determinants of societal life.

Business has a second important role: providing employment. Wage labor is a promise to do what the employer requests in exchange for a monetary payment. The money enables workers to address their concerns in many of the basic domains. Henry Ford may be best remembered as the inventor of mass production, but his social philosophy to create demand by paying his workers enough to permit purchases beyond the bare necessities has had as much or more impact on our world. Ever since Marx's critique of capitalism, this relation between workers and the capitalist owners of firms (now also including much of "management" through the ties of compensation to stock options), has been held up as a source of alienation, deskilling, domination, and more. I have more or less restricted my critique of modernity to its technological characteristic, but as many, many social critics have written, capitalism and technology are completely intertwined.[2] One cannot exist to any culturally significant degree without the other.

Wages impact authoritative resources, providing workers freedom in choosing what they acquire. The more money available to them to spend, the more freedom they have to buy. To the extent that technological equipment has become a necessity, the ability to spend has a significant impact on flourishing. It is virtually impossible today to avoid the use of computers in learning institutions. I visited my six-year-old granddaughter's classroom recently and was quite surprised to find that every child had a computer in his or her cubby. The digital divide, reflecting the inability of much of the world to acquire information technology, is seen to be a serious impediment to flourishing.

Business also has a role in creating wealth for those that have invested. This attribute maintains or changes the authoritative resources that drive broad cultural actions. Shifts in the distribution of wealth as seen in recent years change the relative ability of people to acquire equipment of various kinds and change norms (and expectations) through the structuration process. A reversal in the huge discrepancy between executive pay and worker pay would mitigate or reverse the present, unsustainable trend.

The last effect business exerts on societal culture is a diffusive process whereby the employees export the norms and beliefs of a firm when they enter into other institutional practice. My sense, although largely unsupported by specific data, is that business is not as powerful a shaper of broad societal norms as are other institutions, such as government or churches, but given the large proportion of time spent at work it certainly must have a significant effect. Business-as-usual reflects the prevailing societal norms. The kinds of beliefs and norms shown in my colleague Tom Gladwin's unsustainable-mind presentation (see Table 6) have entered the cultural structure of business-as-usual. The sustainability challenge for business is to adopt a new set of values and beliefs (see Table 7) against the constant pressure to maintain the status quo. If businesses begin to operate with such a set of beliefs and norms, their employees will carry them back home and to other places.

There are ample signs that some businesses are embedding new structure, particularly with respect to care for nature. As I wrote this section, Apple Computer announced that it would join other computer sellers and take back machines when a customer buys a new machine. Firms taking back their discarded products is a codified value in Europe, where the European Union has issued a set of enforceable directives to this end for packaging materials, automobiles, and electronic and electrical equipment. In the antiregulatory mood that exists in the United States, take-back is voluntary and still relatively rare. But the more that firms take the initiative, the more that the importance of lessening the burden on the environment will enter the public consciousness. The norms implicit (or explicit) in this practice, or other similar practices, may be picked up by the employees, who will migrate home with them.

Firms have created cooperative agreements to manage certain scarce resources responsibly out of concerns that overharvesting and use of poor practices have already jeopardized or will jeopardize the health of these resources. Two prominent examples are the Forest Stewardship Council and the Marine Stewardship Council. Both self-interest and concern for future generations are involved. The Marine Stewardship Council was originally organized as an initiative by Unilever (self-interest) and is now a not-for-profit organization with a much broader constituency (shift to other concerns). But no matter where the motivation arises, the notion of cooperation and long-range thinking introduces new values both within the firms and in the general public.

The notion of "Fair Trade" extends business concerns beyond the environment to the social conditions of producers of commodities like coffee or chocolate. Local coffee growers often work under conditions that have often been described as "sweatshops in the fields."[3] In the highly competitive and controlled market for green coffee, small coffee producers are offered prices for their coffee lower than their production, leading to cycles of poverty and debt. Fair Trade labels on retail goods certify that the seller has agreed to pay a reasonable minimum price and avoid environmentally damaging production methods by undertaking practices such as teaching organic farming techniques. The emergence of Fair Trade and other programs directed at labor practices mirrors the growing attention to corporate social responsibility (CSR), especially in large corporations.

Attention to corporate social responsibility in the United States and all over the globe is growing. I conducted a nonscientific search of Web sites using the phrase "corporate social responsibility" as a search string and got over 1.6 million hits. Web pages from consultancies offering some kind CSR service were mixed in with sites of individual companies presenting their own efforts. By far the majority of what I found was aimed at economic development of one sort or another, ranging from increasing the output of sub-Saharan Africa to improving working conditions in Thailand. As meritorious as these initiatives may be, they miss the point about sustainability as flourishing. The focus on the larger dimensions of economic development deflects attention away from the human dimension of sustainability. Being is a property of individuals; it is not a collective term. Poverty alleviation certainly can and will bring many individuals from the brink of loss of even the most fundamental concerns, subsistence. But a development model patterned after that in the West promises a loss of many of the traditional values that have maintained peoples' Being, even in the face of deplorable conditions.[4]

To be consistent with the model of sustainability developed through-out this book, business needs to focus on customers' concerns through offerings, whether the customers live in affluent America or in devel-oping and poor economies. Flourishing requires addressing all do-mains of concerns. Relative attention to the domains at the base of Abraham Maslow's hierarchical pyramid, subsistence and safety, clearly depends on the political economy of a country, but, beyond these two domains, people everywhere have universal concerns about dignity, family, and so on. How they address these concerns depends strongly on tradition and cultural familiarity. In developing offerings for customers in cultures different from the one enveloping the com-pany in its home base, firms should be particularly sensitive and care-ful to respect these local norms and values. Even more, firms can benefit from adopting cultural norms that are more consistent with sustainability than those norms that dominate at present.

Let me summarize this call to business by making a few prescrip-tive comments. First, replace the rubric of sustainable development with that of sustainability as flourishing. This requires more than an analytic exercise to find ecoefficient innovations for whatever a firm has been doing. It requires a close examination of and conversation with customers to discover how they are doing; is Being showing up in the domains of concern being served by the company? Does the company even know about its customers' concerns as opposed to their needs? At the same time, firms should find ecoefficient solutions to stem the tide of unsustainability, but they must recognize and ac-cept that these are only short-term quick fixes.

In a closely related matter, business should stop publishing mis-leading advertisements hinting that ecoefficiency will solve the world's problems and save money at the same time. A Wal-Mart ad-vertisement carried the headline, "Earth-friendly products won't save the earth if they don't save people money."[5] Unsustainability is al-ways costly in terms of social impacts, and almost anything done to reduce it is going to introduce private costs. This kind of statement only adds to the irresponsibility of societal behavior. A second prob-lem with this advertisement is the use of the term "earth-friendly." Very few, if any, human activities of any kind are friendly to the Earth. Some are worse than others, but just a few or, perhaps, none would make Mother Nature jump for joy.

Second (and closely related to the first prescription), use the Tao of sustainability as a strategic and operational template. For sustainability to emerge, all three circles must be attended to. Rather than the dominant emphasis on environment through ecoefficiency, the most important of the three domains, I believe, is the human. The authors I have cited argue the primacy of attending to the human domain. Heidegger pointed out that authentic Being takes responsibility for the world. Maslow, in his later work, wrote that Being creates "a more efficient perception of the world and more comfortable relations with it."[6] Anticipating Erich Fromm's wonderful distinction between having and being, Karl Marx wrote, "The less you *are*, the more you have; the less you express your own life, the greater is your *alienated* life—the greater is your store of estranged being" (emphasis in the original).[7] Without a restoration of human care for the world, we are probably stuck with an unending succession of quick fixes. And without recovering the ethical dimension, sustainability will always be someone else's responsibility and job. In a complex world, that is asking too much and relying too much on technocratic institutional solutions.

When Adam Smith created many of the central themes of classical economics, firms were just starting to develop and to provide the equipment people required to address their concerns. They were replacing craft industries that had traditionally served this function. Because these very crafts had emerged directly from reflections of concerns rather than from capitalist motivations, these protocompanies continued to serve these concerns. Today, recognition of such concerns has receded into the background. Notions of profit and needs have come to dominate the activities of firms, as the institutions of the capitalist system have grown ever more powerful. In today's modern world, societies are virtually completely dependent on businesses to provide the equipment for living. Of the several ways that business influences the culture, providing products and services for Being and sustainability is the most direct and the most important.

Third, firms can and should begin to embody the set of sustainability culture characteristics shown in Table 7. This internal process of structuration within firms has influence on the societal culture. Employees come to work with their concerns and cultural habits, but they also leave each day with fresh memories of the culture of the company. I noted that many companies have adopted programs specifically directed at the environment and at social responsibility. Although these programs do contribute to awareness and norms, they do not have the same impact that fundamental change in "corporate" culture would exert. For example, introducing new management systems reflecting complexity is likely to make the employees more aware of the complex nature of the entire, not merely the corporate, world and more likely to express and practice these new views in other areas.

The process of change is always difficult since, like any institution, firms are driven by a conservative cultural system. Firms, like individuals, will continue to do the same things until something creates a breakdown wherein powerful actors (in Giddens's sense of capacity to change things) become aware of context framing organizational behavior. Organizational change systems—for example, Senge's *The Fifth Discipline*—attack the existing "mental models," a metaphor for the conservative set of beliefs and norms, by introducing routines that force the actors to confront and reflect on these models. *The Fifth Discipline* uses the practice of systems thinking as such a transformational practice/discipline. In a closely related book by Senge and colleagues, *Presence,* the authors probe a more deeply seated practice designed to surface the collective concerns, again similar to the case for presencing, as I have defined it for individual confrontation within the context of action.[8] The argument on which that book is based is the same as that presented here: change will not happen unless the actor or actors stop working and reflect on the context that has been surrounding their work.

Most companies struggle unsuccessfully to adopt learning practices routinely. The structuration process works to transform newly acquired practices into as rigid a set of norms and beliefs as the ones they replaced. If a business is to become competent to adapt continuously to the ever-changing world, it must be able to re-create the learning process just as continuously. The basic idea of organizational learning and adaptive governance is fundamentally the same. A few examples of firms that have mastered the process of continuous adaptation and learning can be found in the literature. Toyota is the example many point to as the model firm to emulate.

Much has been written about the success of Toyota as a manufacturer that does just about everything right. Toyota has been a leader in responding to its customers' concerns. The bulk of the articles attribute Toyota's success to its remarkable "Toyota Production System" incorporating just-in-time, and the elimination of *muda,* that is, waste of labor, materials, space, and so on. The whole system carries a Japanese name, *kaizen,* meaning change for the better. Except for minor variations, the key principles of kaizen are usually listed as:

1. Teamwork
2. Personal discipline
3. Improved morale
4. Quality circles
5. Improvement suggestion

These features relate closely to the above prescriptions and to a few of the sustainability cultural elements. Teamwork is all about cooperation and participation. Personal discipline lines up with authenticity. Improved morale follows membership. Quality reflects a very different understanding from that within the technical, mechanical operations model typical of most American firms.

Quality is seen as how well the customer is satisfied or, referring back to the section about product conversations, how well the product keeps the promises spoken in the purchase transaction. As management system and Toyota scholar H. Thomas Johnson has written, Toyota treats each car coming down the line as an order embodying the desires and expectation of a customer, not simply as a vehicle in a batch to create inventory.[9] Whereas a worker counterpart in more traditional Taylorist, Fordist systems might see her job as simply attaching a car door to the body, a Toyota worker might think about adding quality and keeping promises. If something interferes with the fulfilling of quality along the assembly line, workers can signal a problem or even stop the line by pulling a cord (*andon* cord).

Most of the time a supervisor can intervene and produce a remedy. Occasionally, the line stops and a team that includes both workers and supervisors attends to the issue at hand. Quality circles convene from time to time to reflect on the way production has been going and to develop suggestions for improvement. Hierarchical differences are minimized as supervisors, engineers, and workers all cooperate to make improvements. Again, this process supports concerns for participation and creativity, and reflects the complex nature of an auto assembly plant.

These actions create presencing—a key to the Toyota system. The workers reflect on the entire context of the manufacturing process, including the vehicle, the car, the shop floor, etc. Their shared concerns come to the surface. The whole process is presencing par excellence.

Improvement suggestion refers to the concept of continuous improvement. The kaizen system is not designed for large-scale innovation, but for producing small but important changes arising out of the experience of those closely involved with the process: learning-by-doing. This practice is consistent with the concepts of complexity and adaptive governance. Learning rests on local knowledge, not on dissociated expertise. Change comes in small steps (small-scale experiments) that minimize the chance of moving into a new, unproductive regime. Borrowing again from Johnson, Toyota sees the production system as a "community of interdependent parts that self-organize into a coherent whole that is greater than the sum of its parts. Quantities can describe features of the whole, such as cost or profit, but quantity and measures cannot explain the patterns of nonlinear relationships and feedback that determine such features."[10] A focus on the parts, not the whole, coupled with emphasis on managing by the numbers and targets, eventually lead to rigidity and loss of resiliency— just as managers of natural resources have learned.

Toyota teaches us that it is possible not only to put the sustainability prescriptions I have offered into play, but to do it very successfully and profitably. It is no coincidence that Toyota is leading the way toward new vehicles, such as hybrids, that can reduce environmental loads over their lifetime. In spite of the thousands of pages that have been written about the Toyota Production System (TPS), few U.S. firms have been able to implement it. Some adopt pieces—such as the just-in-time part—and do capture some cost savings, but few have been able to gain the whole set of benefits available. Much of the difficulty, I believe, comes from a failure to understand the substantial differences between the Japanese culture and our own. Kaizen is much more than a set of techniques. It is a cultural system with its own beliefs, norms, and resources that reflects the values and practices in the larger society. Non-Japanese firms cannot simply adopt the apparent factory floor practices and make them work.

When Xerox faced extinction some years ago at the hand of Japanese competitors, CEO David Kearns went to Japan to try to understand what was happening. He saw systems in place that embodied many of the features found in the TPS, particularly involving what then was a new concept in the United States, total quality control. Kearns returned with a commitment to transform the culture at Xerox, but also with the awareness that this was going to be a wrenching, destructive process. He saw the process metaphorically as a war, with the executive core acting as samurai, or as a junta, declaring war on the culture. His efforts paid off, at least for a time, as Xerox returned from the brink.[11]

One possible way to help firms begin to embody a new set of beliefs and norms is to employ new practices based on the emerging field of industrial ecology.[12] Before proceeding further, a disclosure is in order: I have been involved in this field from its recent beginnings and currently serve as the executive director of its primary professional organization. Industrial ecology is founded on the simple but elegant idea that human economic systems can become radically more efficient by mimicking the closed-loop material flow systems of living ecosystems. The relevance of this concept to reducing unsustainability has led to recycling systems and networks of firms interchanging wastes and byproducts with others as feedstocks. Such networks, called industrial symbioses, are analogues to natural symbioses, in which the relationship is mutually beneficial to all parties in the network.

Beyond the potential contribution to reducing unsustainability, these practices, just as equipment with scripts designed in, carry encoded beliefs and norms that fit the sustainability set shown earlier in Table 7. Symbiosis opposes cooperation to the dominant notion of competition. Even more basic, the metaphor of ecosystem conveys a sense of holism, countering the reductionist, mechanistic sense of the current paradigm. Adaptive management springs from the same roots reflecting the complexity of natural ecosystems.

Fourth, businesses should design their offerings to induce presencing and guide behavior toward ethical responsibility, following the product design path developed in Chapter 14. Further, they should consider the nature of the mode of satisfaction and strive for what

Chilean economist Manfred Max-Neef calls synergetic satisfiers, and what philosopher Albert Borgmann calls focal things and practices. Perhaps no more than a handful of existent offerings will accommodate these design notions, but that is no excuse for failure to experiment and innovate. Continuing to employ current design processes based on psychological models of need and functionality is to continue to exacerbate the failures of our technological, consumption-driven culture.

Last, firms should begin to address the issues of right livelihood for their own employees. Social responsibility, like charity, begins at home. Henry Ford recognized the need to pay a wage adequate to create demand for his and others' products. The myth of Fordism does not, however, include any sense that Ford recognized his workers as humans with a bundle of concerns that arrive with them every day as they pass through the factory gates. Work is much more than an activity to bring home money, corresponding to the providing-for essential concern. The workplace brings forth or, better, should bring forth, other essential concerns: authenticity/dignity, learning, membership, participation, and aesthetics/creation seem most relevant.

Deep-seated and lasting culture change is very difficult to produce, as the Xerox example above indicates, but without it sustainability will stay hidden from view. Alternatively, firms can began to adopt the norms and beliefs slowly, one at a time. The earlier Xerox example shows us that this can be done. Using nature as an inspiration, the project director pointed to the emergence of "personal growth, team building, a sense of community, and a much bigger sense of the environment."[13] The group built an island of authenticity within the larger corporate context. But until new business beliefs and norms reach some sort of tipping point, again to use Malcolm Gladwell's phrase, the mainstream culture will continue to dominate. It would be encouraging to say that the culture from the Xerox product development group spread to the mainstream, but it did not. Almost all of the structure that had been built disappeared when the project director left and the machine that focused the group's efforts passed on to the next step in its life.

It should be apparent that I believe that mainstream unsustainable values continue to dominate business. If unsustainability continues to grow in spite of technological efforts to turn the trajectory around, more concerted efforts in the spirit of Xerox would seem to be necessary. In the case of sustainability it is not competition and corporate survival that is at stake, it is the survival of the planet as a place we can inhabit.

Chapter 18 Epilogue

> . . . the test of a first-rate intelligence is the ability to hold two opposed ideas in the mind at the same time, and still retain the ability to function.
> —*F. Scott Fitzgerald,* The Crack-Up

The unsustainability of modernity should be clear by now. But this should not be taken as an absolute rejection of all its underpinnings. Instead, this is a call for the restoration of balance among different worldviews and a more critical choice of where and when to live and act within one or another. The most basic of choices offered herein is the one between objective reality and pragmatic understanding of truth. There are times in one's private life and also in public discourse when one choice will produce the desired results, and times for the other to work its wonderful ways. Like the choices in Ecclesiastes, there is a time for being objective and a time for allowing history and language to shape the world.

In the long run, I believe strongly that sustainability as flourishing can come forth only as the consequences of a cultural upheaval. The present culture with its technological framing of the world stifles Being and creates the addictive patterns that ignore the state of both humans and the world. At the same time, I do not see a revolution waiting in the wings, nor do I believe that such a revolution would necessarily be the best change mechanism. It makes much sense to grasp the idea of upheaval in geological terms, although on a much shorter time scale. Apply pressure that forces small changes continuously, and sooner or later the landscape will look very different. It has taken our modern world three or four centuries to get to where we are now culturally. It may take another epochal time (if we can survive that long) to replace the cognitive and material elements of our cultural structure. To avoid making too many mistakes and too many wrong turns, it is critical to move slowly and to keep learning. Accepting the world as complex should keep our modernist optimism and impatience in tow.

This context for action strongly suggests balance as opposed to a complete shift. We cannot simply abandon the rules and tools of our modern life. They have evolved on a very positive foundation. It is only now that they no longer consistently produce the good life we seek. A better strategy is to begin to recognize more clearly where the structure of modernity and its stories (objective reality, human nature . . .) continue to produce positive results and where the new story (constructivism, historicism . . .) should drive action. If we can accept that the rules by which we live are merely stories that make sense of the world, then we can tell ourselves different stories that may become pragmatically "true." Their truth will be determined by observations after the fact rather than by a priori knowledge. And if we can do this, we can teach ourselves which story to follow in coping. What the proper balance should be between these two stories remains to be determined and always will change to reflect the immediate context. It is futile to try to predict the correct proportion.

Similarly, it is important to balance the way we act in and with the material world. Here the balance should be between the functional and the meaningful. The devices that Borgmann speaks about are essential tools in our modern way of life. We cannot return to the craftsman's way of producing everything we require to carry out our daily chores and spontaneous activities. Most of what we use every day is far too complicated to be made by the user. But that should not preclude craftsmanlike involvement or engagement with these pieces of equipment. By making our material world less transparent through design, and by inducing meaningful relationships with it, we can balance the utilitarian and the meaningful. This means that more time will have to be devoted to activities where results are intermediate to those we seek. For those who already don't have enough time to accomplish everything on their to-do lists, change will not be easy, but is essential to break the addiction to modernity.

Balance is important in organizational strategies, especially in business. Business should begin to balance competition with cooperation. If the purpose of business and other institutions is to serve the basic identities of humans rather than the secondary needs of capitalistic structures, then they need to open up their boundaries. Business has long left Adam Smith's world, where the role of firms was to provide for the concerns of society.

While at MIT I taught mainly in a wonderful graduate program called Technology and Policy. Students with technical and scientific backgrounds came to learn skills they lacked for careers in the public sphere where policy is made and implemented. The founder of the program claimed that those who came left with dual competencies in "technology" and "policy." I always thought that this dichotomy was vague and did not convey what the program really gave them. In my view, the dual competencies sprang from the ability to act in the world of objective reality when appropriate and in the constructivist world when that system of thinking and acting worked. The kind of problems that interested the students were almost always "wicked" in the sense discussed earlier. Positive knowledge and technocratic process simply will not work by themselves in this context.

In a community contemplating if and where to place a bridge within its borders, a constructivist frame would recognize the values and historicity of differing stories and, perhaps, allow a consensus to emerge. The several models of reality I have presented are different stories we tell to keep the action going. They are neither right nor wrong. Ultimately, the "right" story (Cartesianism or constructivism) has to be judged by its effectiveness in maintaining the flow of social life, avoiding "bad" outcomes, and producing flourishing. The critique of the dominant modern view of reality presented here is fundamentally pragmatic, based on questions regarding its effectiveness in producing the common goods and in avoiding the bads.

The same is true of the position taken on technology. Technology per se is not right or wrong. Only statements we make in words or acts can be judged as right or wrong.[1] But technology can be assessed, exactly like reality, as effective or not in addressing the many concerns of humans. My argument is that the dominant forms of technology, for example, everyday consumer goods, produce more bads than goods if judged by some humanistic set of values, as opposed to economic, utilitarian calculus. What we need is a balance between those things that have, more or less, purely utilitarian ends, and those things that can focus us on what it is to be human rather than hide that aspect of our existence from us. Both technology and reality can and do exert dominating power over humans and the world. And as Lord Acton said, "Power tends to corrupt and absolute power corrupts absolutely." Both aspects of his aphorism apply here. One needs to be wary of objective reality as an absolute truth and technology as a panacea for all of our problems, as both carry the potential of dominating power. And when either or both become all pervasive, the system we call world, life, society, or whatever becomes rigid or, worse, corrupted.

Restoring balance is much easier said than done, as anyone who has ever tried to implement a New Year's resolution to overcome a bad habit knows. Once we are dominated by our beliefs and technologies (drugs, for example), even self-awareness of the bads being created is not enough to change the routines by which we live our lives. It takes some sort of intervention to stop the flow and enable us to face the world as it is, to let it become present. The most common intervention is crisis or collapse: an encounter with the world that breaks through previous illusions and false stories and forces onto the consciousness of the actor or actors the reality that someone standing outside might argue is present.

In the case of sustainability, this pathway cannot be counted upon. If we wait until the natural world collapses or degrades to the point that life cannot flourish in biological terms, or until the social world becomes so corrupted that flourishing in human terms is fleeting, it will almost certainly be too late for meaningful action. I have argued, conversely, that it is possible, in the course of everyday activities, to induce almost unnoticeable change through the design of familiar and useful objects.

Balance implies that we stop relying only on one fundamental ontological and epistemological belief system to explain and underpin our actions. Since we have been immersed in this system of modernity for so long, and because it has produced outcomes considered by many to be good, it is difficult to break our habits and addiction to it. And the alternative I am proposing here has yet to gain its historical place in modern cultures. Moreover, critics of constructivism argue that it leads to moral relativism. If abused, perhaps, but my experience is that many more persistent conflicts and problems in life are dissolved by constructivist processes than by calling forth the dominating power of objective reason or other dogmatic systems. Neither way is the right one except in a pragmatic sense. Even these two systems are not the only choices. Other systems of thinking and holding the world are available and may come forth in the future. My choice of these two fits the context of modernity and its largely Western roots.

I have focused virtually entirely on advanced modern industrial societies. This lens reflects my own limits, not the boundaries of sustainability. Sustainability is ultimately an emergent property of the entire Earth and of all its peoples and creatures. The impact of these highly economically developed nations dominates everything else, however. If we do not get our own houses in order, the scourge of unsustainability will continue to spread. Poverty alleviation is urgent, but we should pay heed to Manfred Max-Neef's admonition that what many of the world's poor suffer is poverties in the plural. They are unable to satisfy many of the categories of concerns that make us special beings. But bringing our current modern practices to their still traditionally rooted ways will bring them the seeds of the unsustainability weeds buried in the soil of our culture.

To those who may argue that the definition of sustainability as the possibility of flourishing is much too fuzzy to have any practical value, let me end this book by noting that the same can be said of all our most important values and goals. I believe that sustainability is a newly emergent concept reflecting the precariousness of the perceived world today. Sustainability belongs to a class of distinctions called "essentially contested concepts."[2] These are terms, like fairness, freedom, or liberty, for which there is some common sense of what they mean in the abstract, but which lack the same common sense of how to put them in play. Arguments over the uniqueness and universality of any one construction are doomed to be irresolvable. In this important regard I have offered sustainability as a touchstone to lead us to a place where the most fundamental aspirations of our species can be found and nourished. I make no claims as to its ultimate objective truth but argue, rather, that it has tremendous pragmatic power to break the addiction of modern life without forgoing what that very modernity can indeed produce.

Fitzgerald's aphorism, quoted at the start of this chapter, is a clarion call to all who would seek to stem the tide of unsustainability. Sustainability lives in a world distinct from the present: one with a new vocabulary and cultural habits. As we reach toward that new world, we remain enmeshed in our modern milieu with the vocabulary and stories that have served us so well for centuries. Until the new story replaces the old, we will have to, in Fitzgerald's words, hold on to two opposing models of reality and beliefs about ourselves while we use our intelligence to design the new tools and institutions that sustainability requires.

Notes

CHAPTER 1. IS THE SKY FALLING, AND, IF SO, DOES ANYONE CARE?

1. For more information on the unsustainable state of the world, see, for example: The Millennium Ecosystem Assessment; Wilson, *The Future of Life*; Speth, *Red Sky*.
2. McKibben, *Enough*.
3. Whybrow, *American Mania*.
4. Hawken, Lovins, and Lovins, *Natural Capitalism*, 81.
5. Kurlansky, *Cod*.
6. Gore, *An Inconvenient Truth*.

CHAPTER 2. SOLVING THE WRONG PROBLEM

1. Meadows et al., *The Limits to Growth*.
2. Senge, *The Fifth Discipline*.
3. Kim, *Systems Archetypes I*.
4. Homer-Dixon, *The Ingenuity Gap*.
5. Anonymous, *Our Common Future*.

CHAPTER 3. UNCOVERING THE ROOTS OF UNSUSTAINABILITY

1. White, "The Historical Roots of Our Ecological Crisis." White's article initiated a firestorm of controversy largely from theological critics who argued that he had taken a very narrow view of the Scriptures.
2. Kovel, *The Enemy of Nature.*
3. Dawkins, *The Selfish Gene.*
4. Weber, "Science as a Vocation," 155.
5. Maturana, "Reality: The Search for Objectivity," 29.
6. Ibid., 25.
7. Maturana and Varela. *The Tree of Knowledge.*
8. Maturana, "Reality: The Search for Objectivity," 39.
9. Heidegger, *An Introduction to Metaphysics;* Heidegger, *Being and Time.*
10. Heidegger, *An Introduction to Metaphysics,* 13.
11. Fromm, *To Have or To Be?*
12. Heidegger, *The Question Concerning Technology.*
13. *Philadelphia Inquirer* (2006), June 18: H11.
14. Friedman, "The Taxi Driver."
15. Jonas, *The Imperative of Responsibility.*
16. Heilbroner, "Looking Forward," 313.

CHAPTER 4. CONSUMPTION

1. Ryan and Durning, *Stuff,* 5.
2. Wackernagel and Rees, *Our Ecological Footprint.*
3. Majendie, "Affluenza."
4. Surowiecki, "The Financial Page."
5. Heidegger, *The Question Concerning Technology.*
6. As noted previously, technology interferes with such choice. Philosopher of technology Andrew Feenberg writes, "At the highest level, public life involves choices about what it means to be human. Today these choices are increasingly mediated by technical decisions. What human beings are and will become is decided in the shape of our tools no less than in the action of statesmen and political movements. The design of technology is thus an ontological decision fraught with political consequences. The exclusion of the vast majority from participation in the decision is the underlying cause of many of our problems." Feenberg, *Critical Theory of Technology,* 3.
7. Descartes, "Meditations on First Philosophy."
8. Cognitive science experiments have raised questions about this model of basic human behavior, suggesting that action impulses arise in the brain prior to stimulation of explanatory or intentional regions. See, for example, S. Obhi and P. Haggard, "Free Will and Free Won't."
9. Easterlin, "Does Economic Growth Improve the Human Lot?"
10. Schwartz, "Self-determination: The Tyranny of Freedom."
11. Schwartz, "Too Many Choices."

12. Fromm, *Escape from Freedom*.
13. Borgmann, *Technology*.
14. Ibid., 51.
15. Winner, *The Whale and the Reactor*, 156.
16. http://www.pbs.org/kcts/affluenza.
17. "E-dating Bubble Springs a Leak," *New York Times*, December 12, 2004.
18. Lebow, "Price Competition in 1955," 7.

CHAPTER 5. A RADICAL NOTION OF SUSTAINABILITY

1. Schutz, *The Phenomenology of the Social World*, 63.
2. Mumford, *The Myth of the Machine*.
3. The philosophy of Richard Rorty argues that solidarity with all humans is the fundamental underpinning of a liberal world (Rorty, *Contingency, Irony, and Solidarity*). Maturana, similarly, holds that love is the basic biological emotion that underpins all social relationships. In his view, love is the acceptance of the other to coexist with oneself and forms the basis of all consensual, nondominated social behaviors (Maturana, "Reality: The Search for Objectivity").
4. Maslow, *Toward a Psychology of Being*, 93.
5. Lerner, *The Left Hand of God*, 16.
6. Maslow, *Toward a Psychology of Being*.
7. Keyes and Haidt, *Flourishing*.

CHAPTER 6. THE TAO OF SUSTAINABILITY

1. Giddens, *The Consequences of Modernity*.
2. Aristotle, *Physics*.
3. Cobb, Halstead, and Rowe, "If the GDP Is Up?"; Easterlin, "Explaining Happiness."
4. Marks et al., *The Happy Planet Index*.

CHAPTER 7. CHANGE, TRANSFORMATION, AND DESIGN

1. Kuhn, *The Structure of Scientific Revolutions*.
2. Schumpeter, *The Theory of Economic Development*.
3. Fukuyama, *The End of History and the Last Man*.
4. Harman, *Global Mind Change*.
5. Beck and Cowan, *Spiral Dynamics*.
6. Habermas, *The Theory of Communicative Action*, vol. 1; Habermas, *The Theory of Communicative Action*, vol. 2.
7. Giddens, *The Constitution of Society*, 7.
8. Maturana and Varela, *The Tree of Knowledge*, 26.
9. Kuhn, *The Structure of Scientific Revolutions*.

10. Ibid., 6.
11. Ackoff, "The Art and Science of Mess Management."
12. Ackoff, *The Art of Problem Solving.*
13. Argyris and Schön, *Organizational Learning.*
14. Ibid.
15. Bandler and Grinder, *Frogs into Princes.*
16. Dansinger et al., "Comparison of the Atkins, Ornish, Weight Watchers, and Zone Diets."
17. Lerner, "As Diet Ideas Abound, Is Willpower Obsolete?"
18. Illich, *Deschooling Society.*

CHAPTER 8. CULTURE CHANGE

1. Giddens, *The Constitution of Society.*
2. Ibid.
3. Bolan, "The Practitioner as Theorist," 267.
4. Giddens, *The Constitution of Society,* xxii.
5. Barley, "Technology as an Occasion for Structuring."
6. Gladwell, *The Tipping Point.*
7. Fukuyama, *The End of History.*
8. Weber, *The Protestant Ethic,* 182.
9. Senge, *The Fifth Discipline.*
10. Jelsma and Knot, "Designing Environmentally Efficient Services." Also Jelsma, "Design of Behaviour Steering Technology."
11. See Norton, *Sustainability: A Philosophy of Adaptive Ecosystem Management.* Norton argues the importance of taking a pragmatic stance toward environmental sustainability.
12. Turkle, *The Second Self.*
13. Dreyfus, *Being-in-the-World,* 10.

CHAPTER 9. A NEW STORY FOR NATURE

1. Perrow, *Normal Accidents: Living with High Risk Technologies.*
2. Maturana and Varela, *The Tree of Knowledge.*
3. Daly, *Steady-state Economics.*
4. Odum, *Fundamentals of Ecology.*
5. Koestler, *The Ghost in the Machine.*

CHAPTER 10. THE IMPORTANCE OF BEING . . .

1. Fromm, *To Have or To Be?,* 176.
2. Ibid., 16.
3. Ibid., 26.
4. Rosenbloom, "A Sense of Belonging Among Belongings."

5. Fromm, *To Have or To Be?*, 105.
6. Trilling, *Sincerity and Authenticity.*
7. Patterson, "Our Overrated Inner Self."
8. Heidegger, "Nur Noch ein Gott Kann Uns Retten."
9. Maturana and Varela, *The Tree of Knowledge,* 196.
10. Maturana, "Reality: The Search for Objectivity."

CHAPTER 11. CONSUMPTION AND NEED

1. Ehrlich and Holdren, "One-Dimensional Ecology."
2. Graedel and Allenby, *Industrial Ecology.*
3. See, for example, Benyus, *Biomimicry;* Holmberg et al., "Socio-Economic Principles"; and Hawken, Lovins, and Lovins, *Natural Capitalism.* The Natural Step and Natural Capitalism are environmental management programs that follow specific sets of practices set out in the above-mentioned texts. Closing material loops is a central theme in the latter two systems.
4. http://www.who.int/mental_health/prevention/suicide/evolution/en/index .html.
5. http://www.china-embassy.org/eng/xw/t179428.htm.
6. Maslow, *Motivation and Personality.*
7. Ibid, 22.
8. Max-Neef, "Development and Human Needs."

CHAPTER 12. TO CARE IS HUMAN

1. Heidegger uses the somewhat cumbersome term "ready-at-hand." Hubert Dreyfus, whose work I have extensively drawn upon in this book, translates the term more familiarly as "available." See Dreyfus, *Being-in-the-World.*
2. Heidegger found it important to introduce a new vocabulary in order to avoid confusion with similar concepts arising in the Cartesian, psychological context. I have followed and retained some of his verbiage. "Towards-which" is, for example, not merely the intention of an actor usually construed as some mental state. Although this usage may be unfamiliar and uncomfortable, it will help avoid misinterpretation.
3. Putnam, *Bowling Alone.*
4. Bellah et al., *Habits of the Heart;* Lasch, *The Culture of Narcissism.*
5. Norberg-Schulz, *Genius Loci.*
6. Ott et al., *LAKES.*

CHAPTER 13. CREATING POSSIBILITY WITH PRODUCTS

1. Elgin, *Voluntary Simplicity.*
2. This chapter is not intended to provide a comprehensive discussion of the relationship between humans and technology. This subject is rich and is seen

through many different and often opposing perspectives. For an up-to-date and comprehensive treatment see Verbeck, *What Things Do*. Verbeck argues that Heidegger, Borgmann, Jaspers, and others have taken an overly negative and pessimistic view of the effect of technology on humans, individually and collectively in societies. I agree. This chapter is an attempt to tilt the design of artifacts toward the positive side of the ledger. The earlier critique of technology in this book is a means toward understanding the unsustainable state of the world and the role technology plays therein. I do not mean to portray it as necessarily "bad."

3. This section follows Heidegger's discussion of equipment in his phenomenology of Being. See Heidegger, *Being and Time*. I have again adopted the terminology developed in Dreyfus's authoritative commentary on *Being and Time*. Dreyfus, *Being-in-the-World*.

4. Maslow, *Toward a Psychology of Being*.

5. Borgmann, *Technology*.

6. See, for example, Slow Food USA, http://www.slowfoodusa.org/index.html.

7. For the same reasons that Heidegger used many invented words, I have introduced the notion of presencing. Strange words are useful as signals that the meaning cannot be found in normal conversation. Presencing is the revealing of the ontological context of action (concern, place, identity, etc.). Aspects that are invisible in routine actions come to light. I use the word to emphasize that the design process I lay out is very different from the normal one.

8. Gladwell, *The Tipping Point*.

CHAPTER 14. PRESENCING BY DESIGN

1. Krippendorff and Butter, "Product Semantics."

2. Maturana and Varela, *The Tree of Knowledge*.

3. Latour, "Where Are the Missing Masses?"; Latour, *Pandora's Hope*. Also see Chapter 5 in Verbeck, *What Things Do*, 147–72.

4. Akrich and Latour, "A Summary of a Convenient Vocabulary."

5. Speech acts are utterances that produce outcomes in the world just as physical actions do. See Searle, *Speech Acts*.

6. Heidegger's word for objects that appear out of context is "present-at-hand."

7. Johnson, *User-centered Technology*.

8. Greenbaum and Kyng, *Design at Work*.

9. Rittel and Webber, "Dilemmas in a General Theory of Planning."

10. Walker, "A Journey in Design."

CHAPTER 15. CREATING POSSIBILITY THROUGH INSTITUTIONAL DESIGN

1. Giddens, *The Constitution of Society*, 24.

2. Gladwin et al., "Why Is the Northern Elite Mind Biased?"

3. *Diagnostic and Statistical Manual of Mental Disorders DSM-IV-TR* (Arlington, VA: American Psychiatric Press, 2000).
4. Maslow, *Toward a Psychology of Being.*
5. Fromm, *Escape from Freedom.*
6. This table is also based on Gladwin et al., "Why Is the Northern Elite Mind Biased?"
7. Maslow, *Toward a Psychology of Being,* xi.
8. Dawes et al., "Egalitarian Motives in Humans."
9. Bremmer, *The J Curve.*
10. Lindblom, "The Science of 'Muddling Through.'"

CHAPTER 16. IMPLEMENTING ADAPTIVE GOVERNANCE

1. Holling, *Adaptive Environmental Assessment and Management.*
2. Folke et al., "Adaptive Governance of Social-Ecological Systems."
3. Schumpeter, *The Theory of Economic Development.*
4. Christensen, *The Innovator's Dilemma.*
5. Costanza et al., "Modeling Complex Ecological and Economic Systems," 546.
6. Holling, "Understanding the Complexity."
7. Berkes et al., "Rediscovery of Traditional Ecological Knowledge."
8. Westley et al., "Why Systems of People and Nature Are Not Just Social and Ecological Systems."
9. Aristotle, *The Nicomachean Ethics.*
10. http://www.johnsonfdn.org/conferences/precautionary/finpp.html.
11. Gunderson and Holling, *Panarchy.*
12. Rittel and Webber, "Dilemmas in a General Theory of Planning."
13. Funtowitz and Ravetz, "Science for the Post-normal Age."
14. Rip, Misa, and Schot, *Managing Technology in Society.*
15. Brown et al., "Learning for Sustainability Transition."
16. Perrow, *Normal Accidents.*
17. Jackall, *Moral Mazes.*

CHAPTER 17. THE SPECIAL ROLE OF BUSINESS

1. Friedman, "The Social Responsibility of Business."
2. Harvey, *The Condition of Postmodernity.*
3. http://www.globalexchange.org/campaigns/fairtrade/coffee/.
4. Max-Neef, "Development and Human Needs."
5. "Wal-Mart," *New York Times,* April 22, 2007, 15.
6. Maslow, *Motivation and Personality* (2d ed.), 153.
7. Marx, "Economic and Philosophical Manuscripts of 1844," 96.
8. Senge et al., *Presence.*
9. Johnson and Broms, *Profit Beyond Measure,* Chapter 3.
10. Johnson, "Lean Accounting: To Become Lean, Shed Accounting," 10.

11. Jacobson and Hillkirk, *Xerox: American Samurai.*
12. Graedel and Allenby, *Industrial Ecology.*
13. Ott et al., *LAKES,* 88.

CHAPTER 18. EPILOGUE

1. Rorty, *Contingency, Irony, and Solidarity,* Chapter 1.
2. Gallie, "Essentially Contested Concepts."

Bibliography

Ackoff, R. L. *The Art of Problem Solving*. New York: John Wiley, 1978.

———. "The Art and Science of Mess Management." *Interfaces* 11 (1):20–26, 1981.

Akrich, M., and B. Latour. "A Summary of a Convenient Vocabulary for the Semiotics of Human and Non-Human Assemblies." In *Shaping Technology, Building Society*, edited by W. Bijker and J. Law. Cambridge, MA: MIT Press, 1992.

Anonymous. *Our Common Future*. New York: Oxford Univ. Press, 1987.

———. *Diagnostic and Statistical Manual of Mental Disorders DSM-IV-TR*. Arlington, VA: American Psychiatric Press, 2000.

———. The Millennium Ecosystem Assessment (http://www.millenniumassessment.org//en/index.aspx), 2005.

Argyris, C., and D. Schön. *Organizational Learning: A Theory of Action Perspective*. Reading, MA: Addison-Wesley, 1978.

Aristotle. *The Nicomachean Ethics*. New York: Prentice Hall, 1962.

———. *Physics*. New York: Oxford Univ. Press, 1999.

Bandler, R., and J. Grinder. *Frogs into Princes*. Moab, UT: Real People Press, 1979.

Barley, S. R. "Technology as an Occasion for Structuring: Evidence from Observations of CT Scanners and the Social Order of Radiology Departments." *Administrative Science Quarterly* 31:78–108, 1986.

Beck, D., and C. Cowan. *Spiral Dynamics*. Malden, MA: Blackwell, 1996.

Bellah, R. N., R. Madsen, W. M. Sullivan, A. Swidler, and S. M. Tipton. *Habits of the Heart*. Berkeley, CA: Univ. of California Press, 1985.

Benyus, J. M. *Biomimicry: Innovation Inspired by Nature*. New York: William Morrow, 1997.

Berkes, F., J. Colding, and C. Folke. "Rediscovery of Traditional Ecological Knowledge as Adaptive Management." *Ecological Applications* 10 (5):1251–62, 2000.

Bolan, R. S. "The Practitioner as Theorist: The Phenomenology of the Professional Episode." *APA Journal* (July 1980), 261–74.

Borgmann, A. *Technology and the Character of Contemporary Life*. Chicago, IL: Univ. of Chicago Press, 1984.

Bremmer, I. *The J Curve: A New Way to Understand Why Nations Rise and Fall*. New York: Simon and Schuster, 2006.

Brown, H., P. J. Vergragt, K. Green, and L. Berchicci. "Learning for Sustainability Transition Through Bounded Socio-technical Experiments in Personal Mobility." *Technology Analysis and Strategic Management* 15 (3):291–315, 2003.

Christensen, C. M. *The Innovator's Dilemma: When New Technologies Cause Great Firms to Fail*. Boston: Harvard Business School Press, 1997.

Cobb, C., T. Halstead, and R. Rowe. "If the GDP Is Up, Why Is America Down?" *Atlantic Monthly* (October 1995), 58–77.

Costanza, R., L. Wainger, C. Folke, and K.-G. Maler. "Modeling Complex Ecological and Economic Systems." *Bioscience* 43 (8):545–55, 1993.

Daly, H. E. *Steady-state Economics*. Washington, DC: Island Press, 1991.

Dansinger, M. L., J. A. Gleason, J. L. Griffith, H. P. Selker, and E. J. Schaefer. "Comparison of the Atkins, Ornish, Weight Watchers, and Zone Diets for Weight Loss and Heart Disease Risk Reduction." *JAMA* 293 (1):43–53, 2005.

Dawes, C. T., J. H. Fowler, T. Johnson, R. McElreath, and O. Smirnov. "Egalitarian Motives in Humans." *Nature* 446:794–96, 2007.

Dawkins, R. *The Selfish Gene*. New York: Oxford Univ. Press, 1990.

Descartes, R. "Meditations on First Philosophy." In *The Philosophical Writings of Rene Descartes*, edited by D. Murdoch. Cambridge, MA: Cambridge Univ. Press, 1984 (1641).

Dreyfus, H. L. *Being-in-the-World: A Commentary on Heidegger's Being and Time, Division I*. Cambridge, MA: MIT Press, 1991.

Easterlin, R. A. "Does Economic Growth Improve the Human Lot?" In *Nations and Households in Economic Growth*, edited by W. E. Melvin. Palo Alto, CA: Stanford Univ. Press, 1974.

———. "Explaining Happiness." *Proceedings of the National Academy of Sciences* 100(19):11176–83, 2003.

Ehrlich, P. R., and J. P. Holdren. "One-dimensional Ecology." *Bulletin of the Atomic Scientists* 28(5):16–27, 1972.

Elgin, D. *Voluntary Simplicity*. New York: William Morrow, 1981.

Feenberg, A. *Critical Theory of Technology.* Oxford: Oxford Univ. Press, 1991.

Folke, C., T. Hahn, P. Olsson, and J. Norberg. "Adaptive Governance of Social-Ecological Systems." *Annual Review of Environment and Resources* 30:441–73, 2005.

Friedman, M. "The Social Responsibility of Business Is to Increase Its Profits." *New York Times Magazine,* September 13, 1970.

Friedman, T. "The Taxi Driver." *New York Times,* November 1, 2006.

Fromm, E. *Escape from Freedom.* New York: Avon, 1965.

———. *To Have or To Be?* New York: Harper and Row, 1976.

Fukuyama, F. *The End of History and the Last Man.* New York: Free Press, 1992.

Funtowitz, S. O., and J. Ravetz. "Science for the Post-normal Age." *Futures* 25:1–17, 1993.

Gallie, W. B. "Essentially Contested Concepts." *Proceedings of the Aristotelian Society* 56:167–98, 1956.

Giddens, A. *The Consequences of Modernity.* Stanford, CA: Stanford University Press, 1990.

———. *The Constitution of Society.* Berkeley, CA: Univ. of California Press, 1984.

Gladwell, M. *The Tipping Point.* Boston: Little, Brown, 2000.

Gladwin, T., W. E. Newburry, and E. D. Reiskin. "Why Is the Northern Elite Mind Biased Against Community, the Environment, and a Sustainable Future?" In *Environment, Ethics, and Behavior: The Psychology of Environmental Valuation and Degradation,* edited by K. A. Wade-Benzoni. San Francisco: The New Lexington Press, 1997.

Gore, A. *An Inconvenient Truth.* Emmaus, PA: Rodale, 2006.

Graedel, T. E., and B. R. Allenby. *Industrial Ecology.* Englewood Cliffs, NJ: Prentice Hall, 1995.

Greenbaum, J., and M. Kyng. *Design at Work.* Hillsdale, NJ: Lawrence Erlbaum Associates, 1991.

Gunderson, L. H., and C. S. Holling, eds. *Panarchy: Understanding Transformations in Human and Natural Systems.* Washington, DC: Island Press, 2002.

Habermas, J. *The Theory of Communicative Action,* vol. 1. Boston: Beacon, 1981.

———. *The Theory of Communicative Action,* vol. 2. Boston: Beacon, 1987.

Harman, W. *Global Mind Change: The Promise of the Twenty-first Century.* San Francisco: Berrett-Koehler, 1998.

Harvey, D. *The Condition of Postmodernity.* London: Basil Blackwell, 1989.

Hawken, P., A. Lovins, and L. H. Lovins. *Natural Capitalism: Creating the Next Industrial Revolution.* Boston: Little, Brown, 1999.

Heidegger, M. *An Introduction to Metaphysics.* New York: Doubleday, 1959.

———. *Being and Time.* New York: Harper and Row, 1962.

———. "Nur Noch ein Gott Kann Uns Retten: Speigel-Gespräch mit Martin Heidegger am 23 September 1966." *Der Speigel,* May 31, 1976, 193–219.

———. *The Question Concerning Technology and Other Essays*. New York: Harper and Row, 1977.

Heilbroner, R. "Looking Forward: Does Socialism Have a Future." *The Nation* 257(9):312–16, 1993.

Holling, C. S. "Understanding the Complexity of Economic, Ecological, and Social Systems." *Ecosystems* 4:390–405, 2001.

Holling, C. S., ed. *Adaptive Environmental Assessment And Management*. New York: Wiley-Interscience, 1978.

Holmberg, J., K.-H. Robert, and K.-E. Eriksson. "Socio-Economic Principles for a Sustainable Society." In *Getting Down to Earth — Practical Applications of Ecological Economics,* edited by J. Martinez-Alier. Washington, DC: Island Press, 1996.

Homer-Dixon, T. *The Ingenuity Gap*. New York: Alfred A. Knopf, 2000.

Illich, I. *Deschooling Society*. London: Penguin, 1971.

Jackall, R. *Moral Mazes: The World of Corporate Managers*. New York: Oxford Univ. Press, 1988.

Jacobson, G., and J. Hillkirk. *Xerox: American Samurai*. New York: Macmillan, 1986.

Jelsma, J. "Design of Behaviour Steering Technology." *Proceedings of the International Summer Academy on Technology Studies,* Graz (Deutschlandsberg), Austria, 2000, 121–32.

Jelsma, J., and M. Knot. "Designing Environmentally Efficient Services: A 'Script' Approach." *The Journal of Sustainable Product Design* 2(3–4):119–30, 2002.

Johnson, H. T. "Lean Accounting: To Become Lean, Shed Accounting." *Cost Management* 20 (January/February):6–17, 2006.

Johnson, H. T., and A. Broms. *Profit Beyond Measure: Extraordinary Results Through Attention to Work and People*. New York: Free Press, 2000.

Johnson, R. R. *User-centered Technology: A Rhetorical Theory for Computers and Other Mundane Objects*. Albany, NY: State Univ. of New York Press, 1998.

Jonas, H. *The Imperative of Responsibility: In Search of an Ethics for the Technological Age*. Chicago: University of Chicago Press, 1984.

Keyes, L. M. C., and J. Haidt. *Flourishing: Positive Psychology and the Life Well-lived*. Washington, DC: American Psychological Press, 2003.

Kim, D. H. *Systems Archetypes I*. Cambridge, MA: Pegasus Communications, 1994.

Koestler, A. *The Ghost in the Machine*. New York: Random House, 1976.

Kovel, J. *The Enemy of Nature: The End of Capitalism or the End of the World*. New York: Zed, 2002.

Krippendorff, K., and R. Butter. "Product Semantics: Exploring the Symbolic Qualities of Form." *Innovation* 3(2):4–9, 1984.

Kuhn, T. *The Structure of Scientific Revolutions*. Chicago: Univ. of Chicago Press, 1962.

Kurlansky, M. *Cod: A Biography of the Fish That Changed the World.* New York: Penguin Putnam, 1997.

Lasch, C. *The Culture of Narcissism: American Life in an Era of Diminished Expectations.* New York: W. W. Norton, 1978.

Latour, B. "Where Are the Missing Masses? The Sociology of a Few Mundane Artefacts." In *Shaping Technology/Building Society,* edited by W. Bijker and J. Law. Cambridge, MA: MIT Press, 1992.

———. *Pandora's Hope.* Cambridge, MA: Harvard Univ. Press, 1999.

Lebow, V. "Price Competition in 1955." *Journal of Retailing* 31(1):7, 1955.

Lerner, B. H. "As Diet Ideas Abound, Is Willpower Obsolete?" *New York Times,* July 10, 2007.

Lerner, M. *The Left Hand of God.* San Francisco: HarperCollins, 2006.

Lindblom, C. E. "The Science of 'Muddling Through.'" *Public Administration Review* 19:79–88, 1959.

Majendie, P. "Affluenza: Rampant consumerism erodes us." *Reuters.* Retrieved August 15, 2007, from http://www.reuters.com/article/technology-media-telco -SP-A/idUSL22795523200070126?sp=true.

Marks, N., A. Simms, S. Thompson, and S. Abdallah. *The Happy Planet Index.* London: New Economic Foundation, 2006.

Marx, K. "Economic and Philosophical Manuscripts of 1844." In *The Marx-Engel Reader,* edited by R. C. Tucker. New York: W. W. Norton, 1978/1844.

Maslow, A. H. *Motivation and Personality.* New York: Longman, 1954.

———. *Motivation and Personality.* 2d ed. New York: Harper and Row, 1970.

———. *Toward a Psychology of Being.* New York: John Wiley, 1998.

Maturana, H. R. "Reality: The Search for Objectivity, or the Quest for a Compelling Argument." *Irish Journal of Psychology* 9(1):25–82, 1988.

Maturana, H. R., and F. J. Varela. *The Tree of Knowledge.* Boston: New Science Library, 1988.

Max-Neef, M. "Development and Human Needs." In *Real-life Economics: Understanding Wealth Creation,* edited by P. Ekins and M. Max-Neef. New York: Routledge, 1992.

McKibben, B. *Enough: Staying Human in an Engineered Age.* New York: Henry Holt, 2003.

Meadows, D. H., D. L. Meadows, J. Randers, and W. W. Behrens. *The Limits to Growth.* New York: Universe, 1972.

Mumford, L. *The Myth of the Machine: Technics and Human Development.* New York: Harcourt, Brace and World, 1967.

Norberg-Schulz, C. *Genius Loci: Towards a Phenomenology of Architecture.* New York: Rizzoli, 1980.

Norton, B. G. *Sustainability: A Philosophy of Adaptive Ecosystem Management.* Chicago: Univ. of Chicago Press, 2005.

Obhi, S., and P. Haggard. "Free Will and Free Won't." *American Scientist* 92(4):358–65, 2004.

Odum, E. P. *Fundamentals of Ecology.* Philadelphia: W. B. Saunders, 1971.

Ott, R., C. Kelly, and M. Hotchkiss. *LAKES: A Journey of Heroes*. Webster, NY: Xerox Corporation, 1997.

Patterson, O. "Our Overrated Inner Self." *New York Times*. December 26, 2006.

Perrow, C. *Normal Accidents: Living with High Risk Technologies*. New York: Basic, 1984.

Putnam, R. *Bowling Alone: The Collapse and Revival of American Community*. New York: Simon and Schuster, 2000.

Rip, A., T. J. Misa, and J. Schot, eds. *Managing Technology in Society: The Approach of Constructive Technology Assessment*. London: Pinter, 1991.

Rittel, H. W. J., and M. M. Webber. "Dilemmas in a General Theory of Planning." *Policy Sciences* 4:155–69, 1973.

Rorty, R. *Contingency, Irony, and Solidarity*. Cambridge: Cambridge Univ. Press, 1989.

Rosenbloom, S. "A Sense of Belonging Among Belongings." *New York Times*, September 17, 2006.

Ryan, J. C., and A. T. Durning. *Stuff: The Secret Lives of Everyday Things*. Seattle, WA: Northwest Environmental Watch, 1997.

Schumpeter, J. A. *The Theory of Economic Development*. Cambridge, MA: Harvard Univ. Press, 1949.

Schutz, A. *The Phenomenology of the Social World*. Evanston: Northwestern Univ. Press, 1967.

Schwartz, B. "Self-determination: The Tyranny of Freedom." *American Psychologist* 55(1):79–88, 2000.

———. "Too Many Choices." *AARP Bulletin*, April 14–16, 2005.

Searle, J. *Speech Acts*. Cambridge: Cambridge Univ. Press, 1969.

Senge, P. M. *The Fifth Discipline*. New York: Doubleday, 1990.

Senge, P. M., C. O. Scharmer, J. Jaworski, and B. S. Flowers. *Presence: Human Purpose and the Field of the Future*. Cambridge, MA: Society of Organizational Learning, 2004.

Speth, J. G. *Red Sky in the Morning*. New Haven: Yale Univ. Press, 2004.

Surowiecki, J. "The Financial Page." *New Yorker*, May 28, 2007.

Trilling, L. *Sincerity and Authenticity*. Cambridge, MA: Harvard Univ. Press, 2006.

Turkle, S. *The Second Self: Computers and the Human Spirit*. New York: Simon and Schuster, 1984.

Verbeck, P.-P. *What Things Do*. University Park, PA: Pennsylvania Univ. Press, 2005.

Wackernagel, M., and W. Rees. *Our Ecological Footprint: Reducing Human Impact on the Earth*. Gabriola Island, B.C.: New Society, 1996.

Walker, S. "A Journey in Design: An Exploration of Perspectives for Sustainability." *Journal of Sustainable Design* 2(1–2):3–10, 2002.

Wal-Mart. Advertisement. *New York Times*, April 22, 2007.

Weber, M. "Science as a Vocation." In *From Max Weber: Essays in Sociology*, edited by C. W. Mills. New York: Oxford Univ. Press, 1946/1919.

Weber, M. *The Protestant Ethic and the Spirit of Capitalism.* New York: Scribner, 1958.

Westley, F., S. Carpenter, W. Brock, C. S. Holling, and L. H. Gunderson. "Why Systems of People and Nature Are Not Just Social and Ecological Systems." In *Panarchy,* edited by L. H. Gunderson and C. S. Holling. Covelo, CA: Island, 2002.

White, L., Jr. "The Historical Roots of Our Ecological Crisis." *Science* 155:1203–7, 1967.

Whybrow, P. *American Mania: When More Is Not Enough.* New York: W. W. Norton, 2006.

Wilson, E. O. *The Future of Life.* New York: Knopf, 2002.

Winner, L. *The Whale and the Reactor.* Chicago: Univ. of Chicago Press, 1986.

Index

accidents, 195–96
accountability, 60
Ackoff, Russell, 72–73, 74
acquisitions, 111, 126–27
action: accountability for, 60; and Being, 115; choice of, 38, 83; collective, 78, 79, 88–89; and concern, 156; continuous, 89; historical experience as basis of, 85; and learning, 69, 75, 113, 160–61, 174; moral consequences of, 31–34, 60; objectivation of, 44; predictability of, 121; and rationality, 27, 85; and reality, 26–27; social, 174–80; and strategies, 88; and structure, 83, 84, 85; subordinated to market forces, 33; and values, 41; in world of phenomena, 88
action research, 167

Acton, John E.E.D., Lord, 213
adaptation, 113
adaptive cycles, 184
adaptive governance, 174, 182–96; and awards of damages, 194–96; and complexity, 187–88, 206; general principles of, 184–85; and history, 186; implementation of, 187; and the learning process, 185–86; and participatory design, 191–93; and precautionary principle, 188–91; and risk, 187, 188, 195; small-scale social experiments in, 194; and systems management, 183
adaptive management, 107, 182. *See also* adaptive governance
addiction, 8, 16, 132; of consumers, 8, 12, 30, 36, 37f, 40, 42–43, 46, 110, 127; escaping vs. overcoming,